PROPHETS
IN THE
DARK

PROPHETS IN THE DARK

How Xerox Reinvented Itself
and Beat Back the Japanese

DAVID T. KEARNS
DAVID A. NADLER

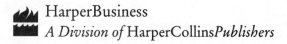

HarperBusiness
A Division of HarperCollinsPublishers

Photographs in insert courtesy of Xerox Corporation, unless otherwise credited.

HarperCollins books may be purchased for educational, business, or sales promotional use. For information, please call or write: Special Markets Department, HarperCollins Publishers, Inc., 10 East 53rd Street, New York, NY 10022. Telephone: (212) 207-7528; Fax: (212) 207-7222.

Designed by C. Linda Dingler

LIBRARY OF CONGRESS CATALOGING-IN-PUBLICATION DATA

Kearns, David T.
    Prophets in the dark : how Xerox reinvented itself and beat back the Japanese / David Kearns, David Nadler. — 1st ed.
        p. cm.
    Includes index.
    ISBN 0-88730-564-4 (cloth)
    1. Xerox Corporation—Management. 2. Corporate turnarounds—United States—Case Studies. 3. Copying machine industry—United States—Management. 4. Copying machine industry—Japan—Management.
I. Nadler, David.   II. Title
HD9802.3.U64X476   1992
338.7'68644—dc20   91–58506

92 93 94 95 96 ❖/HC 10 9 8 7 6 5 4 3 2

This book is dedicated to the more than one hundred thousand Xerox people all over the world and at all levels of the business. They are the ones who truly transformed Xerox into the healthy, viable competitor it is today.

Contents

Photograph insert follows page 208.

Preface

 F OR EIGHT YEARS—from 1982 to 1990—the two of us engaged in one of the most exciting undertakings of our careers. We worked together to alter profoundly the course of a major American corporation bloodied by Japanese competition and crippled by its own mistakes.

This was a partnership, though we assumed very different roles. David Kearns was the corporate leader; David Nadler was the counselor, adviser, and change strategist. Over time, this partnership evolved and deepened as a relationship, and it ended as a warm friendship.

Happily, we were successful. In 1982 Xerox was in danger of going out of business. Today it is a vibrant and growing company. We believe that this is due largely to the quality process that we introduced into the corporation.

To be sure, we were not universally successful. In hindsight, there were many things that we could or should have done differently. We made mistakes, we miscalculated, and sometimes we didn't execute that well. But we learned along the way.

In fact, we felt that we learned enough and were successful enough that we should share our story and the story of Xerox's reinvention so that others could benefit from our undertaking. Our objective therefore is to share both our experiences and our reflections. We feel there is an interesting story to be told of the rise, fall, and then rebirth of an enterprise. We are convinced that there are lessons to be gleaned that can be of use to others who are attempting similar types of organizational change, whether in the area of quality or in other arenas.

We are telling the story and sharing the lessons because there is a critical issue before us today: the competitiveness of American companies and institutions in the global economy. If we are to sustain our nation, our quality of life, and the values that we share, our companies must be reinvented, revitalized, and re-created. We hope the Xerox story will help others learn about the science and art of the reinvention of organizations.

Because we wanted this book to be a device for learning, we made a choice to be candid, at the risk of offending some people. The problems of Xerox were due to the misjudgments or mistakes of various groups and individuals. The story of quality at Xerox also includes some significant missteps and false starts. Sometimes the blame rested with others, and in some cases the blame rested with us. While this book is in no way an exposé, we have attempted to tell it straight.

The book can be thought of as having two parts. In the first half, we tell the story of Xerox through 1982. We describe the origins and phenomenal development of the company through the 1960s. We discuss Xerox in the 1970s, and attempt to unravel the question of how one of the most admired and successful companies of the 1960s could get into enough trouble in the following decade to bring it to the brink of extinction. In the second half, we tell the quality story, relating the development of Leadership Through Quality, Xerox's strategy to reinvent the corporation. We describe how this massive organizational change was conceived, initiated, managed, and led. We take the story through the winning of the Malcolm Baldrige National Quality Award in late 1989. In a final section, we draw some explicit lessons from the story, as well as from our experiences with other corporations through board memberships or consulting assignments.

We've collaborated to tell this story. In reality, you will be hearing the account of two voices, combining our joint recollections of the events. For clarity, we've decided to use one voice, that of David Kearns, to be the narrator, but the account is really a reflection of what we experienced and saw collectively. After the narrative of the story concludes, we switch to a plural voice to talk about the lessons we see.

Writing this book was in itself a learning experience. We found great value in sitting down after the fact, once the dust had settled, to reconstruct the story and learn from it. There's a lesson here for learning, a subject that greatly interests both of us. The capacity to learn and grow arises from the ability to be reflective—to take the time to pause and think back on our experiences, successes, and failures; to develop insight; and ultimately to generalize from this reflection. Organizations, like people, need to reflect if they are to grow and improve.

While we played central roles in this story, the credit for Xerox's success must go to the men and women of Xerox. We have nothing but admiration for the senior managers who participated with us in leading this effort. More importantly, we salute the more than one hundred thousand people—engineers, production workers, Amalgamated Clothing and Textile Workers Union officials, sales representatives, technicians, administrative staff, scientists—who were part of this adventure. In truth, the victory is theirs.

Introduction

ALWAYS LIKED TO RUN. And during the raw mornings early in 1982 I was running a lot—seven or eight miles a day. That was a distance I could handle pretty comfortably, for a few years earlier I had managed to limp through the New York Marathon. I was living in New Canaan, Connecticut, and I would be up by six, when a hard chill was still in the air, and be jogging along the gently winding roads almost empty of cars. I often passed the Vista Market, which didn't open until seven, but the anxious early-morning dreamers would be lined up in advance to buy their lottery tickets.

Exercise was what attracted me to running, but I soon found that it filled a second need: it gave me the opportunity to think free of outside distractions. You never have enough time for truly productive thought, and I had long ago found that my mind was never clearer than when I was in my shorts pounding down a country road. These brittle mornings, though, the unwelcome thoughts that coursed through my head were enough to create a lot of anxiety.

It had been just a few months since I had been appointed the chief executive officer of Xerox, and I suppose I should have been the happiest man on earth. I had always wanted to run a major U.S. corporation and now I had my chance. But a frightening realization had been nagging away at me. I didn't know whether Xerox would be able to survive the eighties. I wasn't worrying about being taken over by some raider; that was something else altogether. I frankly thought Xerox was on its way out of business.

To many in the outside world, we still looked very much like the invincible copier giant and bedrock of the *Fortune* 500 that we had always been. It was evident that we were having a few problems. But, still, we were making hundreds of millions of dollars a year. We were turning out fresh products. We were employing a hundred thousand people. How bad could things be?

Unfortunately, I knew. We were gravely sick. Worse still, it wasn't clear what medicine would make us better. It was tough just to think about it. And every day seemed to bring more bad news.

A lot of our problems boiled down to the Japanese. They were really eating us for lunch. I had made something like two dozen trips to Japan. I went there like a sponge, determined to soak up everything I could to try to understand just how far ahead of us the Japanese were. With each trip, the revelations grew more sobering.

One thing I gleaned from these visits was that the Japanese had consciously made the decision to select our company as a "target." To them, that meant they were convinced they could capture a considerable chunk of our market share and, if all worked out as they hoped, wipe us off the map altogether. They had good reason to think so; they were selling products for what it cost us to make them. Our market share had tumbled from more than 90 percent in the early 1970s to less than 15 percent. Every year, competitors nibbled away a few more share points. We were being decimated. Whether we liked it or not, we were in a war to the death.

Unfortunately, I knew full well that it wasn't the Japanese alone who had brought on this gloomy situation. The place had been sinking for years. Throughout the company, we had lost touch with the customers, the most important constituency out there. We weren't giving them the products they wanted and we weren't giving them appropriate service. The bad feelings between customers and Xerox were shocking.

How bad off were we? To put it bluntly, if nothing were done to correct things, we were destined to have a fire sale and close down by 1990. And the final humiliation for me was that it would be on my watch. This could be my legacy: I had put the company out of business.

The situation was especially difficult for me because I couldn't share these dark thoughts with anyone else at the company. They were far too negative. It would have been fatal for other members of the management team to know that I thought we were headed for the graveyard. They would have either gotten new jobs or stayed on but without motivation.

What also made this realization so disturbing was the fact that Xerox occupied such a magical place in so many people's minds and that more than a hundred thousand loyal employees and their families depended on the company and badly wanted it to be successful. Here was America's thirty-eighth largest industrial company, a major household word in the country, that would be gone. Xerox was one of the best-known names in the world—so well-known, in fact, that it kept our lawyers ever so busy dashing off reminders to outsiders that Xerox was a proprietary name and not a verb that was part of common English. Xerox was the pioneer of a machine considered the most successful commercial product of all time and arguably the most important contribution to communications since the printing press. It is no surprise that, until the recent upheavals, Eastern Bloc countries kept extraordinarily tight control over who had access to copiers. After all, whoever could copy material for dissemination wielded vast power.

About the only consoling factor was that I knew we weren't the only ones in the soup. Global competition had set upon the country, and everyone was vulnerable. American business was threatened not only by Japan and Korea. Europe was mobilizing into a potent force that demanded serious consideration. And yet, as I looked around me, I saw that so many great and admired companies were doing nothing but sitting on their hands. Like us, they were kissing away their businesses and laying the groundwork for their own destruction.

We had tried a number of strategies to breathe some new life into Xerox. We bought some companies that got us into new areas and we did a lot of streamlining and took what we thought were tough cost measures. Successions of motivational ideas were broadcast to employees, so many that top management was losing much of its credibility. We were often derided as being like the Baskin-Robbins ice cream people: every month brought a new flavor. There were no simple answers, and I was running out of time.

After my string of trips to Japan and after deep introspection about Xerox's strengths and flaws, the solution began to point in one direction. Our only hope for survival was to urgently commit ourselves to vastly improving the quality of our products and service. This was something a lot of corporations talked about, but it was extraordinarily difficult to do. It meant changing the very culture of Xerox from the ground up. Everyone from the cleaning people to the chairman would have to think differently. In our near-death situation, I felt we had no choice but to accomplish this. My feeling was, if it hurts enough, you'll get anything done, and we were hurting in a major-league way.

As I puffed down those Connecticut roads and smelled the lovely early-morning air, it was all perfectly clear to me. It was time for a revolution.

1. A New Vista

IT WAS IMPORTANT THAT we pick the right place to meet. My intent was somewhere that was well enough off the beaten track to avoid discovery, which could prove embarrassing. After giving it some thought, we finally agreed upon a nondescript out-of-the-way eatery in Stamford, not at all a likely spot for anyone from either IBM or Xerox to turn up, and that was the key consideration. The last thing I wanted was for one of my colleagues from IBM to see me huddling with someone from Xerox and then to have him start feeding the rumor mills.

After seventeen years at IBM, I was a pretty contented man. I had never worked anyplace else, and never thought of myself as one of those nomadic businessmen who roamed from company to company. I felt I wanted to switch jobs as much as I cared to have my tonsils out. But circumstances had conspired to at least permit me to contemplate the idea, which was why I was on my way to this clandestine rendezvous one chilly evening in the spring of 1971.

Although it may be accepted wisdom that executives move to other companies because they are dangled huge monetary rewards or because they see it as a chance to rise higher up the corridors of power, often nothing of the sort is the motivation. In my case, my meeting was the result of a serendipitous event involving my wife and an old colleague passing through town.

A few weeks earlier, Bill Glavin had been on his way to a Xerox conference in Palm Beach and had stopped in Chappaqua, New York, where he used to reside and where I still lived. Bill and I had known each other for a long time, for he had worked for IBM before taking a good job with Xerox on the West Coast, and we had great respect for each other's abilities. We fit the true definition of friendly rivals. In honor of his visit to his former stomping grounds, the old gang threw him a festive party one Saturday night. Things weren't going all that swimmingly at the time at IBM, where I was vice president of marketing in the huge data products division, and I was working a lot of nights and weekends. I had to hole up at the office that particular Saturday and skip going to the party. My wife, Shirley, was a little steamed. She went alone to the affair, and when she got a private moment with Bill she complained about my merciless hours.

The conversation stuck with Bill. He went on to the Xerox conference and overheard a discussion about me among some senior people there. He told them that if they were interested in me, now was the time to pounce. As he put it, "I can tell you his wife is pretty unhappy with the current environment."

A few days later, Glavin called and asked if I'd like to visit with the top people at Xerox. I begged off, but told him if he were on the East Coast again we might have dinner and chat about Xerox.

Three days later, he phoned and declared, "I'm here." So we agreed to meet at the Stamford restaurant. When I arrived, there were some people joshing at the bar and the place was starting to get active. Bill was waiting with polite anticipation and greeted me with a big smile and a hearty handshake. Bill is a large man with a craggy face, bubbling with energy and enthusiasm. He sort of envelops you. You don't just meet Bill Glavin. You are surrounded by him. At six foot seven, he ranked as one of the tallest executives in American business. He used to remark about how his height proved to be a nifty advantage when he was a salesman. If customers remember you, you always have an edge in sales, and people didn't forget someone who towered over them with a forceful personality.

Our cloak-and-dagger secrecy about where to meet proved fruitless. Any attempt at discretion was just not in the bargain. We hadn't even gotten to our table when an IBM man showed up who worked for the same boss as I did. He had dropped in to have a quick drink on the way home. Straining to keep my cool, I introduced him to Glavin as casually as I could.

Bill and I left and found another spot for our discussion. When we got there, Bill told me how attractive a place Xerox was and how there was some real opportunity long-term. It was a fast-track company, and people went there more for the chance to advance quickly than for money, which was no better than a lot of other places. Glavin made a good pitch. His description of Xerox and the senior management sounded appealing to me. By the time the evening was over, I had agreed to speak to Archie McCardell, then Xerox's executive vice president and the presumed front-runner to become the next president of the company. I ribbed Glavin a little that if I went to Xerox I might wind up being a competitor of his and one of us might even find himself working for the other. That was fine with him, he said. I felt the same way.

Shortly afterward, I went to McCardell's house in Fairfield and had a long discussion with him. He was a heavyset man with a reputation as a tough, financially-oriented executive. But he was all charm with me. He told me they were interested in having me join the company and mentioned some general possibilities without going into specific jobs. I had to attend an IBM meeting in Boca Raton, and on the plane ride back I wrote down the pluses and minuses of joining Xerox. As I studied them, the pluses slightly outnumbered the minuses.

On the Fourth of July weekend, some friends were having a cocktail party. While my wife and I were over there, my oldest daughter, who was baby-sitting our other kids, called and said that Mr. McCardell had called and would like me to phone him. From my friend's kitchen, McCardell offered me a job to come work for him as his assistant. I returned to the party, gathered up Shirley, and said, "Let's go." We went out to dinner and chewed it over. I decided that night to take the job.

From what I knew, Xerox seemed a company with huge opportunities that was growing at a staggering clip, though it needed some managerial help for it to continue to expand. Even for someone coming from a place as remarkable as IBM, aspects of Xerox beggared the imagination. It was the consummate success story, and it cut a very high profile indeed. *Fortune* magazine had recently written, "During the 1960s, Xerox Corp. often seemed like an elevator that could go in only one direction—up." In fact, had Xerox's growth rate of the 1960s persisted for several more decades, Xerox's sales would have exceeded the gross national product of the United States. The company boasted the highest average annual increase in earnings per share of any of the five hundred largest industrial companies during 1960–1970. Both the company and its product had been massive generators of wealth for everyone who came into contact with them. You could have sold Xerox stock in 1970 at a price sixty-six times the 1960 low. The Xerox name wasn't even on the *Fortune* 500 list until 1963, when it nudged into four hundred and twenty-third place. By now, it had soared to number sixty.

Not only did I admire Xerox's success; I also liked the culture of the company. Joe Wilson, the chairman, had a reputation for benevolence and a heartfelt concern for society that was absolutely top-of-the-heap and I had met and heard about Peter McColough, the CEO, and was very impressed with him. All in all, I saw Xerox as a place with remarkably similar objectives and people to IBM. I thought it would be an easy switch.

Soon after I told my superior at IBM that I was leaving, I got word that Frank Cary, then executive vice president, wanted to see me. I had crossed the bridge and didn't want to be talked out of my decision, so I went in with some trepidation. Loyalty was very important to me, and it was traumatic for me to be going somewhere else. I had lunch with Cary and he asked me to think about what I was doing. So I went out in my car and drove aimlessly around Westchester for about an hour. It was a beautiful, sun-splashed day. I must say I did waver a little. But I thought through the whole matter again and concluded that I had come to the right decision. I went back up to Cary's office and told him, "Well, I thought about it, and I'm going."

And so a new vista had been opened up to me, and I was all puffed up about it.

Selling office equipment had always been a part of my life. And because I had grown up in Rochester, New York, Xerox's hometown, Xerox was never all that distant from my thoughts. Tucked away in the northwestern corner of the state in a fertile agricultural region, Rochester was a sleepy place where most people owned unassuming homes separated by squares of well-barbered lawns. It was where the feminist Susan B. Anthony lived and the bandleader Mitch Miller grew up. The once-tempestuous Genesee River wiggled down its center; its falls provided the power that made the place a flour-milling center in the nineteenth century. It was perhaps the nation's first boomtown.

When you grow up in Rochester, you live in the shadow of Eastman Kodak. It seems as if the spirit of Rochester always reflected the cozy paternalism of Kodak, and in fact ever since the early 1900s the city had been known as George Eastman's town. Kodak was easily the largest employer. I remember that the *Saturday Evening Post* once described the city as the largest one-horse town in America, and I guess that was about right. Eastman himself committed suicide in 1932, leaving a note that said, "My work is done, why wait?" But what he created had a continuing impact on every phase of life in Rochester. It was quite an imposing institution and it made a big impression on everyone, including me. As I grew up, I felt I could do worse than to some day wind up working for it.

I came from a moderately well-off family. My mother had belonged to a fairly prosperous family, for her father was an accomplished and ingenious inventor. He created a gum that was pretty popular among kids and he fiddled around a fair amount with box kites. By far, his most important contribution was a check embosser that was marketed as the Todd Protectograph Machine. It would emboss the dollar amount that had been filled in on a check so that it couldn't be altered by crooks. Subsequently, he invented some paper that would change colors when you erased the writing on it or applied ink eradicator to it. He and his brother built a nice little business out of these creations that was called the Todd Company. Later on, the company was sold to Burroughs for a nice piece of change.

On my father's side, my grandfather worked as a station master in Rochester for the New York Central Railroad. My father, Wilfrid Kearns, was a mechanical engineer who graduated from Cornell and worked for the local gas company, Rochester Gas & Electric. When World War II started, he became the first employee of a new company that was formed to make carbine rifles and bomb fuses. The day the war ended, the business essentially stopped. It was transformed into another entity called the Commercial Control Corporation that made one of the first automatic typewriters as well as parts for IBM. My father became its treasurer.

I was fortunate to belong to a decidedly stable family living in a stable environment. And so I had every opportunity to succeed. Years later, I was riding in a car with Dick Munro, then the head of Time Inc., and he said, "Lightning only strikes once in a family and it hit us and the chances of it hitting twice and having one of our kids have a chance to do the same thing are slim. It's a case of how things come together to do well. Understanding that, I think, keeps you out of a lot of trouble."

And yet no one would ever consider me to be a serious student. I always got away doing as little schoolwork as possible and was satisfied to collect middling grades. I played a lot of sports, but not with any great distinction. I guess I just liked to take life a little slow and soak in all the enjoyment that I could.

I went to public high school in Brighton, a nice suburb, and then to the University of Rochester. I had a good reason for my choice of college. I had a girlfriend in high school whom I didn't want to desert just yet.

Even though I didn't like schoolbooks, I was always entrepreneurial and curious. I had a newspaper route for a while and I made a good little business out of raising rabbits. Once they were grown, I butchered them and sold them as meat, as well as to researchers at the University of Rochester. I used to annoy my father because I would jump from one interest to another; he wanted me to concentrate my energies and find something I could stick with. For a while, I was smitten by model railroad trains, and I would begin building a train only to abandon it when it was half-finished. My father, who was as disciplined as they came, would smack his head in disgust. As long as I can remember, though, I've always been a very impatient person.

I was not a model student at the University of Rochester. I guess I saw no reason to change my well-formed and quite comfortable habits. I was usually good for a C and sometimes would eke out a B. The last year I truly outdid myself and cracked the dean's list. In my junior year I decided to join the air force, but my plans were thwarted by a leg injury that kept me stuck in school. As a matter of pride, I told a lot of inquirers that I hurt my leg playing baseball. In fact, I was sleeping in my room at the fraternity house when my roommate bolted in and squirted me with a water gun. That shook me awake and I got annoyed and jumped up and started wrestling with him. During the horsing about, he managed to twist my leg severely enough to leave me limping for a while.

Around this time, I met Shirley, who was to become my wife. She was attending Wells College near Cornell. Unlike me, she was very much a nose-to-the-book type of student. When I would go up to see her, she was always studying, and I found myself forced to become more than casually acquainted with books, too. She couldn't understand at all why you would be in college and not study, whereas I always used to wonder the exact opposite. If you could get by avoiding studying, why not avoid it? Shirley had gone to the same high school but I had only known her then from a distance. I started taking her out that summer and throughout my senior year I saw a great deal of her.

Business was my major at the University of Rochester, but when I graduated I really had no idea what I wanted to do with my life. The Korean War was on and we all had to enter the service. I joined the navy. I was discharged after two years and did nothing spectacular other than washing out of navy pilot training because of air sickness. Later on, I would overcome the problem and obtain a private pilot's license and go on to enjoy flying immensely.

For some weeks I cast about for something to do. Selling seemed immediately appealing to me as my ticket into the world. The Todd Company was still in existence then and was being run by my cousin and uncle. I thought I might go to work there. However, nobody pushed it and I got the feeling that they really weren't all that interested in me. Since I was hemming and hawing, my father paid for me to travel to New York to be tested and advised by a company that counseled people on career choice. By then I had also gone for an interview with IBM at the company's Rochester branch office. As it happens, the counselor pointed me toward IBM and their extensive training program, but I had to believe that this was no coincidence. Since they knew I was talking to IBM, they doubtlessly felt they couldn't go wrong suggesting I work there.

I also tried to get a job at Kodak, as virtually any kid in Rochester would, but I didn't get past the first interview. At that time, Kodak was considerably larger than IBM and must have been looking for someone different. I was interviewed as well at the Haloid Company, the predecessor of Xerox and then a very small office equipment company, and was offered a job as a combination serviceman and seller of supplies. Unfortunately, the job and the location, Philadelphia, didn't exactly get my juices flowing.

So IBM seemed my best bet and I decided to give it a go. I was hired by the Rochester branch as a salesman. This, of course, was before computers. I would be selling electric accounting machines, which worked with punch cards and were the forerunner of the computer. In April 1954, I reported for work. In June I married Shirley.

IBM really did things right. It started you off in an exceedingly rigorous training program that was pretty much equivalent to going to graduate school. In those days IBM was not nearly as prosperous as it is today, and it showed. The first training center I went to was nothing more than an old abandoned garage in Endicott, New York, a damp river town in the western reaches of the state. The class was called machine applications. Thirty-nine of us had enrolled and we were to be there for seven weeks. The training was first-rate and the competition among the students was blatantly cut-throat. It reminded me a lot of the navy, where they posted your scores on a board outside your training room so everyone knew exactly what everyone else had gotten. At this early stage, there were no secrets at IBM about who was making it and who was flunking.

I was a married man now, and I had the fear motivator percolating inside me that if I got fired I wouldn't be able to feed my wife. As I found out, IBM liked to play on that fear instinct every chance it got, figuring that was the way to flog the best out of you. In fact, if you weren't cutting the mustard, they fired you right out of the class. I actually saw that happen. One day, one of the training managers entered our classroom, tapped one of the less-than-stellar students on his shoulder, and beckoned him to follow. That was the last we ever saw of the fellow. When his roommate got back to his room, all of the guy's stuff was gone. He had simply vanished off the face of the earth. It was like the CIA or UFOs or something.

The course taught us how to work the electric accounting machines so that we could go out and sell them. I found the training fairly difficult but manageable. You certainly didn't have to be a genius to pick it up, but it took some smarts. In the end, I wound up ranking thirteenth out of the thirty-nine students, a good showing for me, and I also made some fast friends. A few of them I see to this day.

After the class, we had to spend some time wiring boards. I was sent to the Rochester Gas & Electric Company to do my duty. Then we went to a second school where we were taught sales techniques. I finished thirteenth there, as well. During the classes, you had to do a lot of presentations in front of the other students. It was very intimidating and a real pressure-cooker environment. But I did find it exhilarating when things went smoothly.

In April 1955, I finished my training and was assigned a territory in Rochester. In many respects, I felt I had been born to sell. Ironically enough, one of my early accounts was the tiny Haloid Company. When I came calling on them, they weren't in need of anything beyond the machine they already had, so my work consisted mainly of account service. I sold them nothing at all during my entire sales stint. As it turned out, Charlie Page, the salesman who followed me, did absolutely spectacularly, because that was when the company brought out its first copier and began to grow by leaps and bounds.

I was a salesman in Rochester for two and a half years and I was probably the area's top performer for most of that time. I must admit that I had some bosses who really made a difference. There was a bar next to the office that was known as the longest in Rochester because it filled an entire street. The guys used to go there to have a few beers after work, and I dropped in a number of times myself to join in the fun. One day Bill Ellis, my boss at the time, said to me, "You know, that ship next door is going to sink and if I were you I wouldn't want to be on it when it goes down. If you're not working, you ought to be home with your family rather than wasting time drinking at a bar." That simple advice stayed with me for a long time and kept me out of a lot of mischief. Ellis also taught me how to write crisp, clear accounts, and to this day I write everything in abbreviated bullet form.

Apparently I had performed ably enough in my first test, for I was offered the chance to be the branch manager, as well as to have my own sales territory, in the little IBM office in Jamestown, New York. It was a fairly unusual territory, in that there were a number of Indian reservations we had to call on. But it was a tough territory to sell much in. There were thirty-five people at most in the office, and I would be their boss, my first shot at management. John Raines was the district manager and was probably the best boss I ever had in terms of learning. He was a no-nonsense type who would regularly send me some pretty blunt notes. I'd almost be afraid to open them. My secretary once told me that she didn't know whether he was trying to make me or break me.

As it turned out, I was in Jamestown only a year when I was offered the chance to go into the administrative training program. That was a great opportunity because you got to work for one of the senior executives. We all knew it was a principal way that IBM tried to find and nurture talent. Not that I knew I had any great talent. I was far from cocky about my abilities and was always totally surprised by new job offers. In fact, whenever I was called in to be told of a promotion, I always feared that I was about to be canned.

My assignment in the administrative training program was to work for the eastern regional manager in New York, which was quite a change from calling on Indian reservations. My wife and I bought a house in Chappaqua and I went to work for Elmer Dohrman, as well as taking management classes in an estate IBM was renting in Sleepy Hollow. This was the first time I played a management simulation game, and I was really turned on.

After several years as branch manager in White Plains, New York, I became a district manager in upstate New York, with Rochester part of my territory. I was twenty-nine, and there were branch managers who were forty and fifty, so I felt lucky. I had a very youthful appearance then and I used to buy suits with vests so I would look older. One day I called on Haloid Xerox, because the company was really growing explosively, to see how they were planning to use a lot of equipment they had ordered from us. If nothing else, I wanted to be sure they were prepared to use it. As I reviewed this long list of equipment with one of the executives there, I said, "I am clearly pleased by all these orders but want to make sure you are fully prepared to use it and that we are supporting it adequately." The guy looked me straight in the eye and said, "Sonny, I'll order it and you deliver it. Good day!"

There was a lot of moving around at IBM, and I moved next to New York as sales manager for accounting machines in the office products division and after that to Washington and joined the federal government region. Then I was made a regional vice president in New York, which meant I was really breaking out of the pack. A couple of years later, I became vice president of marketing in the data processing division. I worked on the unbundling task force for about nine months, which was one of the most important learning experiences of my career.

So I had progressed fairly rapidly in the ranks at IBM. Part of it I attribute to the fact that I was a good salesman. Some years, I was the leading producer in my district. I brought enthusiasm and high energy to the job, and I naturally got along with people. At the same time, I liked making decisions. I saw a lot of other people at IBM who studied things to death. They always had to get one more fact. I was never like that.

But I was also very lucky. I could not have been at IBM at a better time. Its growth was just explosive. It was the perfect setting, offering excellent training, good managers, and wonderful people. It was a marvelous company.

Who knows how long I might have remained at IBM if, in 1970 and 1971, business had not begun to sour and Shirley hadn't begun to give me a lot of grief about how many hours I was working. But the economy was bad and there was a significant slowdown in corporate business. The 360 line had essentially run its string out. My boss was shoved aside and someone else was brought in to replace him, adding to my displeasure. I was a little disappointed that I didn't get the job, though I realized I shouldn't have. If you need some change to shake things up, you don't just put the number-two guy in the slot. If I were faced with the decision, I would have done the same thing. Then Xerox came calling, and I was able to put all this behind me.

* * *

If I were going to work for Xerox, I had to make a few bargains. Shirley was very supportive about the new job, but she also had a few not-insignificant concerns, and we talked about them and struck a deal. For some years, she had been troubled by all the moving that is part and parcel of a corporate career, and she was dismayed as our six children got older at how rarely I was around the house to spend time with them. So she said she would enthusiastically support my taking the Xerox job if I agreed to two very explicit conditions. One was that we move just twice more. Since she knew I would probably have to go out into the field somewhere, she would move wherever that was and then she would move back to this area once I was recalled to headquarters. And she made it perfectly clear that that would be it. Any more moves beyond those two would be without her. The second condition was a trickier one, but I could hardly argue against it. She asked that I please be home by six-thirty to have dinner with the children whenever I was not away on a business trip, and whenever I didn't have any true emergency at the office. I didn't need to do any thinking to consent to those conditions. They were the least a family could ask. And I would abide by them, with a little helpful prodding now and then from Shirley, from that day on.

Shirley, I must say, has always been very good at getting me to draw a better balance between work and family. She's a tough taskmaster. One important reason is that she has zero awe of me, which is the way it should be. Once I said something sharp at home without thinking and she turned to me and snapped, "Would you say something like that to anyone at work?" I said no. "Then don't say it here," she said. I've always liked the quip by Harry Truman: "As President of the United States I'm everything. As Harry Truman, I'm just like everyone else." I think a lot of people in business don't understand that, but in our house no one is ever allowed to be a big deal.

When I met with Archie McCardell and Peter McColough, Xerox's chief executive, in preparation for joining the company, I made a point of spelling out what my intentions were, because I didn't want them to have any false delusions about why I was taking the job. I told them I was forty years old and knew with pretty good certainty that I wasn't going to become the head of IBM. I had a promising career going there, but it didn't seem destined to take me to the top. In fact, when I was mulling over the pluses and minuses of going to Xerox, I wrote down on a sheet of yellow paper that on a scale of one to a hundred, my odds were about two of becoming the chief executive. At Xerox, I put my odds at twenty. All the same, I said that I was very ambitious and I would certainly like to run a company some day. But they didn't have to worry, because if I didn't vault to the top at Xerox I wouldn't leave. I made it abundantly clear that I wasn't job-shopping. They just took my little spiel in and didn't really respond. I didn't ask them my odds of becoming chief executive of Xerox and they didn't volunteer any odds.

My feelings about Xerox were positive. I didn't see the company as having any serious problems, and I thought the issues I would be dealing with were eminently manageable. One of my customs was not to try to do other people's jobs. I used to tell people who worked with me at IBM, "We are not strategists for the whole company. We are implementers for our region." So I was going to abide by that same belief at Xerox. I was going to focus on the baggage I was given to deal with and let others worry about the rest of the luggage.

With that little talk with Archie and Peter, I formally changed companies for the first time in my career. I fully expected it to be the last time. For the life of me, I couldn't imagine any reason I would want to leave Xerox. I thought the job would bring some challenges but also tremendous satisfaction. Little did I know how hard those challenges would be and how long it would take to fully realize those satisfactions.

2. The Unwanted Product

EVERYONE TAKES PHOTOCOPYING FOR granted these days, but it's surprising to most people how recent a development the copier is and how only a few decades ago carbon paper and mimeograph machines were the principal means to reproduce documents. Everything about the origins of Xerox and the office copier exude the whiff of the proverbial old-fashioned tale of the lonely perseverance of an ingenious man. The noble yet chance way in which it all came about laid the foundation of the Xerox culture for decades to come.

It's often said that people and institutions become prisoners of their pasts, and, in looking back, much of what happened to Xerox during the years I was there was dictated by what Xerox had once been. Misapprehensions about the past have a way of determining the future. As Xerox's size and reach swelled to almost unimaginable proportions, its former ways continued to tug at it.

There couldn't be a purer Walter Mitty story than that of Chester Carlson. He started life with very little going for him. He was born in Seattle in 1906 to sickly parents. When he was seventeen, his mother died of tuberculosis. His father, a much-traveled barber, was hobbled by both arthritis and tuberculosis and was destined to die young. Rarely was much money lying around the Carlson household. The family tested different climates to soothe the father's condition, before moving to a rented farm in a dilapidated section of San Bernardino, California. The painfully shy Carlson rode a wobbly bicycle to the local school, where at times he was the sole student. During recess, he would sit alone and swat flies. There was nobody to play with. Inside, the teacher would stare vacantly into space.

Carlson took part-time jobs beginning when he was a skinny twelve-year-old, and by the time he was fourteen he was chiefly responsible for scraping out the marginal living his family survived on. He would rise at five o'clock, shake the sleep out of his eyes, and go wash store windows before school began. In the afternoons, he would sweep out bank and newspaper offices. When he was a junior in high school, he toiled as a printer's devil as well as a janitor. In his senior year, he spent his weekends working in a chemical laboratory. Despite the meager resources of the family, Carlson managed to attend junior college at Riverside and then obtained a degree in physics at the California Institute of Technology.

It was now 1930, and jobs were all but impossible to find. Carlson mailed letters to eighty-two companies; not a single offer came back. Finally, he landed work in New York in the patent department of P.R. Mallory & Co., an Indianapolis electrical company. Much of the job consisted of retyping manuscripts and sending out drawings to photocopying firms. This was costly and dreadfully slow, and the process grated on Carlson. As he would later recall, "In the course of my patent work I frequently had need for copies of patent specifications and drawings, and there was no really convenient way of getting them at that time." It dawned on Carlson how useful it would be if offices were equipped with a device that could make copies at the press of a button. With total disdain for the difficulty involved, Carlson, then a large-framed, nearsighted man of twenty-nine, decided he would go ahead and invent just such a machine.

Office reproduction methods did, of course, exist, though none contained the ingredients that swam in Carlson's head. In 1887 the A.B. Dick Company had introduced the first mimeograph machine, which regular users came to remember for making such awful-smelling copies. Mr. Dick, a former lumberman, had been drawn to the machine for reasons similar to Carlson's. He had gotten exasperated copying his price lists by hand. Mr. Dick tried to invent a copying machine himself, before giving up in frustration, and finally acquired the rights to the mimeograph from its inventor, Thomas Edison. Yet other people initially felt differently about the need for such a device, and didn't see the point of making lots of copies of office documents. The first users of mimeograph machines, as it turned out, were churches, municipal offices, schools, and Boy Scout troops.

Fortunately, the lackadaisical attitude toward copying changed rather dramatically in time and office reproduction began to grow swiftly. After 1890, the typewriter and carbon paper became familiar sights. Within another decade, mimeographing was a commonly practiced process. The offset printing press, which was able to produce copies far superior in quality to mimeographs, began to find its way into sizable offices in the 1930s.

Like the mimeograph, the offset press was technically a duplicator, not a copier. To use it, it was necessary to create a special master page before you could begin making copies. This was expensive and took a lot of time, and thus it only made sense to use an offset press when you needed many copies. There were a sprinkling of alternatives. Around 1910, sundry photographic machines had appeared that operated free of master pages. The best-known was the Photostat. But these were cumbersome and expensive, too, and thus they were confined to copying things like legal documents. Until after 1950, in fact, the only truly decent way of making a copy of a letter was by sitting down in front of a typewriter and rolling in a trusty piece of carbon paper.

Chester Carlson was living in a cramped one-room apartment. Nights and weekends, he holed up in a makeshift laboratory in the closet of his apartment. For three years, he investigated how light affects matter, because he became convinced that his copying device would have to revolve around light. Carlson possessed an intensity that never let up. Bent on making more money, he was now going to law school at night, and since he couldn't afford books he studied at the New York library. While there, he also read just about every technical book he could locate on photography, printing, and photostating. The strain on his eyes paid off, for one afternoon he tripped across something called photoconductivity. He learned that you could alter the electrical conductivity of a few materials (including sulphur) by exposing them to light. After that, Carlson started playing around with sulphur on his stove, mostly producing nothing more than copies of pretty repulsive odors.

Carlson meant well, but he was not an ideal tenant. By now, neighbors of his had come to expect bizarre doings from him and wrote him off as a nut. They learned to pinch their nose when they passed by his door. Any time neighbors felt their apartments shaking, they knew it wasn't an earthquake; it was just something exploding again over at Chester Carlson's. Yet his behavior proved a decent way to meet women. A girl who lived in the building rang Carlson's bell one day to yell at him. He sheepishly pulled open the door, dressed in a rubber apron. Before she had fully expressed her rage, she became smitten by the bashful little man with the hangdog look. Before long, they were married.

Carlson's closet was a frustrating place to work in the best of times, and with a wife now in the house, it no longer was practical. Half of the burners on the kitchen stove were reserved for Carlson's equipment, making cooking dinner a challenge. One day Carlson accidentally spilled sulphur all over the stove and both he and his wife nearly passed out. Another night, the chemicals he was working with burst into flames and he and his wife had to battle the blaze for some time before they managed to extinguish it. Enough was enough. He moved his laboratory into a small, drab room owned by his mother-in-law that lay behind a beauty parlor and above a bar in Astoria, Queens.

After a while, Carlson, who was not much of a technician, realized he needed help. He hired Otto Kornei, an unemployed German refugee physicist, whom he located from a position-wanted ad the German had placed in an electronics trade journal. The two of them kept to a grueling pace. Experiment after experiment was tried, as many as could be managed on their budget of ten dollars a month for materials.

One chilly October day, everything came together just right. First they covered a metal plate with sulphur, and then Carlson printed the date and location—10–22–38 Astoria—on a glass slide. To give the plate an electrical charge, he briskly rubbed a cotton cloth across it (later on, he would switch from cotton to rabbit's fur). Then he clasped the slide and plate together and held the two beneath a bright floodlight for several seconds. He separated the slide and the plate and dropped a yellowish powder on the plate. When he blew off the excess, a fuzzy image of the message appeared. Vibrating with excitement, Carlson held a piece of waxed paper tightly against the plate. When he removed it, he beheld the very first electrostatic copy.

Carlson stared at it for a long time, overwhelmed by what it meant. He flashed Kornei an amazed look. To make sure of what they had, the two men carefully repeated the experiment and found it still worked. Then they went out to a modest lunch to celebrate.

Carlson was actually much happier than Kornei. In Kornei's mind there glimmered a pale line of doubt. He thought the image was pretty bad and close to illegible, and thus he was skeptical that the process would ever lead to anything significant. Shortly afterward, hoping to put himself on firmer ground, he took a job at IBM. (Nevertheless, Carlson always felt thankful for Kornei's role, and years later, when Xerox stock was one of the hottest buys on the New York Stock Exchange, he sent Kornei a gift of a hundred shares.)

The Carlson process essentially broke down into five steps. First, a special photoconductive surface was given an electrostatic charge, which it would hold only in the dark. Once exposed to light, the charge would disappear. Next, a printed page was placed in close proximity to this surface and light was shone on it so that an image of the printing was projected onto the surface. (Because of the light, the surface kept its charge only in those places occupied by the dark ink.) The third step was to dust the surface with powdered ink, which stuck to the charged portions, creating a mirror image of the printed page. This image was then transferred to a blank sheet of paper. Finally, to make it permanent, heat was applied, which melted the ink and fused it to the page.

Carlson applied for and received a succession of patents for his invention and then proceeded to try to sell it. Over the next six years, while continuing to work for Mallory, he offered the rights to the process to every important office-equipment company in the country, only to be turned down each time. Among others, he was rebuffed by Remington Rand, RCA, General Electric, and IBM. To be sure, many of the demonstrations Carlson did for technicians left something to be desired. Frequently the images were smudged or the paper developed heat blisters or it was discolored.

Carlson was no stranger to disappointment, and he felt plenty of it now. Adding to his woes, the arthritis that plagued his father struck him as well. He ached constantly. Nevertheless, he pressed on. Then, in 1944, somebody from the Battelle Memorial Institute, a nonprofit industrial research organization based in Columbus, Ohio, happened to drop by Mallory and bump into Carlson. Carlson told him about his invention and showed him a few crude copies. His eyes widened and he said he thought the people back in Columbus might want to hear about that. Soon afterward, Battelle agreed to spend three thousand dollars on further development work in exchange for three-quarters of any future royalties realized from the idea. An elated Carlson took the deal. Of nearly two dozen companies that Carlson had pitched, Battelle alone saw that there might be something to his copying process.

The Haloid Company of Rochester was a very small, very sedate, very undistinguished maker of photographic paper. It had been founded by four businessmen in 1906 (the same year Chester Carlson was born), and in its early days it consisted of a dozen employees working in a grimy shop above the C.P. Ford Shoe factory. The new company's name came from haloid salts, which were an ingredient of an emulsion that was used to coat photographic paper. The company grew, but not by much. By the mid-1940s, Haloid boasted no more than about fifteen million dollars in revenues. Haloid, like all makers of photographic paper, lived very much in the long shadow of Eastman Kodak. Haloid wasn't even located in a particularly good part of Rochester.

Haloid's boss, however, was a remarkable man named Joseph Chamberlain Wilson. I don't know if I've ever met a wise man, but Joe Wilson may have been one. Wilson's grandfather, also named Joseph C. Wilson, had been one of the founders of Haloid (he also occupied his time as a pawnbroker and as the mayor of Rochester), and his father, always called J.R., was the president of the company. The younger Wilson had graduated from the University of Rochester and Harvard Business School, and wasn't overly interested in going to work for someplace as small as Haloid, where children at company picnics were handed T-shirts that read "My Daddy Works at Haloid." But his father persuaded him that because of its small size, Haloid offered many challenges and considerable potential. And so in 1945 he came aboard as an assistant sales manager and, by the time he turned thirty-six, he had succeeded his father as the company's president. He decorated his office with flowered wallpaper and frequently sat at his desk eating peanut-butter-and-jelly sandwiches for lunch.

Wilson was an unorthodox businessman. He cared as much about emphasizing human values as he did about maximizing profits. A vigorous man with a ready smile, he believed that a modern executive had to embody a personal commitment to the good of society as well as to a sound economy.

Wilson was an extremely bright man, who quoted Browning and Keats. He didn't look up the quotes that day to fit them into a speech. He read Browning and Keats every night (as well as James Bond mysteries). While making a sales pitch for his product, Wilson once quoted in Latin a homily from a Montaigne essay: "*Fortis imaginatio generat casum*" (A strong imagination begets the event).

And he was guided by a very simple philosophy. Wilson used to say that most people grossly overestimated what they could do in the short run. The truth was, most people couldn't accomplish much of anything in the short run. But they also grossly underestimated what they could achieve in the long run. He felt that if they put their minds to it, they could accomplish a great deal indeed. And Wilson and Peter McColough really lived according to that conviction.

When Wilson died of a heart attack in 1971, while lunching with Nelson Rockefeller, then the governor of New York, and his wife, Happy, a tattered index card was found in his wallet. He had carried it for many years, for it succinctly summarized his goals in life: "To be a whole man; to attain serenity through the creation of a family life of uncommon richness; through leadership of a business which brings happiness to its workers, serves well its customers and brings prosperity to its owners; by aiding a society threatened by fratricidal division to gain unity."

For a leader, Joe Wilson was not a natural extrovert. In fact, he was strikingly bashful. When he first joined Haloid, he was so painfully shy that whenever the women working there spoke to him in the hallway he would blush. But to be an effective business leader, he felt he had to become more outgoing. It was a treacherous transition for him, but he was determined to succeed. And so, for hours on end, he would practice talking in front of a mirror to try to cultivate a more natural speaking style.

The episode that finally got him over the hurdle and put him at ease before an audience occurred when he was in his early thirties. He had been asked to chair one of the divisions of the Community Chest drive in Rochester and he readily accepted. Good causes were irresistible to him, and, stage fright or not, there was no way he could have said no. The Community Chest practice then was that everyone gathered at the community hall during the week of the drive and for five straight days each division head would give a talk before four or five hundred people. Wilson fretted that he would bore people, and so in the days leading up to drive week, he beseeched all of his friends for their best jokes and anecdotes. Quite a supply came rolling in.

The time came for him to deliver his first address and he proceeded to tell one of the cute stories he had picked up. For the first time in his life, he got quite a nice laugh. The next day, he told one of his other jokes and received another good response. He went home and felt just great. Who knew? Maybe he had a future as a stand-up comic. Things continued well for the rest of the week, until Friday rolled around. This would be Wilson's final talk and he had saved his very best story for the occasion. The anecdote was a little bit risqué, but he sensed that it would be perfect for the audience. He got up there and, brimming with confidence, told the anecdote. There was deathly silence. There wasn't the hint of a smile in the entire audience. Wilson was mortified, and he quickly wrapped up his address and beat a hasty retreat back to his seat. Once he got there, he learned that the Catholic bishop and the Episcopal bishop had come to the head table and everyone in the audience was too uncomfortable to laugh at the off-color joke. Oddly enough, that jolting experience cured him of his terror. After that, he figured there could be no worse experience and so he decided, why be nervous?

After the Second World War, Haloid found itself under pressure from stepped-up competition and rising labor costs. At the same time, the government began drastically cutting back on its substantial wartime orders from Haloid. The company was also jittery about its big-time neighbor, Eastman Kodak. Haloid executives believed that anytime it felt like it, Kodak could put Haloid out of business, and the only reason it didn't was that it was simply too small a speck to care about.

To try to build a secure future for itself, the company began hunting for new products. Wilson asked his chief of research, a man named John H. Dessauer, to stay attuned to all new patents and to read closely all technical publications. Who knew where something might turn up? Dessauer was up to the task. He studied more than a thousand patents and read a hundred-odd technical journals with the same interest that other people read the *Saturday Evening Post*. One day he happened to be looking through the April 1945 issue of Kodak's *Monthly Abstract Bulletin*. It contained an abstract on the electrophotography process invented by Chester Carlson that was under development at Battelle. "Hmmm," Dessauer wondered. "Could this be something?"

Dessauer convinced Wilson to go along with him to Columbus to see the process. Once he had, Wilson was enthusiastic. He figured that if the approach could lead to a reasonably priced office copier that could make copies simply without special techniques it could be a good seller. He related his interest to a new friend of his, Sol M. Linowitz, a young lawyer who was trying to start a new radio station that would air liberal views. The hope was that it would offset the distinctly conservative opinions of the local Gannett newspapers. Wilson asked Linowitz to look into the Battelle research. Several trips to Columbus later, an agreement was reached in early 1947 that gave Haloid rights to manufacture products based on the Carlson process in exchange for royalties to Carlson and Battelle. It also committed Haloid to share with Battelle in the work and the costs of development.

Years later, Wilson would say of that momentous decision: "I would have to be psychoanalyzed to say if I would take the same risk again. It's when you're very young and naïve that you have the courage to make the right decisions."

One of the first things Haloid did was suggest that Battelle coin a new name for the Carlson process, for it didn't feel electrophotography sounded like anything particularly new or exciting. In 1948 a professor of classical languages at Ohio State University was consulted. By combining two words from classical Greek (*xeros* for dry and *graphein* for writing), he came up with xerography, or dry writing.

In 1949, Haloid introduced its first commercial xerographic copier. This maiden machine was known as the Model A or, around Haloid offices, as the Ox Box. It was an immense thing that consisted of three distinct machines. It was not automatic and so incredibly complicated that even a quite adept operator took two or three minutes to make one copy. The operator had to perform some pretty heroic tasks. Every time he wanted to make a copy, he had to lug a heavy plate from one machine to the next. The instruction manual, which described the thirty-nine steps for making good copies, was worse than learning Latin.

A few Model A's were shipped out and they came back practically the next day. Everyone felt they were just too complicated. That might have been the end of the product entirely, except that the Ox Box turned out to be a good way to make paper masters for offset printing presses and so it attracted a small market for that use. Ford Motor Company was among those that found it to be a highly cost-effective alternative.

Over the next ten years or so, Haloid introduced a small number of other xerographic devices. There were the Foto-Flo Model C Photo-Copying Machine, the Xerox Lith-Master, and the Copyflo machine. In one of those odd twists, my grandfather's Todd Company was retained by Haloid to manufacture the Copyflo machine. In terms of sales, none of these products did all that much better than the Ox Box. They, too, were awkward, complex products. The world still awaited the easy-to-use office copier that Carlson's breakthrough had promised.

As Haloid and Battelle continued to work on the development of xerography, a rush of devices appeared that could make copies of office papers without using a master page. They were far more practical than previous devices, since they operated at a cost of just a few cents per copy, and they drew on varying technologies. There was Minnesota Mining & Manufacturing's Thermo-Fax, introduced in 1950, which used heat from an infrared lamp to create images on special paper. American Photocopy's Dial-A-Matic Autostat came out in 1952 and used a process similar to ordinary photography. Kodak's Verifax, which appeared in 1953, used chemical developers.

Yet all of these pioneer devices were badly flawed. First of all, they worked only with specially treated paper that had to be bought from the manufacturer. And the copies themselves were pretty poor. Both the Verifax and Autostat machines produced soggy copies that had to be dried off to be of any use. They didn't smell too great, either. Copies made on a Thermo-Fax were so sensitive to heat that they would get darker and darker as they lay on your office desk.

While Haloid's researchers plugged away, the company tried its best to recruit young and talented people who would help it reap the rewards of xerography. In 1954 Peter McColough was a thirty-two-year-old vice president of the Lehigh Navigation Coal Sales Company in Philadelphia, and, though he was making good money, he was eager to find something more thrilling than selling coal. Thus he came to Rochester for a job interview at Haloid. It didn't take long for the ragamuffin nature of the company to become evident to him. As he was ushered into the office of Jack Hartnett, the vice president of sales, McColough couldn't help being struck by certain details. The first thing he noticed was that Hartnett's bookshelves were nothing more than painted orange crates, and standing on his desk was a working man's lunchbox. If this was the way an executive lived, McColough thought, what kind of company was this anyway? He wouldn't have been surprised if the junior managers worked in tents.

The truth of the matter was that other employees, upon being hired, were typically told that their first task would be to build themselves a desk to work on. The place did normally furnish already-constructed chairs. Almost every spare dollar that Haloid had was plowed into the development of xerography. If employees had to be somewhat inconvenienced, well, so be it.

Later in the day of his interview, McColough was introduced to Wilson, and Wilson totally captivated him. In his boundlessly optimistic way, Wilson told McColough that Haloid was working hard on a copier process that he was convinced would one day compete with offset printing. Xerography was incredibly crude then, but Wilson saw it as having the promise of becoming a truly valuable process. That was Joe Wilson's vision. It was a lot to swallow, and McColough didn't swallow too much of it that day. But he was struck by Wilson's conviction. He was also impressed by Wilson as a person and by his commitment to the community and to his country.

In due course, Wilson offered McColough a job, and he took it. He had to accept quite a substantial pay cut from his position at Lehigh Navigation; he had been making about thirty thousand a year in Philadelphia and Haloid could pay him only about half that much, along with a twenty-five-hundred-dollar annual bonus. But McColough reasoned that he was young and that within no more than five years it would undoubtedly become clear whether Wilson's vision had any merit to it or not. After all, he was only thirty-two; he figured he could afford the time.

The development work on the Carlson process moved along in fits and starts. The scientists at Battelle and Haloid were constantly beset by puzzling technical problems. During one depressed period, in fact, Haloid pondered selling most of its xerography rights to IBM. But the deal never came to fruition. In 1955 a new agreement was drafted under which Haloid gained full title to the Carlson patents in exchange for fifty thousand shares of Haloid stock.

The xerography development costs were mounting to stupendous levels. Between 1947 and 1960, Haloid exhausted about seventy-five million dollars on xerography, far more than it earned during those years. To keep up with these staggering expenses, it had to borrow heavily as well as try to sell newly issued shares of its stock to anyone who would purchase them. To say the least, it was not an obvious buy. Nevertheless, one of the most sympathetic acquirers was the University of Rochester, which snapped up a large bundle of shares for its endowment fund. The price the school paid would equate to about fifty cents today. Meanwhile, Wilson and other company executives agreed to accept the bulk of their pay in stock rather than cash. Some of them made still further sacrifices. They lent the company money out of their personal savings accounts and even offered up the mortgages on their houses. Among those pitching in was Sol Linowitz, who had become one of Wilson's key advisers. (As it happened, when I was in high school, I used to date the Linowitzes' baby-sitter.) He was put in charge of the company's all-important patent arrangements, and would get deeply involved in guiding the company into international affiliations. Eventually, he would serve as chairman of the board. Many years later, Sol and I became very good friends.

In 1955 Joe Wilson made another important decision. He decided the company should develop an overseas business to use the patents there. At the time, the company was principally an American and Canadian company. Wilson felt that if Haloid didn't develop an overseas presence, it would lose its patent protection there, for it held patents in the important European countries. In 1956 he persuaded an English motion picture firm, the J. Arthur Rank Organization, to launch a joint venture with Haloid that was called Rank Xerox. It was based in London, since England was the major market overseas. The venture was granted the exclusive rights to exploit the xerographic patents throughout the world, except in America and Canada. At this time, of course, xerography was far from a proven process. In fact, when Haloid took a machine to London to demonstrate it to Rank executives, it didn't even work.

The machine that would eventually become known as the 914 (because it copied sheets of paper nine inches by fourteen inches) was originally supposed to be small enough to fit on top of a desk. In fairly short order, it was evident that to do all it was supposed to do, the copier would have to be even bigger than a desk.

The problems that cropped up during the development were endlessly frustrating. One was the matter of the sticking paper. When a sheet of paper comes into contact with a charged photoreceptor, something like static electricity is created and the paper sticks to the photoreceptor. The company's engineers were stumped over how to get the paper off. One afternoon, an engineer named John Rutkus was pumping up a bicycle tire at his house when a brainstorm hit him. He thought perhaps the answer might be to have little nozzles emit puffs of air to lift up the edge of each sheet of paper. He placed a piece of paper on the hood of his car. He shot air at it from his bicycle pump. The paper took off. Just like that, Haloid had its solution.

Another difficulty had to do with cleaning away the residue of powdered ink, or toner, that was employed to form images. After a copy was made, a fair amount of toner remained on the photoreceptor. To scrub it off, a rotating fur brush was created. But what fur to use? Raccoon and beaver were tried but neither worked particularly well.

Trial and error finally led the engineers to the stomach fur of Australian rabbits. The length of the fur had to be just so; if it were too short or too long it would foul things up. One of the Haloid engineers found himself lugging a small rabbit pelt to a Rochester furrier accustomed to making fur coats and having him trim the thing to the proper length. The furrier could only wonder: what woman was this for?

Everything about the 914 was technologically complex, and in fact salesmen would tell customers that the copier was more complicated than a car. As a result, a lot of things kept going wrong. The most prevalent malfunction was the jamming of the copy paper. This was known as a "mispuff." Each piece of paper was lifted into position to be copied by a little puff of air, but sometimes the puff went awry, leading to a jam. When a bad mispuff occurred, paper might actually brush against some of the hot fuser rollers. The sheet would catch fire, sending white smoke billowing out of the machine, and causing onlookers to grow rather uneasy.

Indeed, one of the nastier tendencies of the 914 was its periodic insistence on erupting into flames, not an especially strong selling point. (Ralph Nader, who acquired one of the first 914s, was enraged for years about the problem.) Looking for a practical solution, the engineers came up with a fire extinguisher that could be attached to the copiers. When the marketing department caught wind of this plan, it developed apoplexy. How could the sales force possibly tell customers that they needed to have fire extinguishers always at the ready in their offices? They'd imagine their buildings melting down in giant infernos, people stampeding out the doors in panic. The marketing people couldn't even bring themselves to use the word "fire" in conjunction with copiers. Whenever forced to talk about the repugnant problem, they liked to say "scorching." And, in the end, a deal was struck. The engineers could go ahead and attach fire extinguishers to the copiers, but they would be called scorch eliminators.

A lot of things around Haloid were less than ideal for producing a revolutionary new product. And a lot of those things had to do with not having much money. Engineers were testing prototypes of the 914 twenty-four hours a day, which was a good idea, except that the landlord of the building where the testing was conducted shut off the heat at five o'clock in the evening. Haloid didn't care to come up with the money to keep it on. So once the evening rolled around the engineers would shrug into hunting jackets and boots and keep at it. The members of the optical group had to work out of the basement of a Masonic temple.

Finally, Haloid was nearly done with the development of the 914 and ready to manufacture something. However, it had no true factories of its own, for there had never been particularly heavy demand for its early copiers. Worried about the risk of little Haloid bringing the 914 to market by itself, Wilson decided to investigate some more conservative approaches. After all, if the 914 proved to be a flop, the stockholders would be after his scalp. He went calling on IBM and asked it if it might want to invest in a joint venture. Not sure just what the prospects were for xerography, IBM retained Arthur D. Little, a well-respected management-consulting firm based in Boston, to figure out how large the market was for an office copier.

Haloid felt reasonably comfortable that there would be an appetite for its product, though it based this confidence on a few rather informal surveys conducted by some of its salesmen among people who owned earlier copying machines. For the most part, the feedback was positive. The most uplifting response came the day one of the salesmen dropped in on a government office that had a crude copier. He wondered how much paper the office used. "You mean, how many carloads?" he was told. He really liked that answer.

In their own methodical way, the people at Arthur D. Little arrived at a much more sour prognosis. The way they saw it, the size and high price of the copier were deadly drawbacks. It was important for some offices to make copies, the consultants agreed, but that demand could be met by at best five thousand machines. It was their informed opinion that the 914 had no future. That was enough for IBM to hear. It passed on the joint venture. Many years later, Thomas Watson, Jr., who succeeded his father as IBM's head, would say that one of the decisions that his father most regretted was failing to seize the opportunity to become involved in xerography at that early juncture.

Wilson wasn't ecstatic about the response, but there was no way he was going to back off now. And so Haloid would go it alone. In 1959 the first production model of the 914 came lumbering off the assembly line. It was a fearsome thing. It was nearly the size of a small U-Haul and weighed about six hundred and fifty pounds. Workers wondered how it would ever fit through an office door.

By now, the company's name had been changed to Haloid Xerox. Several years before, Haloid had adopted the trademark "Xerox," a word with no real meaning other than being an abbreviated form of xerography. Wilson admitted it was an imitation of another meaningless word, "Kodak." (In 1961 Haloid Xerox would change its name to the Xerox Corporation.) The company had hired a consultant to help it think up a name, but none of those suggested quite satisfied Wilson. So one Sunday morning, as was their custom, Wilson and Sol Linowitz went for a stroll. It was a way for them to chat about the company, public issues, and their families. They came to a clearing and Linowitz spied a big "Kodak" sign. The same thought hit both men. George Eastman had called his company Kodak because it was short and started and ended with his favorite letter. Why not do the same thing with xerography? And thus "Xerox" was coined.

As it happens, quite a number of Haloid consultants argued vehemently against the name change. They thought Xerox sounded weird and feared no one would be able to pronounce it. A few people worried that the name might connote something not tremendously cherished in financial circles: "zero."

In the fall of 1959, Haloid Xerox was ready to demonstrate its 914 to its sales force and engineers. Jack Hartnett, then the chairman of the board, had the honor of generating the first copy. He told the audience that he was happy to see that the engineers had finally gotten around to building something he could work. He laid a document on the copier, closed the cover, and pushed the copying button. When the paper shot out of the slot, he held it up for everyone to see. It was blank.

There was complete silence. Then David Curtin, the head of public relations, came over, lifted the cover off the document, and smiled. "Jack," he said, "you put the document in blank side down."

Hartnett sheepishly flipped it over, repeated the process, and this time succeeded in turning out a perfect copy.

Now Haloid Xerox—its annual sales were running to just thirty-three million dollars—was ready to demonstrate its 914 automatic copier to the world. On September 16, the machine was first shown to the public at the Sherry-Netherland Hotel. Two copiers were on hand. One caught fire. John Dessauer, then executive vice president, nearly had a stroke. But the other one worked just fine, and the company got some good press. *Business Week* put the 914 on its cover.

The following March, the first shipments of the new copier began. Haloid Xerox was about to find out who was crazy: all the other big-name companies who had snubbed the idea, or Haloid.

It was quickly evident that the company was going to have to do more than merely tell people that Xerox machines were now available and then wait while businesses rushed to get out their checkbooks. David Curtin was entrusted with gaining publicity for the new product and the new Xerox name. He found his assignment far from easy. Wherever he went, he was greeted with considerable confusion and even outright derision. In particular, people didn't know what to make of the odd Xerox name. Some thought that the company was selling a mouthwash or an antifreeze or possibly a laxative.

Disheartened by the cruel jokes, Curtin wrote an impassioned letter to Wilson urging him to change the name of the company. He didn't much care what it was changed to, as long as it wasn't Xerox. Name it Haloid again, or call it the Joe Wilson Manufacturing Company.

After he had digested the letter, Wilson summoned Curtin to his office and told him that he was sympathetic to his problems, but he needed to give the new name more time. Then he told Curtin a little story about the celebrated conductor Leopold Stokowski. When he came over to this country, many people advised him to change his name because it was simply too difficult to spell. He refused. "But why?" people insisted. "It will make things so much easier." Stokowski said that the problem would resolve itself. "When they hear my music," he said, "they will learn my name."

"When people see our product," Wilson said, "they will learn our name."

3. Xerox Grows Up

THE INTRODUCTION OF THE 914 was a startling event to behold. It was as if an automobile maker had come out with a rocket car. When the 914 appeared, all the copiers that were on the market were small enough to squeeze on the top of a good-sized desk, and they sold for between three hundred and four hundred dollars. Kodak offered a line of machines, as did 3M, and there was a German product that had achieved respectable market penetration as well. When they went out on their calls, salesmen for these companies would lug the machines around under their arms and would merrily demonstrate them right on the premises. The prices were cheap enough to make them eminently affordable, although the copying itself could begin to add up to some real money. Because of the high cost of the coated paper being used, the expense typically ranged from ten to fifteen cents a copy—and not a very good copy at that.

Now picture the 914. Painted beige and looking roughly like an L-shaped table, its daunting weight and size—it measured nearly four feet high—meant that nobody short of Hercules was going to carry it anywhere. In fact, some people who encountered 914s in their offices complained that the machine didn't work. They actually thought it was something to warm coffee on. Who could blame them? That's what it looked like.

Although the 914 was extraordinarily expensive to manufacture, it used ordinary plain paper and it was remarkably simple to use. All one had to do was place a sheet of paper (or, for that matter, a ring or a Barbie doll) face down on the glass window on top of the machine. By twisting a dial, the number of copies desired was selected, up to a maximum of fifteen. Then one pushed a button, and, in about fifteen seconds, the first copy fluttered into a tray. Subsequent copies took a little over seven seconds. That utter simplicity of operation was what would cause a worldwide revolution in the production, flow, and distribution of information.

The year before the 914 was introduced, the marketing people at Haloid Xerox had already begun doing some spadework to pique interest in xerography. They orchestrated a traveling product show called Copyrama, which brought the latest in duplicating equipment to eleven cities around the country. People got to see the Copyflo machine and flat-plate xerography equipment, and there was a great deal of press coverage. Once the 914 was ready for market, though, Xerox had a puzzling problem. Given the heft of the machine, it was maddeningly difficult to demonstrate to prospective customers. At the same time, there weren't all that many of the machines around to demonstrate. When the sales force first began selling the copier, only a few 914s even existed. The factory turned out a mere five a day. Thus the company's executives turned to television to show off their new marvel, and Xerox became one of the first business equipment companies to be a heavy user of television time to tout its products.

Because the copier looked so forbidding and because competing duplicators were so confusing to work, the main thing that the company tried to impress on customers was the ease of use. It also played up the quality of the copies. The first commercial, which was shown in 1960, depicts a businessman at his desk. He hands a letter to a little girl and asks her, "Debbie, will you please go make a copy of this?"

"Yes, Daddy," she says.

"That's my secretary," the man says proudly.

Debbie hurries off and by pressing a single button manages to copy the letter. She snatches up the copy and is about to take it to her father when she stops and goes back with a big smile to make a copy of her doll.

"Thank you," her father says when she gives him the two pieces of paper. "Which is the original?"

Debbie peers at the papers and scratches her head. "I forget!"

The Debbie commercial was a big hit. One irate competitor, aghast at the claims it made, actually demanded proof from Xerox that Debbie was not a midget. He couldn't believe that a mere child could operate such a complex-looking machine.

Pleased with the reception the commercial got, Xerox went the Debbie spot one better. Somebody said that the company would really open up some eyes if it could show that the machine was so easy to work that a monkey could manage it. Accordingly, the company's advertising agency dug up an animal trainer who managed to teach a chimpanzee to work the copier. The agency then went ahead and shot a commercial where, after being given a document, the chimp scampers through an office and climbs atop the 914 and makes a copy. He delivers it to the boss swinging from a rope. There was nothing faked. The chimp actually did operate the machine.

Everyone at Xerox was delighted with the spot and it appeared on a "CBS Reports" one evening. The next day, calls started pouring in from the field force. Customers were irate. The secretaries who normally operated the copiers had found themselves the butt of rather insulting jokes. Men were leaving bananas for them on the copiers and wondering why they needed to pay them if they could just go out and hire a monkey. The commercial never ran again.

To further build awareness, Xerox ran a two-page ad in *Fortune* and some other national magazines that purported to show two identical paintings of an eagle by Picasso. The copy read: "Which is the $2,800 Picasso? Which is the 5 cent Xerox 914 copy?" The company offered to send any reader who guessed correctly a xerographic copy of the original. Something like sixteen thousand readers wrote in, but not many got the answer right.

Through its advertising, Xerox also tried to educate the public a little about xerography. One of the earliest commercials featured a young woman with her hair standing on end, as if she had just stuck her finger in an electrical socket. It explained that the static electricity that elevated the woman's hair was also one of the key ingredients of xerography.

Another way the company won attention was by putting machines on display in heavily trafficked public areas. For example, a 914 was set up at the bustling Merrill Lynch office in New York's Grand Central Station. Thousands of businessmen and other interested parties stopped there each day to check the stock quotations, so it was an ideal location for attracting interest. Xerox found other similarly congested spots in a number of additional cities in which to place one of its copiers.

Meanwhile, Peter McColough, who had been made general manager of sales in 1959, had adeptly built a national sales force and refurbished the company's dingy service centers, which better resembled haylofts than anyplace you would want a customer to visit. Since the company was unable to bring a machine to prospective customers, McColough knew that it was essential to have spiffy, expansive demonstration rooms to obtain sales.

There was little doubt in the minds of Haloid's executives, especially Peter McColough's, that the 914 would never have been successful if the company had tried to sell it. The price would have been prohibitive. If Xerox attempted to sell a machine that cost some four thousand dollars to produce, as the 914 did, then the company would have to charge many times that if—after maintenance, advertising, administrative, and related costs were worked in—it were going to show any profit. Xerox executives doubted that anyone would sink that large a sum of money into something as yet unproven.

IBM at the time was renting its machines and charging a monthly fee, but that approach wouldn't have worked well either. The problem was that customer needs fluctuated so much. Any rental price would have been too high for many moderate users and too low to earn Xerox a decent return from heavy users. Some businesses with thousands of employees might be making copies almost nonstop, whereas small offices might make no more than a few dozen copies a day. How could one justify charging them the same price?

So McColough conceived the brilliant idea of metered pricing. The company attached little meters on the machines that kept track of how many copies had been made. Xerox then charged a low base monthly rent of ninety-five dollars a month, which allowed the user to make up to two thousand copies; after that, he paid four cents for each copy made. It was a beautifully simple and effective system, not unlike what the phone company employed. It didn't cost much to get a phone into your house, but you paid your fair share as you used it. The upshot was that customers paid slower this way but the revenues were eventually greater. The pricing strategy made the 914 easy to acquire for any size company and for any application. One product appeared to customers as a whole line. It was this canny strategy that really ignited the spectacular growth not only of Xerox but of an entire industry. (Oddly enough, this strategy would come to be a burden and a competitive disadvantage much later on.) When IBM pondered whether it wanted to get involved with the 914, it never imagined that Haloid was going to resort to metered pricing. Had IBM thought of that, Peter felt they would have viewed the project in an altogether different light and may well have seized the opportunity. If that had transpired, the history of Xerox would have been radically different.

As it happened, the gap between buying and renting the copier grew much greater as time went by. In 1966 a 914 could be bought for $27,500 but rented for just twenty-five dollars a month plus a minimum of forty-nine dollars' worth of copies at four cents each.

Good as it sounded on paper, the metering system came with its own assortment of bugs. The early meters frequently failed to register accurately. On some machines, thirty copies would be made and the meter would register four. On another copier, the meter would show fifty copies when just five had been made. As a result, the meters had to be pulled off the machines and redesigned by the meter manufacturers until all the defects were worked out.

Even though Xerox had a proprietary technology and no real competitors, the 914 was hardly an automatic sale. One thing the sales force persistently fought was the perception that copiers could be bought for a couple of hundred dollars. Because it was so ungainly, there was also the matter of where to put it. Often, companies wound up sticking it in the hallway or smack in the middle of a room. Buildings often didn't even have the dedicated electrical line these copiers needed and had to run fresh lines up elevator shafts.

The most delicate problem the sales force had to skate around was Charlie Printpants. Companies had what was called a Central Reproduction Department, or CRD, where their printing and reproduction needs were met. Most typically, the department would be buried down in a basement and consist of an offset press and perhaps a mimeograph machine. Xerox salesmen used to mockingly refer to the guy who would be in charge of the CRD as Charlie Printpants, because his trousers were always coated with ink smears. In fact, the actual Xerox sales training manuals incorporated the nickname. Charlie was considered the enemy, for whenever a Xerox salesman came calling on a business, the manager would commonly ask Charlie Printpants what he thought of a copier. "A copier?" he would say in amazement. "Forget it."

Charlie was no dope. He knew full well that a copier would eventually threaten his job. Thus the objective of all Xerox salesmen was to circumvent Charlie Printpants and try to sell a company a copier without Charlie getting to offer his two cents. Eventually, this strategy worked extremely well. But for a long while Charlie Printpants haunted Xerox and gave salesmen absolute fits.

In time, though, it became unmistakably clear that the demand for the 914 was far exceeding what anyone in the company anticipated. A 914 would be installed in a company's manufacturing department to copy engineering drawings. Then someone from the legal department would notice the machine, and, before long, the lawyers would be dropping in to make copies. Pretty soon, the legal department wanted a 914 of its own. The original projection was that each machine would make ten thousand copies a month. The volume turned out to be forty thousand copies a month, the bulk of these being copies of copies rather than copies of original documents. The company envisioned that people would be making copies of original documents, but not that they would be copying copies to pass on information more speedily.

With the appearance of the 914, personnel issues became of paramount concern at Xerox. Clearly, many of the employees were insufficiently qualified to cope with this new technology. After all, they had spent their careers concerned with photographic paper. Joe Wilson adopted a very hard line on this sticky matter. He would size up, say, Bob Jones, the Los Angeles branch manager. If it was clear he was not fit for the new job that confronted him, then Wilson would block from his mind the fact that Jones had worked for Haloid for twenty years and that Wilson knew the guy's wife and kids. He would summon Jones to

Rochester for a full day, and have him see the head of sales and Joe's father, who probably knew the guy even longer than Joe did. Then Wilson would usher him into his office, and tell him flat out that it wasn't the man's fault or anything but his position had changed and become more complicated and he really wasn't the right fit anymore. There would be far more pressure with the new technology, Wilson would go on, so wouldn't you rather try a different job at the same compensation? Some managers were delighted; others were hopping mad. But virtually all of them took the new jobs. And that was because Wilson treated them firmly, but with dignity. Someone else might have dispatched a junior associate to Los Angeles to tell the man he was out of a job, and then there might have been open rebellion.

For the people who were up to the new challenge, the 1960s were incredibly heady times. I have heard plenty of stories about what the climate was like. Everyone felt there was a mission to be accomplished, and so everyone worked late but never complained. The Xerox offices buzzed with energy and purpose. Senior managers believed they were making the world a little better by bringing about the democratization of information. Steadily, a culture was nourished of pioneers building something destined to become immensely powerful yet also something dedicated to the greater good. That was the conviction that Joe Wilson inculcated in people. He recorded an orientation film in the early 1960s that got played thousands of times for new recruits and succinctly summed up the ambitions of the company. Sitting in a stiff-backed chair, the bespectacled Wilson told the newcomers in his kindly, professorial tone: "We think we are creating a power, a power of finance, a power of marketing, a power of research and development, and, above all, a power of people—the promise to lead this company to ever greater heights than were achieved this past year when for the first time we came to the *Fortune* first five hundred companies of the United States. We're well down the list, way over four hundred in terms of sales. In terms of profits, in the second one hundred. In terms of return on sales and return on investment, though, we were fourteenth and fourth respectively. Do you realize how much this means to you? It means you are part of one of the strongest enterprises in North America. Welcome."

I've often thought about why copiers became so popular and it seems to me there are several simple reasons. Copying is an exceedingly friendly technology. It's easy to use and thus it makes the user feel competent rather than incompetent. Except for five-year-old kids, people who encounter a computer for the first time immediately feel they're dumb. When they come upon a copier, they feel smart. Second, xerography provides clear value. Many technologies have no obvious value. Copying does—and you appreciate that value instantly. Third, the copier harnesses power. By making copies quickly, you can disseminate information as widely as you want to in an inexpensive way. And thus the technology very much became aligned in people's minds with positive thoughts.

Despite all the long hours Xerox employees put in during the convulsive early days, when things went better than anyone expected, there were a few rewards to take one's mind off how hard one was working. In 1962 Joe Wilson told his people that if volume got to a hundred million dollars, he would take the top officers to London for their regular conference, rather than to more customary sites like downtown Rochester or Niagara Falls. Sure enough, sales hit the hundred million mark, and about fifty executives and their spouses jetted off to London, most of them for the first time in their lives. They were put up at the swank Dorchester Hotel, and there was even a dinner one night at one of the houses of Parliament.

Without a doubt, the early heroes of Xerox were the people in sales and marketing. They just drove the company. Xerox was a salesman's paradise, offering something of universal appeal. Salesmen would wander down the street of a city and gaze up at all the buildings and muse about how every one of them contained Xerox customers. Given the circumstances, the spirit of the sales force was tremendous. And people were joining the force as if it were the sure road to the promised land. For many, it was exactly that.

There were people like David Bliss, who spied a little scrap of paper on his college bulletin board reporting that Xerox was hunting for a man in New England. Bliss felt he might as well be that man. He came aboard in 1966, a few years after Xerox joined the *Fortune* 500 for the first time and seemed like it was sure to rocket to the very top of that elite group of companies.

Indeed, the company was growing so fast that its main problem was to keep up with its frantic pace. During these days, Xerox recruiters were literally pulling bodies off the streets of Rochester and assigning them work. Bob Schneider, who worked for Joe Wilson and later became Peter McColough's executive assistant, applied after noticing an ad in *The New York Times* and was hired without even having to supply a résumé, which was a good thing. He had no experience.

Recruits who performed well found themselves rapidly advanced. David Bliss's wife once volunteered to draw a sort of family tree for her husband of all the branch managers and sales managers he had worked for, because they were changing so fast as they got elevated up the ranks. It was like lieutenants being promoted on Normandy Beach.

At this time, Ray Hay was probably the icon for the sales force. Then the head of sales, he was the prototypical fast-talking, hard-charging person who innately understood customers and salesmen. At the same time, he was terribly bored with processes and the structures that became necessary as the company became bigger. All of the early sales models were charismatic, seat-of-the-pants managers. They cared little about processes and analysis and didn't want to learn much more about them. During meetings in which financial plans were reviewed, Ray Hay would invariably fall asleep.

Then there was a fellow named Shelby Carter, an ex-marine who saw everything in war terms and rated himself as one of the greatest salesmen of all time. Even more impartial viewers credit him as being one of the best salesmen they ever laid eyes on. Around Xerox, he became a dashing daredevil of legend. He began at IBM selling typewriters and was a relentless pounder of pavement. His wife would fix him a big jug of lemonade to keep in his car so he could drink it all day and skip lunch. He had a sign affixed to the visor of his car that said, "Calls are the guts of this business." Carter didn't believe in a salesman mold. He figured there were many ways to excel at sales. He called this his "Heinz Fifty-seven Varieties" theory. The one dead giveaway to him of a lackluster salesman, he would say, was a man who had trousers worn out at the right pocket. To Carter, that meant that before shaking hands with a customer, the man was wiping the sweat off his palm on his pants. Anyone constantly doing that was far too uptight to possibly succeed.

Carter did rub some people the wrong way, because he liked to stretch the truth quite a lot. If you didn't like someone like Carter, you'd say he was a blatant liar. If you did like him, you'd say he engaged in hyperbole. I lean toward the hyperbole characterization. Interestingly, there was so much bluster to Carter that many Xerox managers didn't think he was smart. But he was, and he moved a tremendous amount of product for the company. Once I got there, whenever I had a truly complex marketing problem, I would go to Carter and he invariably solved it. If you had a big customer problem, you would sic Carter on it.

Carter eventually worked his way up to national sales manager, at which point he became famous for giving people mementos. He once doled out penknives engraved with that day's price of Xerox stock. He would run contests for the sales force, and as prizes he gave away Kentucky rifles, swords, and, one time, torpedoes. Once a substantial number of women joined the sales team, however, Carter had to tone down a bit as a result of complaints about swords and bombs being given away as honors. So Carter cut back on the torpedoes.

One of his favorite habits was to award bowie knives mounted on plaques to people who had done something really terrific. A whole mythology grew up around those knives and they came to mean a lot more to sales people than getting a bonus. To this day, you see these knives hanging on walls throughout Xerox offices and you know that means another Shelby Carter fan.

Carter was the kind of guy who could really whip up fervor with his passionate oratory. He would stage pep rallies and stand atop a bus with a megaphone and exhort the salesmen to carry the Xerox banner into war. He used to conduct what were known as Jet Squad Meetings. Carter would hop into the corporate jet and fly to two or three cities a day and stir up the troops. In New York they might gather at Shea Stadium. Carter would stand on the pitcher's mound and deliver his spiel, and the salesmen in attendance would be spellbound. Then they would go out and sell copiers with an almost crazed intensity.

Carter took hyperbole to the limit—and sometimes beyond. But he also loved the company and its products with uncompromised passion. If Carter was walking in an office past a Xerox machine and it had paper clips lying on top and was smudged, he would stop and remove the clips, then wet his handkerchief and wipe off the machine until it sparkled. Copiers were his babies, and he adored them.

As they sold 914s, Xerox salesmen continually tried to dream up new uses for the product, and the public seemed to work just as hard at the challenge. The machine was used to copy office jokes, deeds, recipes, book reports, love letters, three-dimensional objects, parts of people's anatomy. The Food and Drug Administration stopped making typewritten copies of the labels on bottles and cans. Instead, it rolled the bottle or can across the Xerox copier and made a duplicate of the labels. One of the odder earlier uses, reported by *The New Yorker,* was to guarantee future brides the wedding gifts they craved. The list of desired presents would be turned in to a department store's bridal-registry counter, which boasted a copier. When she came to do her shopping, a friend of the bride would be given a copy of the list. She would then check off what she bought and return her copy. The master list would be revised accordingly before being given out to the next guest. When police officers had suspects empty their pockets before being put in jail, they didn't bother typing up receipts anymore but simply placed the wallet and keys on a 914 and obtained a Xeroxed receipt. Hospitals started using xerography to copy their laboratory reports. Schoolteachers used them to make enough copies of exams for their classes.

With the success of the 914, the company began developing new models. By 1966, there was the 914; the 813, a much smaller device one-seventh the size of the 914 that could stand on top of a desk and used to be referred to as a 914 with the air let out; and the 2400, a sophisticated reproduction machine that resembled a kitchen stove and could turn out copies at a rate of forty a minute. The 2400 rented for three hundred and fifty-dollars a month rather than the twenty-five dollars that the

914 did, and it took a while for the sales force to become conditioned to saying "three fifty" a month without stuttering.

All the Xerox machines were on rental then, with a fifteen-day cancellation provision. The cancellation policy was a stroke of marketing genius, for it was extraordinarily effective at getting machines in the door. Some people did cancel after the fifteen days lapsed, but not many. More commonly, Xerox salesmen would persuade them to trade up.

There was a constant push to get customers to upgrade to better and faster machines. Roughly half of a saleman's compensation depended on his ability to meet or exceed a budget of points, which were awarded according to the revenues produced by the machine. To convince corporate management to push upgrades, the sales force came up with a concept called "Instant Growth," which argued that with more power customers would do more copying than ever before, even if there was no obvious reason to think that from examining the customer's needs. And thus the company would achieve instant growth. In actuality, this analysis proved to be all too true. Customers did make more copies with faster machines. The reason was that people's needs were much greater than they or Xerox ever imagined. They thought, well, maybe they might run off fifty copies a month, and then they would do two thousand. The idea of Instant Growth became one of the biggest drivers that pushed Xerox to realize it was okay for the sales force to take out older, depreciated equipment and put in newer, more powerful models.

Again and again, customers would agree to trade up. They'd start with the 813 desktop unit and after a while would switch to the 914. When a customer exchanged machines, the desktop model would be returned to Xerox, where it would be cleaned up and refurbished and then rented out again. A machine was said to have several customer lives. Xerox shrewdly set up refurbishing shops all over the country to do the overhauling on used machines to endow them with those multiple lives.

Xerox maintained a computer model aimed at determining the lowest investment Xerox could make to get the maximum number of copies. Xerox had built a three-dimensional chess game. It had different speeds, different capabilities, and different pricing. By creating varying configurations, the company got different returns. It all became a very intricate game. Xerox had to refrain from bringing out new models too early and smothering previous models that were still going well. At the same time, it couldn't wait too long and not respond to customer needs.

Next, Xerox developed line extensions so there were multiple products to sell. For instance, the sorter was added. We take that completely for granted now, but the copier didn't originally come with a sorter.

Largely as a result of xerography, the estimated number of copies made annually in the United States exploded from some twenty million in the mid-1950s to nine and a half billion in 1964, and to fourteen billion in 1966, not to mention billions more in Europe, Asia, and Latin America. Philosophers took to hailing xerography as a revolution comparable in importance to the invention of the wheel, and coin-operated copying machines began turning up in candy stores and beauty parlors.

Meanwhile, Sol Linowitz had been touring the world setting up joint ventures with foreign companies so Xerox could sell its products abroad. Rank Xerox, of course, already existed. In 1962 a venture was created between Rank Xerox and Fuji Photo Film in Japan that was called Fuji Xerox. It was owned on a fifty-fifty basis, though the Japanese totally ran it. New Xerox partnerships were also formed in Australia, New Zealand, Brazil, Mexico, and Argentina. This was an ingenious strategy, though I must admit I didn't initially appreciate it. When I first came to Xerox, I was bothered that the company was sharing its profits with partners overseas because IBM had no partners at all. But in time I came to realize that Xerox could not have grown as fast as it did without help. The company didn't have the capital resources to do it alone. But more important, our local partners were businessmen of character and stature who were key to our growth.

In 1966, thanks in large part to the role he played in developing the powerful Xerox sales force, Peter McColough became president of the company. It was a popular move, though, to some Peter was something of an enigma. He had great vision and great charm. Disdainful of protracted meetings and lengthy reports, he was more of an intuitive manager than a process manager. He was extraordinarily private and confided in few people. It was rare for him to invite people into his office for casual chats. After he had been the head of marketing for two years, Ray Hay once remarked that he had been in Peter's office just three times.

A very smart man and a broad thinker willing to take risks, Peter was probably a better teacher than a manager. In a lot of respects he didn't manage very much. His talent was in getting others to think and do. Peter was always gentlemanly and a real humanitarian. He adopted a policy that no one who had been with the company at least eight years could be fired without written permission from him. What's more, anyone in that unpleasant situation had the right to a personal meeting with Peter. There were times when he did in fact overrule dismissals.

All the same, he had unwavering rules. He told his managers that if they ever came across an employee who lied to them, then he must be fired at once. You can't work with someone like that, he would say. But once that happened, he urged managers to quickly ask how they could help the employee find a new job. He firmly believed in the humane road.

Peter was certainly dedicated to Xerox, but he was also very protective of his leisure hours. He was not one who burned the lamp late at the office. He worked nine to half past six, and then the rest of the hours were for his family, reading, and, as he often said to me, "time to think." Weekends, he was pretty much off-duty. He liked to sail a lot, and when he was away sailing he was often incommunicado. Those trips out to sea, though, gave him plenty of unfettered time to think about the business, and managers were always on edge when he came back, wondering what new ideas were going to be thrust at them.

Thus far, the 1960s had been frenetic but exhilarating for Xerox. As one executive who lived through it said: "The sixties were a decade of just hang on." It was Peter's challenge to keep things rolling along.

In 1959 Haloid-Xerox's sales were $32 million. In 1961, the first full year of 914 sales, they reached $61 million. In 1962 they were $104 million. In 1968 they would hit $1.125 billion. Profits would go from $2.5 million in 1961 to $138 million in 1968. No one, Wilson included, predicted numbers as awesome as these. It has often been said that the 914 is the most successful commercial product in history, and I can't argue with that.

Everybody who held Xerox stock in quantity was getting rich beyond their wildest dreams. Dozens upon dozens of millionaires were made off investments in the company. It is small wonder that, to this day, stockbrokers and financial advisers are always searching for "the next Xerox." Chester Carlson alone held shares worth tens of millions of dollars, making him a very wealthy man. Much of the money he gave away, while he personally fell into somewhat odd habits. He retired to a big house in Rochester, where he used to walk around lugging a straw basket heaped with books and magazines he wished to read. Along with his second wife, Dorris, he became entranced with the occult and spiritualism. They would often conduct seances for friends while relaxing on flat cushions in their living room. In 1968 Carlson died of a heart attack while sitting alone in a Manhattan movie theater.

The profits that rained down on Xerox allowed the company to contribute mightily to many community causes, which it did extraordinarily well. Without a doubt, Xerox was the most spectacular big-business success of the 1960s. It was called the Cinderella story of American business, and everyone envied it.

Nevertheless, the great success of the company brought its own share of headaches. By 1966 employment had risen in seven years from nine hundred to twenty-four thousand. Some managers were hiring fifty to a hundred people a month. There were now twenty-four buildings in the Rochester area. And yet there were no systems or controls to speak of. There was growing concern about the ability of the company to pay people promptly, even Xerox's own salesmen, not for lack of money, but lack of records.

The company found itself unable to bill many of its customers properly. People were switching to better jobs so quickly that they didn't get the seasoning they should have. As the years rolled by, the odds that an order was correct grew very, very low. Sales people weren't being paid the right amounts; customers were being billed wrong. There could be significant differences. Imagine an account rep who handled a major customer like Texaco's headquarters, a building that would have multiple machines and each month would have copiers going in and out, all on different price plans. If a model went in and nothing came out, that meant four or five times more money to a sales rep than a straight trade. So sales people would try to cajole a customer to keep an old machine long enough to make it count as a cancellation rather than a trade.

Myriad honest errors never got caught. Salesmen were overpaid and underpaid, customers were overcharged and undercharged. Major accounts would actually have a dedicated person on their payroll whose sole job was to reconcile Xerox invoices.

Inside the doors of machines were the meter cards on which customers would record the copies made on the machine. Customers were obliged to read them and then send them into the company. There were errors galore. There were hosts of people who never bothered to submit their meter cards at all. Sales representatives had to phone them or personally visit the premises and fetch the cards. Salesmen typically spent a third of their time selling, a third of their time learning new models and price plans, and a third of their time fighting the system.

What's more, managers feared that there would not be sufficient time to hire and train the droves of new people who were needed and to instill within them the same values of the original Xerox workers. Because of the lack of controls, McColough used to worry about bad apples being created. For instance, with no one looking very closely over their shoulders, would salesmen be tempted to do things they shouldn't? There was no telling.

Still, nothing affected Xerox's profits. The product was so astoundingly successful that it negated everything else. Nothing would stop the sales. Eventually, the company even managed to sell copiers to the navy to put on submarines. It had to have engineers cut them in half to get them down the hatches and then reassemble them.

One of the other things that began to invade the thoughts of top management in the 1960s was the fear that someone else would come up with a competing process to xerography that would be cheaper and faster. The executives knew that Carlson's invention had created this enormous market just like that, and they feared that—poof—it could disappear just as suddenly. Management knew that there was a tremendous market for copiers. It also knew that it didn't have a monopoly on brains. Its machine was cumbersome and innumerable things kept breaking down. At any time, someone could come along and do it all differently and better, and xerography would go away. What no one could have imagined was that the xerographic process would prove to be as resilient as the internal combustion engine. Although it improved markedly over the years, essentially it remained the same. Nothing came along to make it obsolete. A century after its invention, it was still the only way to power an automobile.

Because of their anxiety, Wilson and McColough turned to the task of diversification. They began thinking of getting into computers and then into the financial business to finance the installation of the computers. They took a look at several computer companies, including Digital Equipment, Control Data and Burroughs, all without success. Then, in 1968, Commercial Investment Trust, a large financial services firm, was brought to the company's attention by a friend on Wall Street. And, with the opportunity ripe, Xerox decided to buy CIT—for a whopping billion dollars' worth of Xerox stock. At that time, this represented the largest acquisition ever attempted by an American corporation. There was fierce opposition from shareholders. Xerox was growing very quickly and the major institutional holders in particular couldn't see why Xerox would buy a slow-growing financial company and have its earnings dragged down. Xerox ultimately pulled out of the deal, but not because of that dissension. Peter agreed never to reveal the reason, and I myself don't know for sure what it was.

In 1969, running out of diversification options, McColough paid a visit to the home of Max Palevsky, the head of Scientific Data Systems. Palevsky, the son of an immigrant housepainter, had founded SDS a decade before and had enjoyed reasonable success. SDS was located in El Segundo, California, and sold computers mainly to engineering and scientific customers, what were known at the time as the "lunatic fringe." NASA and the Atomic Energy Commission used SDS machines, and there was one at the UCLA Medical Center's Brain

Research Institute that was monitoring the brain patterns of monkeys and men. By now, Palevsky had grown somewhat bored with SDS, and had gotten involved in the peace movement and in producing movies. He was ripe to sell.

In actuality, though, SDS was hardly the most attractive computer company around. It was supposedly earning ten million dollars on sales of one hundred million, but many Xerox executives subsequently doubted it was even doing that well. Like many small companies, it knew the seductive ways of creative accounting that made its results look rosier than they were. Yet McColough felt he had to buy something to get into computers and digital technology, which he was confident would become intertwined with copiers, and so he offered more than nine hundred million dollars' worth of Xerox stock. In two weeks, the deal was done. Everyone was shocked by the price—ninety-two times SDS's 1968 earnings. Of course, Xerox stock was trading at a phenomenal multiple itself. The acquisition did give Xerox knowledge of the computer business, and it was small wonder that stories started cropping up in the press that showed McColough getting ready to duel it out with Tom Watson of IBM. What Xerox didn't know at the time was that the deal to buy SDS marked the beginning of the company's long search to diversify from its core business.

On the heels of the SDS acquisition, Peter hired Jack Goldman, a bouncy, cigar-smoking physicist who was one of the top research people at Ford, to head up research at Xerox. In short order, Goldman recommended to McColough that the company establish a digital technology research center. Digital technology was superior to analog in computing and was unquestionably the wave of the future. McColough and Goldman were convinced the copier business might become vulnerable to computers if Xerox failed to pursue long-range digital research. They envisioned future machines that were based on xerography and on digital technology, as well as integrated office information systems. So Peter hired George Pake, a top-notch, mild-mannered physicist who was then the provost at Washington University in St. Louis, to set up and run what would be called the Palo Alto Research Center, or PARC. Xerox had plenty of capable people in Rochester who were knowledgeable about graphic communications, and Peter could have simply assigned digital work to them, but he didn't want to give them another charter. A fair amount of jealousy flared up in Rochester, but Peter was convinced he had made the right decision.

PARC was formally created in 1970. It perched on a hill overlooking the campus of Stanford University. Palo Alto was where high technology companies were sprouting in the surrounding Santa Clara Valley, an intellectually rarified environment. The PARC building was a gorgeous, first-class facility, a quietly elegant three-story affair with a rock-garden atrium for employees to indulge in meditation. Hundreds of the top brains in the country were recruited to work at PARC—engineers and computer scientists as well as eventually philosophers and anthropologists—and a sort of utopianism developed there. The scientists were extremely well paid and given plenty of freedom to function in a university-type environment. Many felt they had found heaven. It would not be long before the lab became a symbol to the outside world of Xerox's struggle to become something other than a copier company.

As Xerox expanded geographically, it was decided to move Xerox's headquarters from Rochester to Stamford, Connecticut—a sin the local boosters and press never forgave Xerox for—because as the company grew and established operations outside of the Rochester area, it came to be felt that if you didn't work in Rochester you were not important. This was especially true of the growing ranks of Xerox people on the West Coast. So Xerox opted to move to a neutral site away from its two most important operations.

Indeed, by 1970, the shape of the modern Xerox had become clear. The corporation had grown to a large enterprise with roots in a great many places. It continued to have a substantial presence in Rochester. Only a couple of years before moving the headquarters to Stamford, the company had built a twenty-nine-story skyscraper headquarters smack in the heart of downtown Rochester, in what was called Xerox Square. People used to talk about how they were "going to the Square." That building continued to be occupied by scores of Xerox people. A dozen miles east, in the farm town of Webster, were the company's sprawling campus of copier engineering and manufacturing facilities. In northern California there was now PARC. In the El Segundo area of southern California, SDS anchored a growing Xerox presence. And, of course, there was Rank Xerox in England and Fuji Xerox in Japan. So Xerox was becoming a significant multinational operation. And to many people, the headquarters move from Rochester down to the environs of New York City symbolized the fact that Xerox felt it was now going big time.

Dealing with the new challenges of Xerox was not going to be easy with the people on hand at the company. Joe Wilson was a great visionary, but, despite his Harvard training, his interest in day-to-day operations was never great. There would be times when someone would come up for promotion and he would say, "No, I'd like to move so-and-so up because I'm more comfortable with him." Rarely is the best person to promote the one who makes you most comfortable.

By now, Xerox began encountering a measure of external adversity as well. There were now more than forty companies in the office copier business, many of them producing xerographic devices under license from Xerox. Significantly, however, Xerox refused to grant a license for the selenium drum that allowed its own machines to make copies on ordinary paper. All competing products still required specially treated papers. Low-priced latecomers were swarming into copying. One company even envisioned the day when copiers would be so cheap they could be sold as toys. Other soothsayers spoke of some future date when copiers would be given away to stimulate sales of paper, in the same way that razors are handed out to promote razor blades.

In considering ways to cope with the multiplying demands of the business, Wilson and McColough decided that they needed help. They concluded that the internal people were not sufficient to the task of managing the company's breakneck growth and decided, in a rather unpopular move, to hire outside expertise. Eventually, they brought in upwards of a dozen top people from Ford, IBM, and GM. Like the heads of other fast-growing companies of the day, they primarily decided to tap the talent base at what was perceived to be the best-run industry in the country: the automobile industry. And the biggest number of recruits came from the highly successful Ford Motor Company, most notably Archie McCardell, who arrived as group vice president in charge of finance and control and swiftly became an executive vice president and the leading candidate to become president; Melvin Howard, who joined as the chief financial officer; Gerry Bennett, who became another key financial executive; Don Lennox, who became a senior manufacturing manager; and Jim O'Neill, who was put in charge of the copier group.

Most of the Ford men came from the finance area. When they left Ford, the car maker's chief financial officer was so miffed that he forbade his staff from using a Xerox machine anymore, despite the staggering quantity of copying the department did. They were forced to make do with a decidedly inferior substitute called Ozalid. With the arrival of the new recruits, a major change was about to take place at Xerox. It found itself headed for a fitful decade that would prove every bit as troubled as the 1960s were marvelous.

4. Life with the Ford Men

MY FIRST BIG ASSIGNMENT at Xerox came about because of somebody's bad eyes. I reported for work in July 1971, and the very next month Archie McCardell and Ray Hay asked me to go up to Rochester to fill in for a key executive who had been sidelined with a cataract problem. The man was Jack O'Callahan, who was in charge of the domestic marketing operations, one of the crucial jobs in the organization. So I went up and sat in for him. As I understood it, it was supposed to be a temporary assignment until his cataract operation was successfully completed. After I was in Rochester a mere three weeks, however, Jim O'Neill called me in and said that he wanted me to stay in the Rochester organization and work for him. I couldn't help but suspect that the whole thing was a ruse to begin with and that the intention had always been to install me in Rochester.

Whatever the case, I readily agreed and took the job. My thinking was that the sooner I fell into a true operations position the better off I would be. So my family moved up to Rochester and I took over responsibility for the U.S. marketing group. I very much liked working for O'Neill. He was an extremely tough manager, as anyone who dealt with him would tell you, but he taught me a lot.

I had other odd initiations to Xerox. I was at the company just a short time when I was invited to a big management meeting in Paris. I remember that Yotaro "Tony" Kobayashi, now the inspired head of Fuji Xerox, gave me a Seiko watch as a gift there and I wear it to this day. I was scheduled to make a presentation, my first before this august group. I didn't know it then, but meetings at Xerox, while they were important forms of communication, rarely saw anything much come out of them. Peter McColough and Archie McCardell were running this particular session, which was held in the International Hotel. I was very nervous. To this day, I always get a little anxious before I give a major speech. The top executives sat in swivel chairs on a stage, so they could twirl around and see the audience and then swing back and see the screen where slides were shown. When my turn came to speak, I gazed out across the rather forbidding room and saw a contingent of people from Fuji Xerox in the third row. Every one of them had his eyes closed. I wasn't aware that the Japanese frequently liked to shut their eyes when they listened to presentations, and it didn't necessarily mean they were asleep, though that was always a possibility. I took a deep breath and delivered my speech, which I thought was going pretty well. During a pause, I stole a quick glance at Archie and Peter to see if I could read their reactions. Both were sound asleep.

I had only been at Xerox about four months, when the entire company was plunged into a period of grief by the sudden death of Joe Wilson. Even for people like me, who never really got to know him very well personally, Wilson was a larger-than-life figure who symbolized all the wonderful values that Xerox stood for. It was a black day for the company and for anyone whose path Joe Wilson had crossed.

Wilson's death also triggered some significant managerial changes, although I suspected that they were planned already. Peter McColough became chairman and chief executive and, to no one's real surprise, Archie McCardell was elevated to president. At the same time, Peter began to withdraw more from the daily operations of the business and focused his attention on future planning. He did, however, remain actively immersed in pricing decisions, for he felt he had a special knack for that area.

McCardell's ascension brought to the forefront the group of executives who came to be somewhat derisively known by many Xerox veterans as the Ford Men. Their substantive and stylistic differences from longtime Xerox managers were considerable, and would lead to a whole range of problems.

It was unmistakably clear that some change was needed. Already, Xerox was not the company it had been in the early 1960s. And how could it be? The place was growing so fast both in revenues and people that some basic things simply had to change. In the early days, for instance, everyone knew Joe Wilson personally. He reserved a day around Christmastime to shake hands with each employee. Then he found he needed three days to pump all the hands, and it soon became obvious that the chief executive could no longer be so acutely familiar to the entire organization. More sophisticated sales, service, and management training was clearly a requisite for the company's employees, and so Peter created a marvelous world-class training center in Leesburg, Virginia, to tackle that.

But the Xerox employees who had been inculcated with Wilson's values and managerial style were not ready for what did come about, and they became wary of and guarded around the new management. The old-timers didn't feel the auto people shared the same values. The eager Ford Men had manifest ambition but they were not copier men. They were not rooted in the business and instilled with an adoration of the 914. Perhaps more important, they were not marketing men smitten by the aroma of selling. Their knowledge was about management systems and processes that they felt could govern any company—whether it made cars, bottle caps, or copying machines. Their language was the peculiar mumbo-jumbo of financial wizards. Among other things, the Ford Men introduced rigid controls and a sense of authoritarianism that didn't exist before. A very hierarchical structure was put into place that had been unknown and to some extent was unfortunate. I was used to more formal controls coming from IBM, but even I was taken aback by the rigidity that evolved. As a result, a rather severe culture clash, which would grow in intensity, developed between the Ford Men and the Xerox people.

McCardell himself was something of a puzzle. He was unquestionably a smart guy. In college he had been an economics major, and he earned an M.B.A. from the University of Michigan. Despite his rise up the ranks, he was a fairly introverted man who rarely let down the bars. You dreaded meetings going on too long with Archie, because he was a big cigar smoker. Some interminable Xerox meetings were five- or six-cigar events, and you had to fight your way through the smoke to leave the room. Archie didn't engender teamwork, and under him we didn't have much collegial behavior. Everyone was always trying to protect his own turf. McCardell was a very orderly thinker. He had a habit of sitting in his office and writing out all his memos longhand as a way to collect his thoughts. Having spent seventeen years at Ford, he learned the managerial uses of statistics introduced there by, among others, Robert McNamara, one of the famous Whiz Kids who became president of Ford and later secretary of defense in the Kennedy administration. Extraordinarily bright, McNamara was a man totally bewitched by numbers, and I think McCardell caught the spell. To him, trend analysis and financial controls were the most important tools in guiding decisions. He felt numbers shone a spotlight into the belly of the corporation and revealed everything. All that went on could be boiled down to a set of statistics. Jim O'Neill, equipped with a similar background, managed in much the same way.

Among other things, McCardell transferred his fascination with odds and percentages into a fondness for poker. He was an inveterate poker player, and often whiled away the time on plane flights by breaking out the cards. There were some famous, apocryphal stories about how when his plane was approaching its destination, Archie used to order the pilot to circle the airport because he was still trying to recoup some savage losses.

Archie could be warm and affable—and I always got along well with him—but he could also be obstinate. Although I liked him, it became obvious that a lot of other people at Xerox didn't share my sentiments. The perpetual complaint was that he was a bean counter and his own analyst. Even I began to think we were going too far and measuring too many things. And I did feel meetings with Archie were inconclusive. Time after time, the relevant people were in the room who could make a decision but they didn't get the chance to make it. Instead, Archie would retreat to his office, make up his mind, and then later inform the others. McColough told me later that Archie just didn't like to debate things with him in front of the rest of the management team. Part of the problem was that there was a distinct surface politeness at Xerox. During group encounters, it was a much more genteel place than IBM. At IBM, when someone was unhappy about something, you knew it right away in a meeting because he would speak his mind. That didn't happen at Xerox. With a few exceptions, people were consistently civil to each other's faces. As a result, meetings would end on a polite but inconclusive note, and when you later heard the decision, you never knew what the thought process had been in reaching it. I used to think it might have been better if there was more fiery debate and we all got to know how each other felt. Meetings at Xerox, in fact, came to be labeled "Home on the Range" meetings. Never was heard a discouraging word.

Civil or not, the Ford Men were not always easy guys to be around. One particularly vituperative person was known for throwing things at people—pencils, paper, whatever was at hand—and sometimes hitting them. But he was shrewd enough to throw only at subordinates, never at superiors. He behaved well around me, and I never had to duck flying objects. Though I found his behavior a touch extreme, I must admit I wasn't sure I had achieved the right management mix either. I sometimes thought I was too eager to accept less than perfect work. It's hard to know where the line is.

Jim O'Neill, who was another McNamara protégé, was an intimidating figure in his own right. Beanpole thin, he was very smart but also very acerbic, and he could make mincemeat out of peers and subordinates alike. He used to say that McNamara was brilliant but couldn't decipher good input from bad input. Some people would say the same about O'Neill. But he had a remarkable McNamara-like mind and could calculate to the seventh decimal place in his head.

Though some Xerox people would hate to acknowledge it, McCardell and the Ford Men introduced urgently needed financial controls that brought the company into the twentieth century and prevented it from totally veering into disarray. They imposed order on the most unimaginably disordered company. The place sorely needed discipline and benefited from it. It now knew what it was spending and what it was spending it on.

But the Ford Men never really assimilated. Rather than buy into the culture that was there, the Ford Men began to change it. For instance, the rigid managerial structure they subscribed to was driven by cost savings and not by what the customer wanted. It was something Xerox was not used to and never did absorb, and it showed that you can use numbers too aggressively. In the long run, it was not wholly helpful to the company.

To take one example, we were going to build a second factory for one of our new copiers. All the financial analyses showed that we needed the plant. But everyone in marketing knew we didn't. I told O'Neill that we would never fully use the factory we already had, but he brushed that off and snorted, "No, the numbers show it. Where's your quantitative proof?"

"Jim, we don't need any proof statement," I replied. "Just plain common sense, talking to our customers and sales reps, will make it clear we just can't sell that many machines."

In the end, fortunately, we didn't build the factory and the one we did have was pretty empty for years. We were able to hold the annual meeting in it one year because it was not being used.

And so I'm not sure the financial measurements fully achieved their objective of telling management everything that was happening in the company. Not that the Ford Men didn't give it their best shot. One classic computer model that they came up with was christened Shazam. It was built by the finance department to calculate the impact of price changes or new product introductions. To say the least, it was unwieldy. It had something like thirty-five hundred input assumptions that were necessary in order to make a forecast. If the marketing department wished to make a price change, it had to furnish this massive list of assumptions—average copy volume, how much Instant Growth, how many customers would have cancelled their own machines if the new price did not exist, and so forth—and then some seemingly precise answer would spew forth. Shazam would dictate that the new price would cause a 1.782 percent drop in sales but a 7.451 increase in profits—or something like that.

Believe it or not, Shazam was merely an early incarnation of the handiwork of the financial men. They moved on to significantly more complex and intricate models. It was akin to doing weather forecasting for a hurricane. You had to take your best guess at what the water temperature was and what the cloud movements were. Eventually the finance department began to distrust the assumptions offered up by marketing. Thus it would run the model inputting the numbers from marketing and then run it again using its own assumptions—all to debate how many angels could dance on the head of a pin. To many, it seemed like highly manipulated nonsense, and to some extent it was. Who, after all, knew these unknowable underlying assumptions on which everything was based?

As a result of things like this, incredible intramural jousting began. The fighting became like an untreated infection. The marketing and financial departments were continually at war over prices and models. To win these battles, some of the business centers recruited finance people to their ranks who knew how to present assumptions to get what marketing wanted. It was a case of recruiting enemy soldiers into one's camp. But an unfortunate side effect of this was that nonmarketing people less knowledgeable about the customer were filling up marketing jobs.

Under the new management approach, a lot of power was stripped from the branch managers, and there was much more centralization. If things weren't going well, managers would be summoned to a conference room in Stamford that was referred to as the Red Room because of the color of the walls (some said it was blood red) and, in sessions sharply different in tone from our normal Home on the Range meetings, get thoroughly chewed out. Some managers complained that they would be in the Red Room for hours as the Ford Men debated the shape of a price curve.

The marketing people who were actually in touch with the customers and were taking the temperature of the market felt that their information was roundly ignored. Instead, McCardell believed only the rows of numbers he saw on what were known as the Bennett White Papers. Gerry Bennett, the head of finance, would prepare these White Papers with all the essential numbers that the finance department had put together. The marketing people might arrive for a meeting with totally conflicting information that they had gleaned directly from the marketplace, but McCardell, who wanted growth above all else, had his quantitative analysis from his staff, and the "feel" of the marketplace was not enough to carry the day. As far as he was concerned, it couldn't possibly be right. After all, whatever the White Paper said was unassailable fact.

In a lot of ways, what was happening at Xerox was not unique. Many companies are the victims of their own success. When you have tremendous success, it conceals a great deal of sins. As a result, you learn the wrong lessons.

Some years ago, there was a compelling study done at a major university concerning learning among pigeons. A mechanized device was arranged that would randomly toss pellets into a cage of pigeons. After a while, if you looked in on the pigeons, some of them would be flapping their wings, others would be scratching at the bottom of the cage, and still others would be wandering around in circles. That was because when the pellets came flying in, that is what those pigeons happened to be doing and they associated those actions with the reward of being fed. This behavior was called superstitious learning. It was a matter of being locked into chance and actually irrelevant beliefs.

In the aftermath of World War II, American industry found itself in a uniquely powerful position. Many leaders of American corporations could have stayed home and done well. Unfortunately, they came to work. They experimented with all manner of management strategy: they created steep hierarchies, they implemented extensive financial controls, they distanced themselves from the customer. And they continued to do well. Much like the pigeons, they believed that these practices led to their success, when in fact they succeeded despite them. Thus was superstitious learning of the worst kind embedded in American corporations. Once the balmy times receded, these strategies began to strangle American companies, but they couldn't disabuse themselves of their superstitious learning. In the 1970s, Xerox was on its way to developing as bad a case of this affliction as anyone.

The rise of the Ford Men spelled the beginning of the end for some of the old Xerox heroes. For the genetic code of the place changed. The sales stars of the 1960s, the hip-shooting Shelby Carters and Ray Hays, weren't listened to as much at meetings anymore. Carter would say, "I have this hunch about this," and everyone would respond, "No way. We don't act on hunches." People griped that you had to arrive for meetings with your computer printouts tucked under your arm. The place changed from being market-focused and natural to highly complex and financial. In a world that became analytical and began to pray at the altar of process, Carter had no patience. He couldn't do it. The culture became less and less tolerant of the absurd act. The process was everything. If it couldn't be analyzed, it couldn't be true. That was the new motto of the company. This was devastating to Carter. He was always grumbling about how long it took to get things done. It was like someone had given him a frontal lobotomy. He could still walk around, but he was no longer effective. He wasn't the same Shelby Carter.

Though he remained at the company for some time more, at age fifty-five Carter felt his career had flattened out and he left to return to his roots in Texas, where he worked at a Texas bank and did some teaching at the University of Texas at Austin. He did well financially and things turned out just fine for him.

Nobody seemed able to solve the problem of the warring factions and individual ambitions at Xerox, and so in March 1972 a new card was played. A corporate reorganization was undertaken and McCardell made me a group vice president in charge of marketing and the service side of the business. Meanwhile, Jim O'Neill was put in charge of engineering and manufacturing, and my old friend, Bill Glavin, was to oversee program planning and product management. All three of us reported to Ray Hay. As a result, what came to be known as the troika was formed. Some years before, the management structure of the Soviet Union had a troika at the top of its system, so the Xerox structure was likened to the Soviet example by many people in the company. The point of the comparison was that they felt nobody was in charge, we were moving along at the same pace as the Soviet Union, and we were becoming a dinosaur that couldn't get out of its own way. There was also a sense of betrayal and that interlopers were killing the organization.

The criticism was well justified, for the troika wasn't a particularly good management structure, and I certainly wasn't too excited about it. I thought dividing the business into three pieces was not the way to get things done. O'Neill and Glavin had very different approaches to managing the business and thus didn't get along all that well. O'Neill was tough-minded and would say what he thought and do it publicly, and Glavin had a problem with that. O'Neill once went to a meeting at Rank Xerox, which wasn't doing well, and totally humiliated one of the top executives. After the meeting, the lambasted man said he had to get away from the office and go for a solitary drive. He said it was the worst business day of his life. Soon after, he left the company.

Meanwhile, I tried to tend to my own knitting. I really liked the sales force. The people were high-spirited and they had a sense of adventure. They were always cooking up ways to inspire more sales. One of the wackier ideas came out of the business products branch in Minneapolis. The manager of the Twin Cities branch, Duncan LaVigne, bought a Hampshire pig and named it Millard Fillmore after the lackluster thirteenth president of the United States. He then told his salesmen that the manager whose team had the worst record each month would play host to the bovine for the subsequent thirty days. On the other hand, any month that the branch surpassed its sales quota by 50 percent, LaVigne would be stuck with the pig.

Before Millard arrived, LaVigne's six sales teams ranked fourteenth among the fifteen branches in Xerox's Midwest region. But the fear of getting Millard had a powerful effect. Within eight months, the branch had catapulted to fifth place in its territory. As it turned out, the first Millard got so fat during a year of being boarded at a nearby farm by losing teams that he had to be slaughtered. But he was instantly replaced by another Millard. The first recipient of him was none other than LaVigne. The Twin Cities branch had achieved 150 percent of its monthly sales quota.

Despite these sorts of motivational ideas, a basic shortcoming of the sales force was that it had evolved in a noncompetitive environment and adopted a noncompetitive outlook on the world. Salesmen dealt mostly with internal issues. Moreover, while the Ford people brought in an analytical discipline, they didn't bring along a heavy competitive drive. Not everybody likes competition but I felt our sales force didn't cope with it very well at all.

One other thing that bothered me was that, despite the missionary fervor of the sales force, there was an unusually high turnover rate, much higher than I was accustomed to at IBM. Part of the cause was a poor image. New sales representatives had to endure long days of "cold calls" seeking unsolicited business, and the brush-offs could pile up and get to you. Most rookies were assigned to geographic territories where they visited a wide array of businesses—accountants, boating companies, lawyers, medical offices. To upgrade the image of the salesman and make his lot more intellectually challenging, we began shifting to a vertical market structure. Under this approach, a salesman would specialize in a group of businesses with similar traits. For instance, we created the ACE group (architecture, construction, and engineering). We found that the turnover rate of salesmen working vertical markets was one-third that of territorial representatives.

Another problem was that the fast-track reputation of Xerox was working against us. Newcomers expected to become a manager after a couple of years of knocking on doors. Those who didn't were frustrated. But the promotion opportunities weren't as bountiful anymore. So we worked hard to moderate the high expectation levels and to make the sales job more satisfying. For too long, we had talked too much about quick promotions.

Nevertheless, nobody, myself included, was terribly worried. On the surface, everything still looked great. Profits continued to be robust because in the rental business you had healthy inflationary gains. The company essentially took inflation and just passed it through to the customers through price increases.

In mid-December of 1972, a new and explosive factor entered the picture. The Federal Trade Commission spoiled our Christmas by filing a complaint against Xerox charging restraint of trade and alleging that Xerox had illegally monopolized the $1.7 billion copier industry. Among other things, the FTC said Xerox had stamped out smaller competitors, used its market clout to reap outsize profits, and sought to perpetuate its patents by reregistering slightly different versions of those about to expire.

The case was unusual to say the least. It represented only the second time in many years that the FTC had sought to dismantle a monopoly; normally that was the work of the Justice Department. What's more, the commission didn't base its case on either of the two standard antimonopoly statutes—the Sherman and the Clayton antitrust laws. Rather, it relied on a broad and seldom-used section in the FTC act outlawing "unfair methods of competition in commerce."

According to the complaint, Xerox controlled 60 percent of the overall copier market and 95 percent of the business in plain-paper copiers. To redress this dominance, the FTC suggested some sweeping measures: that we sell off our controlling interests in Rank Xerox and Fuji Xerox, that we radically alter our pricing policies, and that we offer all our patents, royalty free, to licensees. The latter demand would mean throwing open one of the most tightly protected patent systems in the world. You don't often see such a basic patent position as Xerox's, since there is usually one way or another for companies to get around patents. But the five original patents of Chester Carlson were so basic that there was absolutely no way to get around them.

A central target of the FTC case was our Machine Utilization Plan, what we referred to as MUP. It was our pricing approach that involved our biggest and most important customers, and was not something we took lightly. But perhaps the worst fear of senior management was losing our foreign affiliates. At the time, Rank Xerox and Fuji Xerox were contributing nearly half of our earnings. If we complied with the FTC's demand, we would basically have to cut ourselves in half.

Peter McColough now faced a fundamental test of his leadership. If the FTC succeeded, it could do immense damage to the company. The very action itself had a definite chilling effect. It imposed significant restrictions on what we could do with pricing, and therefore we did not act aggressively to match some of our growing low-priced competition. How much impact it had on our running of the business in general is difficult to quantify. But I feel it caused us to take our eye off the competition, and we were not the aggressive organization we had been.

Among other things, the action was a blow to our image. When it came to image-building, Xerox had built one of the best. It was known as an enlightened employer and as a responsible corporate citizen, which was not the result of any black magic or hocus-pocus but of Joe Wilson's and Peter McColough's philosophy that the corporation is an integral part of society and has inherent social responsibilities. We worked hard at hiring minorities and at cleaning up the environment. We regularly sponsored some of the best programing on television, including *Death of a Salesman, The Glass Menagerie,* an eight-part series on blacks in America, and a controversial four-part series on the United Nations at a time when it was under sharp attack. Just the previous year, the company had begun a unique sabbatical program in which at least twenty of our employees each year would be paid to work full-time on anything they wanted to that might contribute to a better society. Employees could work in the areas of civil rights, parole reform, drug addiction, and teaching handicapped children—and many did.

The antitrust suit cost us in other intangible ways. It tired the company out and cast a pall over things. It made our employees peevish and testy. The stock market didn't like us anymore, either. The whole matter imposed onerous demands on the time of McColough and the other senior executives. And the lawyers rose to the top and got involved in almost everything. We all spent time being deposed. The company became traumatized and it lost its confidence.

The FTC case also spawned a large number of private antitrust suits by our competitors, so many of them that we became known as the most sued company in America. We had a huge in-house legal staff, plus we were forced to spend millions of dollars a year on outside counsel. McColough decided to settle some of these antitrust cases because the time requirements on the legal staff and our executives were just too great. It wasn't possible to fight everybody. At the same time, he stiffened his resolve and decided he had to fight some of them to vindicate Xerox's position. But the company had to be careful who it settled with and who it fought.

It was several long years before, in July 1975, Xerox and the FTC came to a settlement of the antitrust action. We agreed to forfeit much of our patent protection through licensing arrangements, because McColough believed that the erosion of our hold on the market would not be that significant. After all, there was our unrivaled sales force to contend with and the two decades of experience building our brand in the marketplace. The patents were simply less important than when Xerox was small and fragile. We also agreed to adjust our pricing policies and to allow customers to buy toner from other suppliers. But Rank Xerox and Fuji Xerox were left alone.

Even though it took a long time coming and was a tremendous pain in the neck, the FTC settlement wasn't an altogether bad deal. We already realized that if we didn't license people new competition would come into the business and infringe our patents anyway. We would sue and they would countersue, claiming antitrust. And the litigation would go on and on. We couldn't conduct a business like that. So once we decided we needed to license people there was no reason not to settle the FTC suit.

Even after the settlement, we remained entangled in pending private suits for years to come. We paid ten million dollars to settle a suit brought by the Addressograph-Multigraph Company, and we resolved an action from Litton Industries for another ten million. In both instances, there was no admission of guilt.

We elected to contest a suit brought by SCM, and it went to trial. We had no particular animosity toward SCM. But it bothered Peter to settle any of the cases because, though it was not said or admitted, there was the feeling that if Xerox weren't guilty, why would it be settling? So we felt we had to fight some of them.

We chose SCM because we didn't think they could prove in court that they could have succeeded in office products if we had licensed them. Their sales record was simply too poor. Also, Peter had interviewed the present head of SCM some years before for the job of chief financial officer. During the course of the interview, he told Peter that he wanted to come to Xerox because he felt that SCM was not willing to make the required investment in research in office copying to succeed. These factors convinced us that SCM was the one we should fight tooth and nail to the end.

The SCM battle was a long and bitter one. Peter alone spent forty-two days giving depositions. We were compelled to provide SCM and its lawyers with more than a million documents. And, of course, they were written by people who had no idea that some day they would be subpoenaed as part of an antitrust case. Some of the papers were very embarrassing. One sales memo read: "This is the week to attack, attack, attack IBM. We're forming killer squads to go after IBM."

SCM was seeking five hundred million dollars in damages from us. Xerox was suing SCM, too. The trial was held in Hartford, Connecticut, and lasted fourteen months in 1977 and 1978, making it one of the longest courtroom confrontations between two companies. Xerox used twenty lawyers and nearly a hundred aides. SCM had fifteen lawyers and another hundred aides. So many of the people lived in two of the local hotels they were dubbed the Xerox Sheraton and the SCM

Hilton. Peter was on the stand as the lead witness for Xerox for two weeks. Our lawyers needed an additional thirty days with him to get him ready to go on the stand. After thirty-eight days of deliberation, the jury awarded SCM $111.3 million only to have the U.S. district judge set aside the award. His reasoning was that patent law allowed companies to guard their inventions without financial liability. SCM appeals were unsuccessful. We fought a suit brought by Van Dyke Research in New Jersey, and similarly prevailed.

We felt we could have settled the SCM thing for a hundred million dollars or so. We spent twenty-five million defending it. More important, by winning we felt we would send a signal that we were not guilty and deflect further suits. And after SCM there were no more cases against us.

We also had a legal tussle with IBM. In the spring of 1970, IBM told Xerox that because we would not license them in plain-paper copiers (they had asked for years and we kept saying no), they said they were going ahead and introducing a plain-paper copier anyway, what became known as the Copier I. They gave Xerox diagrams of it and the lawyers decided that some two dozen Xerox patents were violated. An internal meeting was called to decide whether to sue. Peter said that Xerox certainly should, not only for patent infringement but also for misuse of information. Xerox had given them some information for computer applications and they were clearly using it for copier applications.

When the Copier I was introduced, it wasn't all that remarkable. It was pretty slow—making only ten copies a minutes—and couldn't do things like copy from a book. Still, IBM was the glamour company, and the new machine resulted in a lot of 914 cancellations. The day the product was introduced, Xerox sued IBM, charging infringement on twenty-two of its patents, as well as with misuse of trade secret information. IBM countersued.

Frank Cary was head of IBM at the time. Much later, Peter went to see him and said that he thought we should settle this because it was unseemly for two respected companies to be suing each other. But Cary wanted to settle for something like a million dollars and Peter had fifty or seventy-five million in mind. So he couldn't get anyplace.

The case was first tried in Canada on patent infringement, and Xerox won, which was a good indication that it would prevail on American soil. Peter went to see Cary again, seeking a settlement. He told Peter that he couldn't see how they could settle, for it was apparent that they had different choke levels. He wouldn't pay too much and Peter wouldn't accept too little. Peter said, "Maybe our choke levels are not that far apart." And he suggested a little choke test. Each of them would write down on a slip of paper what they would honestly settle for and then they would compare the numbers to see just how far apart they were. Peter wrote down thirty million dollars and Cary wrote down twenty million. They shared the papers and Peter said, "We're not that far apart. Why not split the difference?" And so the matter was settled for twenty-five million dollars and an ugly courtroom battle was averted.

I wasn't deeply involved in the antitrust actions because the activities Xerox was accused of took place before I came to the company. Peter had very strong feelings about the severity of the impact on the company, though in my own mind it's hard to quantify the specific effect of all the legal action. Peter felt we might have staved off the competition better without the suits. He complained that his hands were tied. I do know I got turned down on a number of price plans because of the FTC case, and wound up losing the business. One of them was a big order for the Social Security Administration.

And, of course, the FTC made us license the Japanese. The Sony television was already making a splash in this country, but the government and the lawyers and the economists didn't see what was brewing over in Japan. The auto companies were fretting more about Volkswagen than the Japanese. That's why what the FTC did to us was absolutely stupid. The FTC was chasing the horse after it left the barn. They weren't even thinking of the specter of international competition. It's clear to me that Xerox lost its aggressiveness during this period.

Though it was not yet evident to us, something was going on over in Japan that was destined to have a profound impact on our future. Xerox was being identified as a "targeted" company. That meant that the Japanese had decided that the copier business was an industry extremely important to Japan and they were determined to marshall their collective resources to launch an all-out offensive against Xerox. It has always been murky how the Japanese actually come to target industries, though the belief of many American companies is it happens with the involvement of the government through the Ministry of International Trade and Industry. There has been quite a history of targeted industries, dating back to the 1950s, that has included steel, chemicals, motorcycles, televisions, cameras, computers, semiconductors, and automobiles. In each instance, U.S. corporations would discover themselves battling a ferocious wave of Japanese products that were invariably priced lower than U.S. products. Starting in the early 1970s, the Japanese began zeroing in on us. It would not be a comforting development. For when the Japanese target your business, it means a war that can end in annihilation for the loser.

I don't like to dwell too much on the ramifications of the FTC case and the private suits it fomented, because I don't like to make excuses. The real problems that afflicted us—though we were just beginning to realize it—were that we had lost touch with our customers, had the wrong cost base, and had inadequate products. The barrage of suits took something out of us, but the true challenges to the company lay outside the courtroom. They lay in corporate boardrooms across the Pacific and they lay in our own managerial suites, where our mind-set was causing us to drift into what would become a battle royal for our very life.

5. The Stormy Times

WHENEVER YOU WANTED TO say the popular and correct thing at a Xerox meeting, all you needed to do was draw a deep breath and go on about how much growth you were going to achieve. Then everyone's ears would perk up. For growth was the buzzword that permeated Xerox and just about strangled it. Sometimes it seemed as if it was all we ever talked about. Almost every meeting we had boiled down to some sort of discussion about growth and how we would reach a bigger and bigger scale. We believed we were aboard a quarter horse that had to be ridden full speed ahead. When I first came to Xerox, there was a task force devoted to growth. We did everything including put growth under a microscope to try to figure out ways to get more of it.

This fixation was understandable. After all, since the formative days, the company had done nothing but grow, and grow explosively. So everything was "Get the growth and get the profits." In the business world, this may sound like a perfectly normal and intoxicating objective to have, but the truth was this was a deeply troubling mind-set. The swelling profits that kept pouring in blinded us from everything else. They took over and possessed us like a demon.

In fact, Xerox was such a fast-expanding and profitable company, with such extensive patent protection, that a lot of managers began believing their performance as managers was as good as their financial performance. Few Xerox managers were burdened with modesty. And yet at least half the reason for their success was because there wasn't much competition. To sell a Xerox copier was not exactly the world's most formidable task. It was almost as if you were the only person selling milk or the sole heating-oil man in town. All in all, it was not really difficult being a "successful" manager.

Given this environment, it was easy for managers to get a little arrogant and to stop paying much attention to what the competition we did have was doing and to drift out of intimate contact with the customer. We got into big trouble mostly because we stopped listening to the customer. Sooner or later, that sort of deafness can be fatal.

But it was nowhere near that simple. There also was no real quality control to speak of in the company, no all-pervasive attitude that the products must be as good as humanly possible. Quality in these days was considered nothing more than an expense—and who wanted extra expenses?

Even our pricing policies were alienating our customers, and you could hardly blame them. Our pricing was about the most bewildering strategy I had ever come across. It was like discovering calculus for the first time. In these days, we were selling some machines outright, but copiers were still predominantly a rental business. The sale price was always very steep, and people usually prefer to rent something new. Then if they don't like it, they can send it right back. Yet there was never a straight rental price, but instead one that rose the more the customer used the machine. Xerox was always intent on making copiers as easy to acquire as possible, and that meant keeping the up-front costs low. So a customer would pay a base monthly rental and then would get charged for each copy he made. The ingenious thing Xerox managers had come up with was a whole raft of pricing configurations based on usage. The appeal of this approach was that it make one machine seem like a lot of different machines. The drawback was that we got carried away. The pricing plans became more and more complex. You would pay a certain price for the first five copies, then a different price for copy six through twenty, then yet another price for twenty through fifty. You'd get dizzy looking at the permutations.

When I first came to Xerox, there were literally thousands of price plans. And with such an outlandish number, the whole strategy had become a distinct negative. Our billing systems couldn't keep up with all the alternatives. What was worse, customers couldn't possibly keep them straight in their minds. For that matter, I wasn't able to keep them straight. It was maddening trying to explain them to our sales force, which, after all, was supposed to be the final expert on pricing. I remember asking one of our senior sales executives once about the price of a certain product and, as he explained it, the numbers began running together in my mind. When he was finally finished, I scratched my head and said, "That's pretty complicated. What do we say when a customer asks about the price?" And he said right back, "Ask him about his mother-in-law." In other words, the sales people knew the prices were virtually indescribable.

IBM woke us up in a hurry. IBM had entered the copier business in 1970 with Copier I, which was not all that impressive a product and failed to make a big splash. A few years later, it brought out Copier II, a considerable improvement, and when it did it unveiled a new pricing approach. It was labeled Top Stop Pricing. The way it worked, after a customer had made a certain number of copies there were no further charges. In other words, IBM put a cap on these pricing schedules—and customers ate it up. That was when we emphatically realized how dissatisfied businesses were with our complex schedules.

Although we actually continued to take orders for the 914 into 1976, we knew well before then that we had to introduce an ever-broader array of products if we were to continue our relentless growth. And, in fact, there was a great deal of work done to determine the future product constellation of the company. The development people actually went through a list of permutations that were referred to by the letters of the alphabet: A, B, C, D, and so forth. Strategy Q turned out to be the one that was adopted. It prescribed various products that were to be built over a period of years. The most notable was what would be named the 9200, a duplicating machine that would occupy an important niche in Xerox history. During development, it was first called Gamma and later renamed Ardrie.

The goal was a marvel that could make a hundred and twenty copies per minute—two per second—and that would incorporate several impressive advances. Instead of a selenium drum, it would employ a seamless belt as a photoconductor, and it would use a special process to fuse toner to paper almost instantaneously.

There were myriad problems in creating the 9200. This marked the first time that Xerox had tried to deal with building true reliability into a copier, and it turned out that nobody knew how to specify for reliability. We had to build test chambers. It was like putting a man on the moon. There were perpetual technical problems. Since this was the first time imaging was being done on a flexible belt instead of a drum, a plant had to be built to make the belt. The "developer" for the toner—the small beads that carry the toner—needed to be made out of a different material because the old developer didn't work well at the faster speed. At one point, we felt we would have to use nickel, and when we looked into that possibility it turned out we would essentially have to corner the world market in nickel. Talk about daunting tasks. Something else was ultimately substituted.

After eight years of research and development, we finally introduced the 9200 in late 1974. By the time the first copy came out of it, its cost had approached $500 million, a figure that was widely likened to the cost of creating Du Pont nylon or the Boeing 747. The expense had escalated tremendously over what had originally been budgeted, in part because development took two years longer than expected. As some consolation for the mammoth investment, the machine was expected to produce the revenue to catapult the company forward. Internally, it was viewed as a bet-the-company project. If it didn't succeed, the company would have been gone.

The original marketing plan had been that the 9200 would serve as a replacement product for older models, but that strategy was revised several years before the 9200 was even finished, because the cancellation rate for existing copiers was running much lower than had been predicted. Hence the 9200 would never make it as a replacement product. We wouldn't have gotten the orders. Therefore, the product was repositioned to directly assault the offset machine and be put into central reproduction departments, the domain of our old foe, Charlie Printpants. Customers who relied on in-house print shops were heavy users, making thirty thousand or more copies a month, so they were awfully nice customers to have. Most of our high-volume machines were used in the twenty-thousand-copy range.

But this strategy posed a treacherous marketing challenge. Having spent decades circumventing Charlie Printpants, a guy who had built up a lot of enmity toward Xerox, we were not going to find it easy courting him, no matter how many flowers and sweets we brought along. We wanted him to love us, when he still felt like hating us.

Probably the thing most people best remember about the 9200 is the advertising campaign we launched to promote it. It marked the introduction of Brother Dominic, who became perhaps the best-known monk in the world.

In the now-famous television commercial, Brother Dominic is depicted duplicating information with a scribe. Once he's finished, he faithfully delivers his work to his supervisor.

"Very nice work, Brother Dominic," the superior says. "Very nice. Now I would like five hundred more sets."

Brother Dominic walks off, head down, shoulders hunched. Then he has a brainstorm. He boards a bus to town and journeys to a copier store, where he asks, "Can you do a big job for me?"

The attendant takes the pile of paper and runs off copies on one of our 9200 duplicating systems.

Copies in hand, Brother Dominic returns to his superior and says, "Here are your sets, Father."

"What?"

"The five hundred sets you asked for."

The superior looks heavenward and says, "It's a miracle."

The creation of Brother Dominic also represented a miraculous rejuvenation of the career of a man named Jack Eagle. Eagle, a fifty-year-old comedian, was hired to play the clerical figure—even though he's Jewish. Although he continued to perform occasional stand-up comedy in the Catskills, he coined most of his money from the Xerox commercial and some hundred and fifty personal appearances a year he made for us at trade shows, branch openings, and product demonstrations for important clients. All the while, he never touched a copying machine, an act we felt was un-monkly. With the popularity of the ad, we began handing out free Brother Dominic T-shirts, posters, and coffee mugs. Eagle was really smitten by the attention. At the height of his fame, he cracked, "People are beginning to think I'm real. They called me up to Lake Placid for the Olympics when there was no snow. When I left there was five inches."

Even with the help of our lovable monk, sales of the 9200 were sluggish at first. There were about a hundred thousand company printshops in the country, and we hoped to place one 9200 in each of them. That was an unrealistic expectation. The CRDs proved hard to crack. Our salesmen had serious trouble persuading printers that the greater expense of the 9200 was justified by its increased automation, which made possible a reduction in the number of skilled employees in the printshop. Addressograph-Multigraph and A.B. Dick mounted major campaigns to push their new, automated offset machines. In time, however, we won Charlie over or found ways to work around him. We also got a lot of 9200s installed with customers who were less intensive users than those with CRDs.

One of the things that concerned us about the 9200 was the fact that its complexity was sure to give rise to particularly difficult and unique service problems. Accordingly, we set up a small, highly specialized group of technical troubleshooters that we called the Tiger Team. It subsequently evolved into the Field Engineering Organization.

The revenues from the 9200 never hit the plans we had sketched out, but it became a hugely successful product and produced a tremendous revenue base. It spawned other products and allowed us to deal with competition. Without question, it was a winning bet.

But it also masked to some extent festering problems that were spreading throughout the company. The 9200 was like a transfusion that kept the company alive, but the organism was not changed.

Friction had increasingly developed among McCardell, Ray Hay, who headed U.S. operations, and Joe Flavin, who ran the international operations, which served to blunt the effectiveness of top management. A lot of it had to do with the fact that Hay, who had been shaped in the old Xerox culture, felt McCardell wasn't a good marketing man. Hay, of course, was a stellar salesman and a first-rate marketing person. At the same time, he could be rather harsh and sarcastic. People who worked under him were scared of him. Hay once told me that I allowed people to know too soon in the process how I felt about something and that discouraged input. On the other hand, I always thought Ray played too many games. He would do things to purposely put people off guard. He would lacerate someone for how he dressed, or he'd review some numbers presented to him and say, "Why'd you put that in the chart?" Once he was sitting next to another manager's wife at a dinner affair, and he turned to her and said, "Boy, you're gaining weight."

The chill among the trio worsened, and Hay and Flavin ended up quitting. In the fall of 1975, after Flavin departed to head the Singer sewing machine company, McCardell and McColough asked me to come to Stamford and take command of the international businesses that Flavin had been running. As a result, I began to oversee Rank Xerox and Fuji Xerox. I began flying over to Japan fairly regularly and got my first glimpses of what our upstart Japanese rivals were like.

Competition was really beginning to heat up on a number of fronts. IBM, of course, was already battling us. Kodak, our local rival, had entered the copier industry in late 1975. It had a product aimed at the large business user that was every bit as good as ours, and it introduced the phrase "Kodak quality" into the copier business. What's more, Kodak was delivering notably better service to the customer than we were. And to the customers' eyes, it was therefore better. The big question was how soon Kodak would jump into the more profitable mid-range copier business. For reasons that always seemed inexplicable to me, it never did explore that market as much as we thought it would or as much as it should have.

With two of the behemoths of industry angling for a piece of our market, we were plenty worried. The Japanese were also nibbling away, making far more headway as it turned out than we realized at the time, but we were totally blinded by IBM and Kodak. The two of them could throw an awful lot of light into someone's eyes.

In fact, Ray Hay used to say to me over and over: "IBM, IBM, IBM." It was as if it were some sort of mantra. With the improvements IBM had made in its second copier model, we all knew that IBM was in the market to stay, and that gave us major shivers.

It's wrong, however, to think that we were oblivious to the Japanese. My very first summer at Xerox, I remember going to meetings where the Japanese came up for discussion. People would say, "The Japanese are coming. The Japanese are coming." So it wasn't a matter of Xerox not knowing about Japan. In fact, we predicted the Japanese would arrive sooner than they did. But what no one at Xerox seemed to have any good grasp of was the level of quality and the low cost of manufacturing that the Japanese were destined to achieve.

So we talked about them a lot, but we certainly didn't fear them.

It wasn't only our intense focus on IBM and Kodak that kept us from spending more time contemplating the Japanese. It was also because the Japanese were producing coated-paper machines. We had this fixation on plain-paper copiers. We simply perceived that we were in the plain-paper business and that was the market that mattered. Anyone fooling with coated paper was shooting for small fry. Who, we asked ourselves, wanted coated-paper machines? The answer, unfortunately, was lots of people. But at this time we didn't pay much heed.

Part of the reason for our narrow focus was the general attitude of top management. McCardell ran the business very optimistically. He was always looking to the moon—and sometimes beyond. He expected us to grow every second of every day, Sundays not excluded. As a result, he had no tolerance for anything that seemed small in scale. If a project was proposed that involved less than a billion dollars in revenues he wouldn't touch it. It was beneath his thought process for growth.

Don't get me wrong. Archie was a very smart guy, and because he came up the financial side, he was extremely analytical. But we used to tease him about being his own analyst: he'd make a decision and then go ahead and perform the analysis to support it. As all too many people have found out, that can be a highly dangerous way to operate.

One thing that was always unmistakably clear was Archie's conviction that everything we made would sell. As a result, we were continually announcing things too fast and overbuilding products. And we were always fixing them in the marketplace, creating a base of customer dissatisfaction.

From the very beginning, Xerox had built an organization that wasn't centered on the quality and reliability of the product. The early emphasis was on ease of use, because other duplicating equipment was anything but easy to use. As you recall, the company's first advertisements, featuring the little girl named Debbie, all focused on ease of use. There was little concern about quality or reliability, and to this day the copier is the least reliable piece of equipment in the office, though it's a lot more dependable than it used to be.

Any understanding of a copier made it clear how difficult it was to have a reliable machine. Few inventions are as complicated as an office photocopier. It is part chemical plant, part optical device, part paper mover, and part computer. You are trying to move this black toner (or dry ink) around the machine and you are dealing with paper. Paper contains moisture. As the paper went through a Xerox machine, the moisture was extracted and that caused it to curl. Moisture-free paper was not easy to handle. All the toner you were trying to put on the paper wouldn't stick and would float around the machine. The xerographic process was very dirty. So we had an unstable process that we were trying to make go faster and faster, and as we did we just added to the constellation of problems that could arise. Almost every model we came out with developed its own scrapbook of horror stories. One of the most famous was the 3600-3, which was plagued by frequent fires, one of which flared up at the White House.

As copiers became more important to office workers and were used in greater frequency, their lack of reliability became much more evident. A paper jam didn't matter much if you were using your copier once a week. When it was being used every hour and for important applications, a paper jam became a huge annoyance. Also, as offices grew more dependent on copiers, they did away with backup modes of duplicating material. They didn't keep carbon paper around any longer, and so if the copier broke the office was stuck.

We were getting a lot of complaints about service by the mid-1970s, and I remember a management conference in Acapulco where the service question really reared its head. It was one of the first times that service was discussed as a prominent item at a Xerox top-management meeting, and so it was clearly beginning to move to the front burner. But our solution was to hire 700 more service representatives. That was a bad thought process, because we weren't addressing the source of the problem. We weren't going to try to make better machines. We were going to have more people floating around fixing bad ones.

With our bulging service force, the concept of retrofit became an increasingly common part of the Xerox culture. At the auto companies, there would be periodic recalls where car owners would be advised to bring in their Fords or Buicks to their nearest dealer for a new brake lining or fuel pump. It was a similar story at Xerox. Tech reps were frequently being shipped new parts that had to be installed to remedy a problem in a copier. And we were always bickering over retrofit dollars. First we would tackle anything that impinged on safety; then we would do the things that affected the major machines; and finally we would get around to the less-important models. Unlike the way things worked at the auto companies, Xerox retrofits were basically on-premise rebuilds. The work was virtually always performed at the office where the machine sat. It was as if you got a call from your GM dealer saying he was going to send a mechanic over to replace the engine in your driveway. The tech rep would show up and dismantle the machine wherever it sat, scattering parts and dirt all over. Needless to say, it looked awful.

As often as not, once we did a retrofit, the machine was improved but it still broke down a lot. Some retrofits were so extensive that we would have to do a "like for like," a trade where we would take out the machine and swap it for a similar model.

In those days, Xerox was still a very successful company. While profit margins were decreasing in the early seventies, many of our products still had gross margins as high as 70 to 80 percent—but with customer dissatisfaction on the rise the company was becoming very vulnerable.

If there was ever a product that symbolized the Xerox of the 1970s, it was the 4000 copier. A medium-speed, mid-range copier designed for moderate-sized companies, the 4000 was the first machine that would do duplex, meaning it could copy on both sides of a sheet of paper. Page one of a booklet would appear on one side, page two on the next, and so on. The 4000 came out in 1971, which was maybe a year sooner than it should have. In some people's minds, it came out a lifetime too soon.

We did win two Clios—the most prestigious television advertising award—for our commercials for the 4000. They featured football benchwarmer Kolodny, who was able to bring in the winning play to the rest of the football team only with the help of a 4000 copier. But that was about the only good news surrounding the product.

I have to admit that the 4000 was a mighty impressive piece of machinery on paper and physically looked great. The trouble began once you tried to operate it. There must have been several hundred things that went wrong with it, more things than people probably realized could even go wrong with a copier. For a good year after the product was installed in the marketplace, there were hundreds of engineering change orders—things that had to be fixed. Never before had Xerox had a product so riddled with flaws, and it marked a sad turning point in the quality of what we produced.

The problems were as basic as you could get. For instance, the very frames of the copier were out of square. They simply didn't fit together properly. Copier fit is absolutely crucial. If you're off even a tenth of an inch on a piece of the frame, that's more than enough to bring about drastic problems. If this happens, you need to force components together, and over time they will start to separate, opening up a real Pandora's box. Among other things, the bad fit led to the toner escaping from the copier and then showing up on customers' walls and rugs. Toner is pretty filthy stuff, and you can be certain that toner stains all over the place are not something that make a business call up and tell you it's a customer for life.

The machine's shortcomings just went on and on. It was such an unstable machine that it was forever jamming. Meter cards were still being used and customers would be forced to keep boxes of worthless copies to give to tech reps when they came so they would be credited against their meter cards. We subsequently learned from one engineer that during the development process he had never been able to get any time in the humidity test chamber to work out kinks in his sub-system. Sure enough, when machines were installed in the South, the high humidity there triggered a spate of failures. The copy quality itself didn't hold up. It would be great when the machine was installed, but in time the copies would get lighter and lighter until you could barely read them. Another irksome defect was snake deletion. If you've ever seen a copy that had a sort of washed-out portion meandering down the middle of the page, as if there was a white snake wiggling across the sheet, you've seen snake deletion. The 4000 produced more snakes than the Amazon jungle.

Fortunately, many of these problems we sorted out, mainly through some heroic effort by an obscure and unsung fix-it organization we had created. Some years before, we had developed a skunk works over in the working-class area of East Rochester, New York, actually just a block from where my father once worked for the gas and electric company. The skunk works began with just a couple of guys who would build tools for the tech reps to use when they went out on their calls. For instance, they developed a tiny but powerful vacuum cleaner that the reps used to clean dirt out of copiers.

The skunk works was located in a leased loftlike space on the second floor of an apartment house. It was a pretty creepy place. It was always messy and there were scads of dirt scattered about, which gave the unmistakable impression that a lot of work was going on. I used to wonder if they would rustle up bags full of dirt just before I came there for a visit and then spread it around to impress me. When you arrived, the entrance would invariably be locked and it was the sort of situation where you rapped on the door and then someone slid open a panel and you saw just a pair of eyes, like in some secret after-hours club.

The guys who worked there were true individualists. They liked the clutter. They really worked at maintaining a disheveled image. Everything was makeshift. Their environmental chamber consisted of a big polyethylene wrapper that was draped over a copier. They used to like to test copiers for endurance, and the way they did it was by shoving a yardstick between the machine and the wall so the start button was continuously kept pressed on. The real brains of the place was a fellow named John Webb. He loved copiers about as much as anyone humanly could. I once happened to visit him at his house and, instead of Ping-Pong tables, he had two of our copiers sitting in his basement so he could tinker with them while he was waiting for his wife to summon him for dinner. He must have been the only man in America who had two copiers in his home for recreation.

The skunk works group grew to about nine in number, and it expanded its reach and began to tackle actual Xerox products that were screwed up. In many instances, the team really saved the day, because we were shipping out product after product that was not meeting our own expectations much less the customer's.

There is an art to fixing copiers, and these guys were masters of it. Among other things, they managed to stamp out the snake deletion in the 4000 by discovering a wax that you could coat the drum with. It was a commercial wax that they had picked up at a local hardware store and used to coat the drum. But it did the trick. It was certainly great having the skunk works, and I always got a kick out of visiting it, but dumping a lot of problems on it that should have been solved long before a product came out was no way to run a company.

Frank Pipp, who joined Xerox as a manufacturing executive in the summer of 1971 after twenty-two years at Ford, reminded me again and again about how dumbstruck he was by the lamentable quality at Xerox.

Frank was a glaring exception to the mentality imported from Ford. He was not from the financial side of Ford but from the manufacturing ranks, and he took on the same role at Xerox, providing unquestionable benefit. He was the classic manufacturing manager in the best sense of the word. He had a real down-to-earth approach to things and an abundance of street smarts. Because of his folksy nature, a lot of people would underestimate the advice he had to offer. He was never bashful about speaking his mind. When he disagreed with me, Frank would write things down on sheets of yellow paper informing me of my errant thinking. I always felt Frank was wise beyond his years, and later on when there were tough problems, I often leaned on him. I remember going to his house one night and asking him to go up to Rochester to tackle an assignment. I thought he was the right person but he wasn't sure he was the right person. Nevertheless, he went. He had a very disciplined mind and was a great implementer, though he would get terribly frustrated when he wasn't able to implement something.

I vividly recall an anecdote Frank told me that occurred while he was running a Ford assembly plant in California in the late 1960s. The West Coast was where the first true penetration by the Japanese car makers took place, and where small Japanese cars began chugging down highways long before they sprang up throughout the rest of the country. Consequently, Pipp had far more awareness of the threat they posed, and of how good the cars were, than did the top executives in Dearborn. For the most part, the Dearborn brass thought the Japanese were a joke.

Pipp wasn't laughing, and he had invited some Dearborn people out to try to convince them that there was nothing flimsy about the Japanese products. When they got there, he had a Toyota truck up on a hoist. Pipp's plant had bought the truck and disassembled it to get a feel for how well made it was. At that time, Ford, along with the other American automakers, didn't believe that you could assemble a car without a rubber mallet handy to bang together the parts that didn't quite fit right. The rest of the parts—the ones that came out engineered and manufactured properly—fit together easily. They were known as snap-fit parts. When Pipp's crew got done taking apart and reassembling the Toyota truck, they were speechless. They hadn't once needed to pick up a mallet. The truck was entirely snap-fit. They had never seen anything like it. To make sure they weren't hallucinating, they took it apart a second time and put it back together. Incredibly enough, it was a snap-fit vehicle. The Toyota parts were made to far more exacting dimensions than Ford was making them.

The Dearborn people were told of this discovery and invited to look over the truck itself as it drooped from the hoist. Everyone was very quiet, until the division general manager cleared his throat and remarked, "The customer will never notice." And then everyone excitedly nodded assent and exclaimed, "Yeah, yeah, that's right," and they all trotted off happy as clams.

Much to Pipp's displeasure, this attitude of denial at Ford wasn't any different at Xerox in these days. And pointing it out got you in trouble. Pipp was only at Xerox two months when he nearly got fired. Ray Hay came around one day and asked him why he wasn't improving the quality of one of our latest products. "I can't improve the product at all," Pipp told him, and Hay grew enraged and his face turned beet red. "Why not?" he demanded. "That's why we hired you." And Pipp explained that once something gets to manufacturing there's not much that can be done to improve it. "All manufacturing can do is take what it gets from engineering and hopefully make it as good as the design," he said, "or often there's a good chance we'll degrade it. But we can't correct design problems created by engineering." In other words, the problems were that basic. We were coming up with lousy designs.

Part of our difficulty was unquestionably our mind-set. Certain beliefs would become part of Xerox thinking and there was almost no way to shake free of them. From the very beginning of the company, for instance, Xerox was consumed by the idea that the worst thing a machine could do was damage a customer's original sheets of paper, so it was important to minimize manipulation. We felt that the originals that were placed in copiers to be duplicated had to be protected against any sort of damage. After all, there's a big difference between crumpling up a copy that is smudged and having a copier eat up your only copy of a script or your will. This notion of not damaging the original was embedded in everyone's head and became part of their vocabulary. People would walk the halls of Xerox practically mumbling to themselves: "Remember, don't damage the original."

This conviction meant that we would do everything possible to avoid moving the original, especially having it actually enter the machine and thus be put at risk of being marred or mutilated. Consequently, using our machines could get fairly cumbersome. If someone wanted to make fifty copies of a ten-sheet original, then the first sheet had to be photographed fifty times and the fifty copies shot into fifty sorting bins. Then the next sheet would be photographed and the copies directed into those same bins, and so on. If you had a fifty-page booklet to copy, the way you did it was you copied pages one, three, five, and the rest of the odd numbers, then fed the pages back through the machine to do two, four, six, and the other even numbers on the other side. The shortcoming of this method was that the copies went through the machine twice. If the paper got jammed, it was destroyed and you had to begin all over again.

The technology existed to allow you to create what was known as a recirculating document handler, in which the original sheets would whisk through the bowels of the machine and therefore would eliminate the need for these gargantuan sorters, but we avoided it. We knew perfectly well how to make recirculating document handlers and considered doing just that, but we convinced ourselves that customers would never accept them because they increased the risk of damaging originals as they shuffled them through the machine. We even undertook some marketing studies in which customers told us they didn't want machines that put the originals at risk, though I have to wonder if our bias caused us to phrase the questions so we got the very answers we expected.

We did have a secret development project, code-named Moses, that was begun in 1972 and was largely aimed at developing an alternative to the clumsy sorters. It was also intended to match the speeds of the copiers Kodak and IBM were planning to announce. Moses constituted our first attempt to try to physically move the original through the copier. The idea went like this: a web was created to hold the original. To envision what it looked like, think of a quarter of a mile of Saran Wrap, two sheets stuck one against the other. The Saran Wrap would be curled around a roller, and the original would be clamped between the two sheets. As the web held the paper, copies of both sides would be made simultaneously. It was a cumbersome way to do things, but it protected the originals.

We sank a ton of money into Moses, and more than a thousand people worked on it. We hoped it would produce something that would absolutely blow away the competition.

Much to our chagrin, in April 1976 Kodak introduced a recirculating document handler for its Ektaprint copier, and it looked like a first-rate product. It had a document handler that was restricted to twenty-pound paper, not anything like what Moses was trying to do, but it appeared reliable and of high quality. And it was as if the atomic bomb had been dropped at Xerox. We were dumbstruck. The Kodak machine was simpler and much less costly than Moses, and it didn't break down much. At the time, I was on the marketing side of the company, and when I saw the Kodak machine I realized for the first time that you could make a more reliable copier than ours. Up until then, I thought our engineers were doing as well as possible with a complex technology.

We wound up losing a lot of very important customers to Kodak. And when you lose customers, you have to respond in some fashion.

So we had our East Rochester skunk works take our 9200 machine and hurriedly transform it into what we called our 8200. We downsized the speed and reduced the "footprint," which was the space on the floor the copier actually occupied, to make it competitive against Kodak. But the machine encountered reliability problems and in some ways it heightened the customer perception that we were pushing products we hadn't bothered to perfect.

For all our dark fears, it turned out that the recirculating document handler rarely did any harm to originals, certainly not often enough that customers needed to go through sleepless nights worrying whether they would ever see their originals again. By 1977, with Kodak and IBM selling machines that were cheaper than Moses to make and equipped with superior features, there no longer seemed any point in throwing more money at the project. And thus we made a highly controversial and much debated decision: we decided to cancel Moses. We now knew that if the customer would accept some risk to the document, then Moses wasn't worth it. It was a big decision, and it took us a lot longer to make it than it should have. It was, however, the right decision. To say the least, it was a dismaying outcome. When you stop something that large, you get a double whack. Not only is the investment washed down the drain, but you have no new product coming out for a while and have to substitute derivative models, hardly a satisfying way to do business.

Thus we had been defeated by our own constrained thinking. And that sort of mind-set against damaging the original probably was similar to thousands of other little things that cropped up throughout the company. You wind up freezing your thought process because of these stubborn attitudes.

Another example of constrained thinking was the long-held fear of top management that xerography would one day become obsolete. There continued to be the deep-seated concern—certainly Peter McColough shared it—that some day somebody would invent a new technology that would eradicate xerography as quickly as a magician made a person disappear. As a result, we became reticent about indulging in much research and development aimed at further refining the xerographic process. Jack Goldman, who was the head of research, used to constantly remind the top executives about the RCA debacle. For years, RCA kept plowing money into research intended to improve on the vacuum tube. Meanwhile, others were engaged in the development of the transistor, which, when perfected, made the vacuum tube a museum piece. It was a scary lesson. It scared me.

For one thing I long believed was that many of the great ideas are not precipitated by the customer. While the customer knows what he wants, he doesn't always know what's possible. And that first dawned on me in my very earliest days in business. When I was new at IBM, working in sales and taking a management training program in Sleepy Hollow, New York, I was rooming with a development engineer. One evening, I came back to my room grumbling about the lack of speed and reliability of the tape drives, and wondered why the engineers couldn't do something about it. My roommate stared at me with a look of total exasperation. "Boy, you guys in sales are all the same," he said. "You remind me of the farmer in 1850. If you asked him what he wanted, he would say he wanted a horse that was half as big and ate half as many oats and was twice as strong. And there would be no discussion of a tractor."

I always remembered that. Because if all you do is respond to the current users of your product, that is what they will tell you. They want the same thing that they already have but they want it to be more reliable and to cost less. It's only through an interaction of your ideas with your most forward-thinking customers that fresh concepts emerge. And so, the way we looked at things, twenty years from now we didn't want to end up making a better horse. We wanted to have some tractors.

There was just one difficulty. We were too single-minded. Our research efforts became fixated on other technologies to the almost total exclusion of our copier business. And that's where we made a mistake, because this hurt us badly with our bread-and-butter customers.

There's no more instructive illustration of this than the problem of "dirt." An inevitable shortcoming of early copiers was that some of the toner inside the machine always got loose and escaped. This loose toner was known as dirt. Some of it would wind up on copies in places you didn't want it. If a copier stood against a wall, a film of dirt would build up on the wall. Dirt would also seep into the workings of the copier and foul things up. So, to the extent that you controlled dirt, you saved a lot of money on service calls. In the mid-1970s, in fact, we figured dirt was costing us hundreds of millions of dollars a year. But because of our mind-set that xerography was mature, we were not investing in development for improvement. Therefore, we didn't spend much time trying to eliminate dirt. Meanwhile, the Kodaks and Canons and IBMs of the world were investing considerable sums of money improving the xerographic process, including dirt, and were creating machines that had a lot less of it. And they were making thousands of customers much happier. They took our xerographic process, reduced the cost, and significantly improved reliability and quality.

We were encountering serious problems with our noncopier interests, too. SDS, our billion-dollar acquisition, had begun to look a little rotten. One obvious problem was that its government business, which accounted for something like 40 percent of its revenues, had begun to slow. A lot of its sales were tied to the space program, and once a man walked on the moon the government moderated its investment in space, including computers. But the ills of the company went deeper than this. I believe XDS, as Xerox renamed the enterprise, was always a poor company through and through, and I'm not sure it ever really earned any money. Shortly after I came to Xerox, the decision was made to break XDS into functions, so XDS as a unit disappeared. The folklore around the company was that now that you didn't report the company's results collectively it was possible to conceal how badly it was doing. If it was losing a lot of money, that all got mucked in with our other results. I was at IBM when Xerox bought SDS and I happened to own some Xerox stock. I promptly sold it because I thought the decision made no sense. I had had a nice run-up with the stock and made some decent money off the trade.

In the spring of 1975, with XDS hemorrhaging money, McColough convened a computer task force named Odyssey to figure out what to do about it. Its conclusion was that no one would buy it, no matter how cheap the price. The best path Xerox could follow was to shut down the business and stanch its losses, selling whatever assets were worth something. McColough followed the advice. At the July 1975 board meeting, Xerox voted to terminate the business. At a press conference announcing the action, Peter admitted that the acquisition was a mistake.

The press came to mock SDS as "McColough's Folly," and it did turn out to be a financial disaster. For a billion dollars, Xerox got a hundred-million-dollar company that, as far as I can tell, never made any money for the corporation. To be fair, we did get some excellent people from it as well as digital technology and expertise that we badly needed. I had nothing to do with getting out of SDS. I was running U.S. marketing at the time, but I agreed with the decision. SDS had been bought for stock worth fifty times earnings, but Xerox could have used the shares to get something else.

With the demise of SDS, Xerox decided to stop making mainframe computers. We were forced to take a whopping $84.4 million write-off to cover the expense of discontinuing the computer business. That huge charge resulted in Xerox's first quarterly decline in profit growth since the company had become Xerox in 1960. Xerox stock, which hit a high of $179 a share in 1972, plunged to fifty dollars in early 1975. There were a lot of long faces on Wall Street.

While we dealt with this bruising setback, some fairly unsettling things were going on overseas and we got a good glimpse of them in the summer of 1975. In July at the annual National Office Machines Dealers Association, a totally new type of Japanese copier was unveiled. Known as the Savin 750, it was destined to have an electrifying effect on the copier industry and on Xerox.

The long effort to create the 750 was spearheaded by a man named Paul Charlap. Charlap, who was an American, was aware that Xerox was not especially interested in slow copiers that made less than twenty copies per minute. Though we sold equipment of this sort, it was large, high-priced, and not particularly dependable. There was another good reason why we didn't care much for slow copiers. We weren't selling machines; we were leasing them. And our profits came from how many copies customers made on those machines. If a copier was slow in generating copies, that was money plucked out of our pocket.

We didn't make much money off the low end of the market and thus we figured, so what, let them have it. We realized the bulk of our profits in the medium and high end. Even though there were unmistakable signs that the Japanese liked to start in the low end of a new market and then move up, we still didn't care. By this time, we were expert at rationalizing away problems.

I suspect that because of our lack of interest in this portion of the market, Charlap sensed that there was a ripe opportunity there just waiting to be exploited. So he cobbled together a team of Americans, Germans, Japanese, and Australians dedicated to building a small machine that would outdo anything Xerox had to offer. The result was a real dazzler.

Liquid toner, a technology invented by an Israeli named Benny Landa, was the crucial ingredient that made the Savin machine so different. Xerox machines worked with powdered toner, which required a tricky process. In order to create a copy, the copier had to first melt the powdered toner into a liquid. After the liquid was fused onto the paper, it had to be cooled off. Liquid toner didn't require these steps. That made for a less expensive machine to build, as well as one that was less susceptible to breakdowns.

Savin hooked up with a Japanese manufacturer named Ricoh, and they approached the market with an altogether different strategy. Since their machines broke down less often, they underscored dependability in their sales pitches. Rather than following our policy of leasing the copiers, they sold them outright. And the prices they set were well below Xerox's. The first Savin 750s were priced at five thousand dollars. A Xerox 3100, the closest machine to the Savin, cost two and a half times as much (though we subsequently lowered our prices). Needless to say, with the advantages it had, the Savin was a smashing success.

One thing Savin didn't stint on was marketing dollars. They advertised their copier as heavily as we did ours. The ads were brash—and occasionally embarrassing. One of them that cut particularly close to home maintained that the "call key operator" button on a Xerox machine, the one that meant something had gone amiss, was the "feature that works best." While that wasn't literally true, it had more truth in it than we cared to admit. For during the mid-1970s, our customer cancellations were rapidly on the rise, and our response to the problem was to try to outrun them. In other words, we pushed harder to get enough new orders to offset the customers we had lost. It was not the smartest strategy ever conceived. Instead of trying to understand the root cause of the cancellations, we simply ignored the old customers. But the root cause would haunt us for a long time. Customers were fed up with our copiers breaking down and our service response.

It was small wonder, then, that in 1976 more than a hundred thousand Japanese copiers were bought worldwide, both Savins and those of others.

The promise of the Japanese had slowly begun to penetrate my own consciousness. I was making periodic trips to Japan, usually to visit our Fuji Xerox joint venture. The first time I visited Fuji Xerox, I thought, "How is this company ever going to be successful?" In its first ten years, Fuji Xerox took what Xerox and Rank Xerox had to offer, reengineered it and manufactured it for the Japanese market. Sometimes it was obvious that these machines weren't created with the Japanese in mind. When the Xerox 7000 arrived in Japan, secretaries had to stand on a box to reach the print button. It had been designed for the taller American secretary. Then Fuji Xerox began to take our American designs and make some changes to them for the Japanese market, extending the design time significantly and increasing the costs. By now, though, Fuji Xerox was starting to develop its own products, and I heartily encouraged them to go full speed ahead. I doubt my encouragement mattered all that much, because I know they would have followed that course anyway.

In 1976, deeply concerned about survival in the Japanese marketplace, Fuji Xerox began what was known as a Total Quality Control program, dedicated to steeping its workers in a drive to produce products of the very best quality. It called it the "New Xerox Movement." The first goal of the movement was to design and build a copier in half the time and at half the cost of previous machines.

Later that year, I flew over to take a look at the result. It was a new mid-range copier known as the Ace project, and it couldn't have been more aptly named. When I got over there, they did a demonstration of an engineering model of the product for me, and I was mightily impressed. As I stood there, surrounded by a group of Japanese executives, I started clapping enthusiastically. I felt sort of silly later on when I reflected on my action, but it was just a spontaneous outburst indicating how delighted I was. It was a truly stellar machine, notably better than anything we had in the States. Fuji Xerox showed me its objectives in terms of cost, reliability, and performance, and they were very lofty. When I shared those goals with some of my people back in the States, many scoffed and told me there was no way the Fuji Xerox people could ever meet them. And they were right. They didn't.

But Fuji Xerox had made a product that was better than anything Xerox had come up with, even though the engineers fell short of their goals. Up until now, I used to come to Japan convinced I had information that could help Fuji become more competitive. The Ace project was the first time it really sank in that I had much to learn from Fuji Xerox and could take things back rather than the other way around. It was an eye-opening realization.

Despite what we were beginning to learn, however, we saw no reason to take any significant action. From a financial standpoint, the early penetration by the Japanese was not all that important, and no alarms went off in our heads. The brisk business we were doing at the medium and high ends of the market made the low-end business that most Japanese products were aimed at look trifling. What we failed to grasp sufficiently was that it meant an important toehold for the Japanese. It got Japanese products into American offices, where customers could sample them and, if they proved to be reliable, come to like them. They were slowly but surely building customer credibility and loyalty. Some analysts came to call the low end of the market Xerox's soft underbelly. In a sense, they were right. Once the Japanese got into our belly, it was only a matter of time before they began gnawing away at our vital organs.

The important point is that we saw the Japanese coming but did not understand their ability to build good, reliable products at significantly lower cost. It was a similar situation to what American automakers went through. We continually rationalized that we were investing in R & D and that we had plans that would keep us competitive.

* * *

One thing was always true at Xerox: we never hit our sales targets. All through the 1970s—and on into the 1980s, for that matter—we constantly established unrealistic goals. Setting your sights too high was something not at all uncommon in the business world—you're always hoping for the best—but we were worse than most. Since our whole mind-set was growth—15 or 20 percent growth in sales and earnings every year—we automatically expected too much. You ought to establish reasonable targets, to take into account things that can go awry. But we didn't.

A major debate I had early in my career at Xerox was with Archie McCardell over the production volume of the 4000 copier. Driven by the 20 percent growth objective, Archie directed us to build and plan to sell unrealistic numbers of 4000s. When I saw the numbers I shook my head in disbelief because I knew we would never sell that many. His plan was utterly preposterous. I knew we didn't have the marketing organization to sell that many machines and I knew the customers weren't out there in that kind of quantity. And this was before I realized the seriousness of the product's reliability and quality problems. I probably should have laid my body down on the railroad tracks, but I didn't. I argued about the forecast, but at that time Xerox people breathed big forecasts every minute of the day. They ate them for breakfast, lunch, and dinner. So we built those machines and they sat and sat in the warehouse until we finally had to bleed them out. We had hired all these production workers and geared up to crank out the machines and now we had to effectively shut down production, get rid of the workers, and sell the copiers for whatever we could get for them.

In the mid-1970s, the American economy suffered the worst inflation rate since the end of World War II and a brutal recession. It was exacerbated by the ineffective wage and price controls begun under the Nixon administration, international crop failures, and the first of the Middle East oil shocks. Copying itself proved pretty impervious to the slumping economy. People made as many copies as they did during boom times. But while our revenues kept climbing, profits fell. Costs were rising and we weren't doing a good job of controlling them. While people made ample numbers of copies, they did them for the most part on the machines they had in place, and put off leasing new ones. In the miserable year of 1975, we installed just 1 percent more copiers than we removed, a fraction of a normal year.

Everybody who participated in the decisions of the 1970s must accept some of the blame for the errors in judgement and strategy, and that includes me. We were terrific at communicating and planning. But we were terrible at implementing solutions. As I saw it, we had too much vision and too little substance at Xerox. Maybe we simply weren't good enough to pull off the vision. We were clearly trying to do too much—more than we could do well.

Nevertheless, despite little in the way of good new products, Xerox continued to grow because of its powerful sales force. Also, Xerox was fortunate that Kodak moved slowly in developing its Ektaprint line. And the IBM Copier III fared badly as a result of major reliability problems. Although it was rebuilt and did better later on, IBM's momentum and reputation were hurt, and I believe the experience caused IBM to rethink its copier strategy.

Still, how long could the situation continue? Throughout the 1970s, we introduced only three completely new copying machines in the United States—the 4000, the 3100, and the 9200. As Shelby Carter aptly remarked: "I was out there with a rusty bayonet and an empty rifle."

6. The Coyote Eats the Road Runner

WHEN ARCHIE MCCARDELL talked to Peter McColough one afternoon in August of 1977, my life abruptly changed. He told Peter he had been offered the chief executive's job at International Harvester, the giant farm equipment company, and he was going to take it. The job would mean running a company that was bigger than Xerox, plus I think Archie was growing increasingly impatient that Peter hadn't yet stepped aside and given him a chance for the top post. Peter accepted his resignation, which left a conspicuous vacancy.

Archie never discussed the matter with me, and I don't know for sure what happened. But for some time afterward the scuttlebutt around Xerox was that he was not actually all that keen to pursue the Harvester job, and thought that by telling Peter about the offer he would receive the assurance that his elevation to chief executive was imminent. According to this water-cooler talk, Peter didn't extend that reassurance and so Archie left.

Whether that was true or not, there was no question that Archie's star had fallen quite a bit in the time he had been at Xerox. His unrelenting style of tight controls and of measuring everything that moved or stood still had made him highly unpopular with a lot of people in the company. No chief executive is ever the conquering hero to everyone, but too many employees no longer exuded confidence that Archie could stimulate the business. Frankly, I thought Archie was criticized for far too many things, some of which he had nothing to do with. He even wound up being blamed for things that didn't happen until after he left. Be that as it may, it's certainly true that many Xerox people didn't mourn his departure. While some of the Ford Men remained in power for years to come, Archie's leaving marked the beginning of the end of their dominance.

It was late in the day and I was in my office huddling with some executives on pricing problems. By now, I was executive vice president, international operations, and I hoped to some day occupy one of the top two spots. Whenever he dropped by to visit someone, Peter McColough had an impish habit of banging loudly on the person's door with his fist. It sometimes made the occupant of the office jump out of his skin. As we sat there talking, I was jolted to hear this thump, thump, thump on my door. I immediately knew it was Peter and called out for him to come in. He poked his head in and said he'd like to see me in his office immediately. "All right," I said, and I turned to the men I was chatting with and told them to wait. "No," Peter said. "Don't wait. David and I will be awhile."

I had no idea what was up. When I got to Peter's office, he asked me to sit down and straightaway told me that Archie had resigned to go to Harvester and he wanted me to become president. To say the least, I was rather taken aback. I had heard nothing of Archie's plans until that very moment, and my mind was moving a mile a minute as I absorbed all this. Collecting my thoughts, I said I would be proud to accept the job.

I wanted to hurry home and tell my wife the good news, but I had a business dinner that evening with Sidney Stiglitz, the chairman of Xerox of Mexico, that I probably couldn't miss. I didn't want to relay the news over the phone, and so I sat through dinner eyeing my watch, anxious to get home.

As it happened, I had scheduled a vacation starting the following day so that Shirley and I could take the boys camping in the Adirondacks. I had mentioned that to Peter and offered to cancel the trip, but he insisted I go ahead and not disappoint the family. He did ask me to check in with him so, if necessary, I could return when the special board meeting approving my appointment was held. I remember having to take a boat to get to a phone to call the office, but it turned out everything went smoothly.

In assuming my new role, I wanted to set an informal tone and make it known that I was always approachable. People who didn't already know it quickly picked up on the fact that I tried hard to balance family and work, and that I found the time to do things like coach Little League. I am informal in nature and have always worked hard to make people feel relaxed and at ease. What's more, I told Peter that, unlike the way Archie comported himself, I felt we should express ourselves openly in front of the other senior managers during meetings and come to our conclusions in their presence so they understood the decision-making process. He said that was fine with him, and that's the way I've always done it.

When I took over as president, I clearly did not understand the depth of the problems that plagued Xerox. It was perfectly plain that the company suffered from a confluence of problems, but I simply didn't appreciate their severity. They were slowly choking the life out of the company, just as surely as if an assailant's hands were around our throat. It would be awhile before I finally came to realize this.

It was around this time that I remember meeting with a group of securities analysts and talking with them about pricing. In the course of the discussion, I laid out the sort of price increases we were planning on getting. One of the analysts stared at me and asked point-blank what would happen if we couldn't get those increases. I was a little startled by the question, and it struck me as awfully naïve. Not get price increases? That was like not getting any more daylight. Who in the world would think that you could not increase prices to cover inflation? As politely as I could, I responded that if we got no price increases at all, then that would certainly alter our predictions rather significantly. But I said I just didn't see that happening. We simply didn't plan around the possibility of not being able to make price increases stick.

The senior team knew that employee morale was beginning to sag, and sag badly. Peter, in fact, had become gravely worried that various company failures and disappointments might cause a lot of managers to bail out. He was right to be concerned. People were unquestionably losing confidence in the business and many felt the company had no more than an unremarkable future ahead of it.

For some time, Peter had been using the phrase "the architecture of information." It was supposed to capture the essence of where Xerox was headed. Peter's whole idea was that the company had to engage in research outside of basic development in copiers and try to understand how information was organized and how it worked. He wanted to find an architecture of information that could computerize the office. Some day, Peter imagined, the company would manufacture a host of office products that would be connected together to speed the flow of business information. This ambition reflected his determination to build a truly great and big company as well as his concern that xerography alone would not be sufficient to accomplish that goal. So a diverse array of office systems became one of the key underpinnings of Peter's vision. Later on, a lot of people criticized Peter for not having a vision or a strategy. The truth is, Peter very much had a vision. Unfortunately, a lot of people who followed him, myself included, failed to carry it out.

Xerox employees heard this catchy "architecture of information" phrase over and over. But they never saw any true manifestation of it. All they saw were copiers. And they began to wonder if Xerox would ever be more than a copier company. And here we had Kodak whaling away at us in our most profitable portion of the business. The Japanese were kicking us at the low end. Our cost structure was totally out of whack, and we didn't even fully understand that. We had done a lot of studies of the Japanese cost structure that ultimately turned out to be dead wrong. I don't know if we were looking at things with rose-colored glasses or what. But we didn't see that the Japanese were already ahead of us and speedily drawing away.

With all these clouds looming over us, Peter came up with an idea that he hoped would prop up people's morale by showing them the future he envisioned in actual hardware and software products. The company would stage a huge worldwide conference of the top two hundred and fifty managers and their spouses, the first such convocation for the company in six years. The last time the managers had jetted in for a meeting of this scope, Xerox was still very much a high-growth, high-profits company in control of its destiny. This time around, the situation was altogether different. From the moment Peter thought of the idea, it became clear that it would be one of the most important gatherings in the company's history. He also hoped to continue the tradition and hold another conference six years hence and then six years beyond that. Little did we know this would be the last time one would be held.

The Xerox World Conference was scheduled to occupy four days during the beginning of November 1977. The site that we picked was Boca Raton, Florida, and Peter made clear that the event was to be first rate. True to his vow, it would be carried off on an incredible scale. It was extraordinary.

The planning for the conference had begun before Archie McCardell's sudden departure, and so some roles had to be hastily changed. Originally, Archie was to have delivered one of the keynote addresses, and I, as the top marketing officer, was scheduled to discuss our competitive posture in the copier business. But my new role as president and chief operating officer offered me an excellent opportunity, and so I hurriedly got cracking on a speech that would be both broader in scope and sufficiently uplifting. This would be my first appearance before such an elite group of Xerox people in my new role, and I badly wanted to make a good first impression. I also wished to deliver an unmistakable message about what I stood for and what I hoped to accomplish.

The two hundred and fifty managers and their wives gathered in Boca Raton on Sunday, November 6. The following morning, everyone attended a presentation of Xerox's complete product line. Many of the machines were familiar, but Peter took a big gamble. He decided to show a number of Xerox products that weren't yet ready for market and, for all we knew, might never make it out of development. But he felt that if managers were going to take seriously our intentions to shape up the company, then they had to witness some new and exciting stuff. All told, there were something like three dozen devices and software on display—copiers, printers, duplicators, word processors, and, most notably, the Star workstation from PARC. Some of the machines didn't even have their actual marketing numbers yet, but were referred to by their code names.

Probably the niftiest device in Boca was our 9700 laser xerographic computer printer. When laser products first began to emerge in the early 1970s, people were hardly in agreement about their promise.

Some felt they were dangerous to be monkeying with; others felt they were the future, pure and simple. No one really knew, though, what sort of market there would be for an expensive laser printer. Over the turbulent years of its development, the 9700 was nearly jettisoned several times. But the company stuck with it, and by the Boca Raton conference we had a product ready to be demonstrated.

There were lots of other things to marvel at. There were desktop workstations, facsimile machines, high-speed reproduction devices. There was the Star workstation, for which we had very high expectations. A television hookup to Palo Alto had been arranged so that on a big screen we were able to show the scientists there demonstrating laser printing and transmitting information to Boca. No doubt about it, it was a technological extravaganza.

But Peter didn't overlook opportunities for fun. There were organized tours of the area, a chance to see a safari land, and time set aside for deep-sea fishing. One evening, the company took over five of the best restaurants in Boca and dispatched everyone in prearranged groups for dinner. The idea was to have people mingle with colleagues from other parts of the world, and so we made sure the guy from Japan ate with the guy from Brazil and the fellow from Britain dined with someone from Germany.

On another evening a big tent that Ringling Brothers would have been proud of was set up in the parking lot. There was a lavish buffet and sundry games of chance. Everyone was handed play money to gamble and if luck was with you and you ran up your allotments, you could exchange the fake money for prizes that were none too shabby. One of the choicest was a motor scooter.

On still another afternoon there was a formal luncheon at which Henry Kissinger was the guest speaker. That really impressed people. Kissinger had only recently left office as the secretary of state, and to get him to show up at a corporate conference was a true coup. The way we managed it was a fortuitous connection. Ernst Vander Beughel, a remarkable professor who had headed KLM and was former foreign minister of the Netherlands, was on our board and happened to be a very good friend of Kissinger's, good enough to persuade him to come. He also wheedled a nifty discount. When he rose to talk, the audience was spellbound. Kissinger spoke at some length about the world and the Soviet Union and was marvelously witty and entertaining.

On Tuesday morning we got down to the serious business of the conference. Peter McColough delivered his Real World speech, and it was a blunt appraisal of the marketplace and Xerox's position in it. In no uncertain terms, he made it clear that Xerox was being "out-marketed, out-engineered, outwitted in major segments of our market." He underscored the fact that Xerox would never have it the way it did when it was protected by its patents, when it could take its sweet time developing and introducing products and when it made no difference how much it cost to make something because the company could charge almost whatever it wanted. Peter stressed that he didn't wish to incite panic among the managers, but that it was evident that everyone, and Peter included himself, had waited too long to confront these issues publicly. "We are now faced with the urgent need for change within this company!" he declared. And he made it clear that we would succeed.

By any measure, the conference was a great immediate success. People told themselves that they had seen the future of our technology and it was impressive. They had seen the top management of the company and they were all quite articulate. They had been pampered beyond belief with first-class airfare, swank hotel rooms, and delicious food—and they liked it. As the hotel emptied out, there hung in the air a euphoria, a widespread arousal of corporate emotions, as if all the doubts about the company had been beaten out of everyone. Xerox not have a future? Now that was all a laugh.

And yet there was just one problem. From that day on, everyone measured everything by the grandiose promises made in Boca Raton. People kept wondering when they were going to see all that fabulous stuff that they were shown in Boca. Where's that facsimile machine? Where's the laser printer? Months went by. Years. The dream didn't materialize.

In the end, the world conference was like so many meetings that Xerox held. Lots of things were promised. Few were delivered on. So what at first looked like it would give the company a sorely needed boost turned out to be still another negative. Morale at Xerox began eroding even further. We were sinking toward the bottom of the sea, and I doubt anyone yet knew how dark and gloomy it would be down there.

These were confused years at Xerox. Important problems were surfacing out of every crack. Indeed, in the months and years that followed the Boca gathering, an ever-growing fissure had begun to get on a lot of people's nerves, including mine. The clash between the Ford Men and the Xerox veterans had been draining enough. Now a war intensified between the West Coast and East Coast segments of the corporation that, to Xerox people at least, seemed every bit as bitter as the Civil War.

The seeds of the confrontation go back to the acquisition of SDS in 1969 and the formation of the Palo Alto Research Center in 1970. From the very beginning, a culture distinct from that at the rest of Xerox flourished at PARC, particularly among the members of the Computer Science Laboratory. People there dressed and behaved differently. Shaggy, unkempt hair and beards were not uncommon sights. People sometimes worked barefoot and shirtless. Weekly meetings were held in the "beanbag room," where everyone sat on big pellet-filled hassocks. During those meetings, the designated speaker was allowed to determine the rules for conversation, like a dealer set the rules in a poker game, and these gatherings came to be called "dealer" meetings. The PARC researchers decided to dub themselves Xeroids.

In mapping out where they wanted to go, the Xeroids adopted an antimainframe strategy, which could also be construed as an anti-IBM strategy. At the time, the center of gravity was IBM and the mainframe computer. PARC saw no reason to confront that behemoth, and so it chose to delve into anything but the mainframe and the data processing center.

It was certainly true that PARC was marvelously successful in developing ingenious ideas and product concepts. The things that came out of the labs fundamentally altered the nature of computing. PARC eventually developed Ethernet, which allowed workstations to talk to one another; the first graphics-oriented monitor; the first hand-held "mouse" inputting device that could be used to point to selected portions of a document; the window concept that enabled different sections of text to be compared simultaneously; the first laser printer. PARC technology wound up in Apple's Lisa and Macintosh computers, and provided the seeds for a number of Silicon Valley start-ups. Lots of computers offered "bit mapped" displays that PARC originated as a way to create very fine grained images. Apple's Lisa incorporated a display that could be divided into windows as well as a mouse pointing device for delivering commands. In fact, all the help we gave competitors caused outsiders to joke that PARC was really a "national resource."

The list of PARC accomplishments went on and on. PARC invented a computer language for children that sought to bypass the abstract thinking often necessary in computer programing and called it Smalltalk. Much later, PARC developed a motion detection system inspired by frogs' eyes, since frogs can see things only if they are in motion.

At one point, PARC scientists wanted to create a software program modeled loosely on the famous science-fiction thriller *The Blob,* that creepy tale about a mysterious organism that assumed a life of its own. A researcher named John Shoch, who later became my assistant, was largely responsible for developing the Worm, a series of programs that moved through a data network almost at will, replicating, or copying itself, into available machines. In this manner, the Worm could coordinate the operation of multiple computers joined via communications lines into a network. The Worm came in lots of shapes and sizes. There was the Existential Worm, whose sole mission was to stay alive within a network, and the Billboard Worm, a program that flashed cartoon drawings or messages onto the screen of the computers it had taken over. Then there was the Alarm Clock Worm that not only took over empty computers but then dialed up the absent operators over telephone lines according to a list of wake-up calls. Then there was the Animation Worm, in which a single program automatically created program segments in other machines to accomplish real-time animation. Interestingly enough, the Worm was essentially what more recently became famous as the computer virus.

Probably the most heatedly debated project at PARC was Alto, which was intended to be a less expensive computer as powerful as the leading minicomputer. It had some of the attributes of a personal computer, though it was far more sophisticated. A prototype of the Alto was completed in April 1973. The first picture displayed on its screen was the Cookie Monster from Sesame Street, which had been programmed as a test pattern. Viewers were able to watch Cookie Monster wolf down a cookie.

The Alto became competitive with a rival machine called the Star, which would reach the market as the Xerox 8010 workstation. Unlike the personal computers of today, which work with other manufacturers' equipment, the Star functioned well only when linked with other Xerox equipment. PARC's Alto adherents tried to take on the Star contingent, and managed to get prototypes into the White House, both houses of Congress, and several companies and universities. Despite those lofty accomplishments, we scrapped the Alto in 1980.

Crucial to the PARC story, however, was the fact that the work there was not connected to a firm business strategy, which was the fault of senior management. The place just sort of drifted along on its own course. Interestingly, one piece did get connected—laser printing. That had a more natural fit with the business, which is probably why it ended up getting connected. And that was one of the major successes for Xerox to come out of PARC. This was a big breakthrough for the company and turned into a very good business.

What didn't work was the workstation strategy. And that came to be one of the big Xerox knocks. There were several reasons and they were not complicated: we had settled on an antimainframe strategy, so our workstations were not compatible with large customers' mainframes; secondly, we never supported the PARC work with a total business strategy and the required marketing support. Though this continues as a business to this day, it never was what Xerox hoped it would be and we never made any money from it.

One of the oddities of all this is that later on we tried to tie PARC's strategy more to the main business. This caused a major flap with Bob Taylor, who ran the computer science lab, and he and a whole group of his people—thirteen in all—left to go to DEC. We had expected some people to leave, but we didn't count on so many going to just one company. I thought it was a bad deal and I went to see Ken Olson, the head of DEC, about the situation. I wanted to make sure he was personally focusing on this and to make clear that as a corporation we were very concerned about it. I didn't insinuate that we planned to sue them, but I was concerned about DEC stealing resources. Years later, at a Business Council meeting, Ken walked over to me and said, "Dave, I'd like to get a couple of minutes with you." When I stepped aside to talk with him, he said, "We're having some difficulty with the group now that we're trying to tie them more directly to the business strategy," and I chuckled and said, "That's how you got them in the first place."

SDS and PARC were only the beginning of Xerox's effort to become a force in information systems. A number of acquisitions were made to put flesh on the bones of the "architecture of information" strategy. In the early 1970s, we acquired Diablo Systems, which had created the daisy wheel printer, and Century Data Systems, which made computer hard disks. We bought Shugart Associates, a highly successful floppy disk drive company; Versatec, which made plotter printers; and EOS, a maker of sophisticated military electro-optics. Unfortunately, none of these acquisitions ever really got connected to Peter's vision of the architecture of information.

But there was a deeper problem that arose. For one of the significant ramifications of assembling these noncopier companies was the creation of a brutal clash of cultures. It became the West Coast systems gang pitted against the East Coast copier-duplicator people. Neither had much, if any, love for the other. The copier-duplicator gang vehemently wouldn't accept outsiders. They viewed the West Coasters as people who spent their time coming up with sophisticated ideas that never made any money for the corporation. The West Coasters, on the other hand, regarded the copier people as the past, a group of stodgy individuals completely out of touch with the future path of the world.

There are politics in any company or any family, but there certainly was a political issue at Xerox that affected the company in a most unfortunate way. There was tremendous competition for resources. Lots of tough fights and acrimony evolved, even at the field level. These weren't just philosophical battles that all got worked out nice and neat. There were real hard feelings. The head-knocking between some of the people got quite bad and quite personal. In the end, we lost more than a few good people over it who simply wouldn't put up with it any longer.

For many Xerox people, the clash could be boiled down to one man— Don Massaro. At first blush, Massaro seemed like an ideal guy to have around. He was a very charismatic, aggressive, risk-taking aeronautical engineer. He came to Xerox in 1977 when we bought Shugart Associates, a firm that Massaro had cofounded, and he continued to run Shugart for us quite impressively. The firebrand that he was, Massaro made it clear that he had no respect for corporate shibboleths. Friends would tease him that he was a bull in a china shop, but he would just laugh. I liked him immensely.

In 1979 we put Massaro in Dallas to run the Office Products Division, which was responsible for developing office products other than copiers. He was thirty-six years old, and he had his hands full. Set up in 1973 in Dallas, the Office Products Division was going nowhere. It started off by trying to sell the 800 series of word processors, which came to market more than a year behind schedule and used magnetic cards, an old IBM memory technology that was fading fast. There were a few additional design problems of note. To control the editing functions, you needed to strike one of twenty-two different combinations of keys. Baffled by the preposterous complexity, secretaries used to burst into tears. The 850 series, launched in 1977, did only mildly better in the marketplace. Annual revenues from office products were never more than a drop in the bucket for the corporation.

This was the mess Massaro tried to fix. In his early days in the job, Massaro once told me that he felt like the cartoon character Road Runner, who was always trying to stay a step ahead of the wily coyote. The corporate staff of Xerox, Massaro said, was like a pack of coyotes nipping at his heels and setting endless booby traps for him. Liking the analogy, Massaro decided to adopt the Road Runner as the division's mascot.

To his credit, Massaro tried hard to patch together a business strategy linked to PARC. He immediately hired Dave Liddle, one of PARC's top researchers and manager, to help construct the business strategy. Under Massaro's stewardship, the division began to move. In three years, it unveiled seven new products. Among them were PARC's Ethernet and an updated word processing system called the 860. Then there was Star, our professional workstation that featured a video screen, keyboard, and large box holding logic circuits and desk memory. It had a mouse to control the cursor. The machine was aimed at users new to computer workstations—like chemists or financial analysts. There was also a fifty-five-hundred-dollar desktop computer called the Xerox 820 but known internally as "Worm," a nod toward the Apple computer. The Worm, we vowed, was going to eat the Apple. It represented the first personal computer from a *Fortune* 500 company. Next came a line of low-cost electronic typewriters code-named Saber. We thought these products would cut a swath through the competition.

To the copier people, however, Massaro represented money gone mad. It grated on them that corporate funds were being diverted to him. An exuberant, audacious man, he operated according to a sort of spit-in-your-eye management philosophy. In meetings, he would insult his boss and run things with seeming impunity. The systems people who worked for him were cocky and flashy. They loved to one-up copier people. The big thing for sales people was the President's Club, when the top performers got to take their spouses to Hawaii or Puerto Rico for several days of awards and good times. But when the business turned sour, the events would be scaled back to distinctly less exotic locales. One year, when the business was pretty poor, the copier people had to settle for Daytona Beach. Meanwhile, Massaro, whose business was losing millions of dollars, took his team to Hong Kong. He was flaunting it.

People would tease me mercilessly about Massaro. "Why doesn't Kearns wake up?" they'd say. "What's Massaro got on him?"

The warring factions should have brought some good differences of opinion to the table, but they didn't. Because it was all totally dysfunctional.

In the end, Massaro couldn't pull his strategy off. Product after product fell well short of our expectations. When IBM entered the personal computer market, it blew away our computer. Neither Massaro nor me nor anyone else at Xerox understood how to market the PC, and

THE COYOTE EATS THE ROAD RUNNER   107

that was our undoing. When IBM introduced its PC, it made two crucial decisions. One was to sell through dealers in addition to its own
sales force. The second was to create software and hardware that was
not tied to their mainframe strategy and thus opened software development to the world. And the company made a huge marketing investment. Soon afterward, Apple introduced the Macintosh, which PARC
and Massaro had ridiculed as a toy.

Had IBM not come along, it might have been a different story. But
to take on IBM with a huge investment when the copier market was
sinking was not possible. We tried to take it on a little on the fringes
and finally got out after a couple of years at a huge cost. It was a disaster for us. We would have been smarter to have pulled out immediately.
Within two years of its introduction, the IBM machine supplanted
Apple as the best-selling personal computer.

That left us with Star, a first-class, very sophisticated and expensive workstation for a niche market that we were unable to make
money out of. As for the Saber typewriters, they were first-rate, the
customers liked them, and we were able to capture a significant market
share. However, the stand-alone typewriter market was declining and
being supplanted by the personal computer.

I have to admit it: I put my money on the wrong horse. I believed
Massaro's plan. I wanted it to happen. In retrospect, Massaro way over-
stated what he could do. And I bought the goods. That was a flaw. You
need to plan a business not around what you would like to happen. You
need to plan on the most likely outcomes. That was a general defect of
mine. It makes no sense to plan for worst-case scenarios, nor can you
be ludicrously optimistic. But you do need to strike a balance, and I
hadn't yet.

Massaro's star swiftly dove into eclipse. His operation was losing
money, and we had to cut back costs. Massaro is a grower of a business, and this was an intolerable way for him to operate. So, in 1982,
he left with Dave Liddle to form a new company. At Massaro's
farewell party, he was given a bronze statue of the Road Runner. The
irony was that the coyote had already eaten him.

In the end, Massaro offered a glimpse of what might have been if a
few other things had been different. He was on the right track in trying

to integrate PARC with the rest of the business, but the timing proved wrong. Quite simply, the "architecture of information" vision was too big for us. Too many ideas were coming at us to be properly dealt with. A major mistake that I very much participated in was to allow more technology to be developed than we could launch with all the immense marketing costs involved. We just couldn't afford all the new ideas we were developing. So we did a number of things half-baked. We should have done fewer things better. As a result, our goal of being seen as an office systems company, and not just a specialist in copiers, was not realized.

Meanwhile, we continued to have our share of difficulties in the copier side of the business, including our first really public disaster. The culprit was the 3300, a small copier that came out in October 1979.

The 3300 made twenty-three copies a minute and sold for seventy-three hundred dollars. It was intended as the answer to the flood of low-cost Japanese copiers. We had been continuing to try to find better and better ways to handle the document, and the 3300 also had an unusual document handler called the Doghouse that sat on top of the machine and enabled the operator to feed the document through it without opening the top. To come up with a low selling price, the designers of the 3300 were forced to use the most inexpensive parts they could possibly get away with. Among the sorry choices they made was a cheap motor that greatly exceeded the noise specifications. I'll never forget the day the machine was first demonstrated for me. It was switched on and a loud noise reverberated through the room. I thought something had gone horribly wrong and instinctively moved back. "What's that?" I exclaimed. I wasn't too happy to find out that it was nothing more than the normal motor noise.

Despite some flaws like that, we were all pretty excited about the 3300. We were able to offer it at an attractive price and we thought for sure we would snatch some market share from the Japanese. I remember going to a launch party and we were all high as kites.

But not long afterward, I made a visit to Chicago and I got an earful from the tech reps and sales force that the product was no good.

They said it had disturbing reliability problems and did not have the feel of a quality product. I came back and poked around and found that they were absolutely right. The machine was incredibly unreliable. The most prevalent problem was jamming. Paper would enter the machine, jam, and then scorch, producing this noisome burning smell. There was just no way we could keep the product out there. We finally had to suspend production in April 1980. Roughly four thousand of the copiers had been placed, and we had to recall them. Boxcars full of unshipped 3300s sat in the parking lots at the Webster plant. It cost fifty million dollars to complete the recall, and it was a shattering public relations disaster.

We didn't abandon the 3300, though we might as well have. A crack team of engineers was assigned to fix it, and in April 1982 we reintroduced it at a price of $5,495. But the damage was done. It was never the successful product we had planned.

The whole episode was awful. Here we were going to get our costs down under the Japanese and instead we came up with a total dud. In our surveys, we always found that the first month's reliability sets the tone for the customer's perception for the next year. So it was crucial that a machine work well when first installed. And yet, time after time, we were failing in that objective. The idea is to find problems before they find you. We were always having problems find us. And one thing you learn as a top executive: when the bad news starts, there's never a good place to hide.

For the 3300 debacle produced one of the more embarrassing moments of my own life. Each year, after we hold our annual shareholders meeting, we conduct another meeting for our employees. In 1980 the meeting was held in a big tent that was pitched out in the parking lot in Webster. During the session, I made a few remarks about the unfortunate problems we had encountered with the 3300. After I was done, Frank Enos, a man who worked on the final test in the factory, got up and said that he had a question. "Fine," I said, "fire away." Then, in this booming voice of his, he said, "David, why didn't you ask us what we thought about it? We could have told you it was a piece of junk."

Of course he was absolutely right. Why didn't I ask the employees? I was stupid. We were not using our people in a way that would make a difference.

Enos, who is now a shop steward at Xerox, became one of my personal heroes in the company. He showed the kind of spunk that all employees ought to. And he had his priorities straight. He didn't care one bit about me or about offending the president of the company. He cared about the company's products and its customers. I've always remembered Frank Enos in that tent. After that encounter ended, I swore to myself, "I'm not coming back to this meeting next year and have this happen again." I told Enos, "From now on I will ask you." And I was good to my word.

There was beginning to be a sickening self-doubt within the company that we were basically living on borrowed time. We knew this in a lot of ways, including by simple osmosis, but one of the more visual ways was in the infamous Jaws Chart.

Before I came to Xerox, almost all of the company's revenues derived from the lease base. There were virtually no outright sales of Xerox machines, though naturally the company did sell copier supplies like toner, developer, and paper. At IBM, as late as 1956, there were only rental prices. Your only choice was to rent. But then the government forced IBM to change the practice. Xerox customers always did have the option to buy. But in the early days of the 914, purchase prices were extremely high. They were so high very few customers were likely to take them seriously. Purely and simply, Xerox wanted to encourage the rental business.

By the early 1970s, however, purchase prices were significantly lower, and there was a reasonable connection between the price to buy and the price to rent. But since customers were long accustomed to renting and the sales force was clearly accustomed to renting, few sales transpired.

In drips and drabs, though, sales slowly began to develop. There were a number of reasons. Sale prices were more reasonable, the market was growing accustomed to the idea as the computer market shifted from all rental and lease to a significant amount of outright sales, and

Xerox management saw the opportunity to move profits forward in time and improve cash flow. If you were staring at a lackluster quarter and managed to increase actual sales, you could improve your short-term results.

Once enough managers caught on to this little deception, the pressure slowly built to change the rental mentality. I vividly remember that when I became the head of the U.S. marketing division, the pressure arose to get sales as we rolled toward the end of the year. That was the means to make the profits look all the better. "Outright sales" is the terminology we used to refer to the sales. For short, we said "ORS." All during the final months of a year, everyone was scampering around trying to bag some ORS.

Within the company, there was a lot of spirited debate over the prudence of emphasizing sales. The most vehement opponents were the financial people, for they, better than anyone else, saw where escalating sales would lead—and it wasn't pretty. If in a given year we were to rack up a certain amount of outright sales to improve our numbers, then we would be compelled to accomplish even more sales the following year if we wanted to show further growth in our earnings. It didn't take a genius to realize that the exercise becomes geometric. And once you get into this game you can't get out of it. If you were to suddenly shut off the sales, you'd be setting yourself up for a major downer of a year.

Another difficulty with outright sales was that they made it ever more difficult to project revenues for the year. Each January you basically started over from scratch. On the other hand, our rental business was extremely predictable. We knew how many machines we had out there and how much rent was to come in every month. Then we would factor in a certain number of cancellations and factor in new installations and upgrades and have a good handle on what sort of numbers to expect. Rental is a very nice business to have. But with the growth mind-set we had and the changing market requirements, outright sales became an irresistible mechanism to get that growth in a more difficult market.

For a lot of Xerox managers, the idea of outright sales was equated to eating your babies or eating your seed corn. Managers would get into pretty ugly shouting matches with one another. They would scream at the top of their lungs, "How can you do this? How can you eat your own babies?"

My own feeling was that outright sales were an inevitability. One of the things that really concerned me was that there was a great deal of churning of the leased base. We'd get customers to trade up from copier A to copier B and then up to copier C. I felt that we were doing more churning than was absolutely necessary. Not to the disadvantage of customers. To our disadvantage. The sales force would go ahead and churn a machine for a small incremental advantage, and it was inefficient for us to remove a copier and install a new one for such a tiny gain. This hurt the company. Within a year of my arrival, I started to advocate sales as a way to put a stop to the churning and solidify the base. And so we would try to really impress on customers who had a machine that they could buy their installed leased copier as an economic alternative.

Another reason for outright sales was the hot breath of competition we felt everywhere we turned. In such a competitive marketplace, we were getting too vulnerable. With all those leased machines out there, if a competitor came out with a blockbuster of a product, or even nothing more than a roughly equivalent product with a cheaper price tag, our customers on the shortest possible notice could just return our copiers and switch. What's more, product life cycles were getting steadily shorter and that diminished the appeal of leasing. As it was, I was constantly startled by the cancellations we had. Compared to my experience at IBM, the cancellation rate was much higher at Xerox. To make matters worse, even as late as the 1970s, we were still offering a lot of fifteen-day cancellation guarantees. So there was a good case to be made for outright sales, as long as we coupled that with a steady supply of new products.

It was in the late 1970s that managers began to appreciate the direness of our predicament by studying the Jaws Chart. On paper, the Jaws Chart consisted of two lines that started from the same point on the left-hand side of a graph. One line rose sharply upward and one swept sharply downward. That afforded the chart the look of the open mouth of a shark, which was how it got its name. The intent of the Jaws Chart was to indicate what was happening to our copier business. The upward sloping line represented profits. The downward plunging line stood for the lease base. Since we had begun converting the lease base to sales beginning in the middle seventies, our annual profits looked a lot better than the fundamental strength of the business. The shrinking lease base foretold the future: if the trend persisted, there would no longer be a lease base to convert and profits were destined to decline. It was a scary thing to look at. Unless new machines came along to generate additional profits, Jaws was going to have the meal of its life by gulping down our earnings.

New products, of course, gave the lie to the Jaws Chart, and that's what we were banking on. In 1975, when I picked up management responsibility for Rank Xerox and Fuji Xerox, I strove to do a lot more outright sales. To me, this was the opportune time, and it had nothing to do with chasing higher profits. We were due to come out with a fresh product line, and it wouldn't have been a good idea to have leased products coming back. Unfortunately, my strategy was done in. The new product line was delayed substantially and we were stuck with nothing additional to offer and shrinking lease revenues. While we waited for the new machines, Jaws had a field day on Rank Xerox's profits. The operating earnings tumbled from 255 million pounds in 1979 to 200 million in 1981 to 105 million in 1982. Talk about pain.

In the United States, the conversion of the lease base lagged behind what was going on overseas, so Jaws had to contain his appetite a bit longer. But he would get what he was after.

And so the die was cast. There was an unmistakable hardening of the position to do more sales. The momentum had begun and there was no stopping it. Unfortunately, our understanding of the requirements of an outright sales business versus the leased business was incomplete to say the least. And the capacity to generate enough product introductions to keep the revenue flowing was beyond our ability.

As we entered the 1980s, things were getting bleak. Margins had dropped from 70 percent to 10 percent. The company could no longer fund its own future and grow without borrowing. Still, even with the Jaws Chart floating around, many managers refused to acknowledge just how sorrowful things were. They kept drafting overly optimistic predictions and saying things would level off. There was a lot of denial.

And it was a particularly bad time not to be on our guard. Already having established a powerful position in the low-volume end of the market, the Japanese had begun to expand their horizons. Canon struck first by introducing a line of middle-volume copiers in 1981. The Japanese designs were in many cases simpler and used some interchangeable components, which allowed for ease of servicing. We still didn't know it, but by now the Japanese had decided to make Xerox a "target" company, homing in on us in the same way that they had with American videocassette manufacturers and American motorcycle makers. They were convinced we were so vulnerable that they could drive us out of business and claim the copier market for themselves.

The problems of the company were definitely coming to a head. Clearly, there was a need for some fresh solutions. The question was where to find them.

7. The Odd Couple

NO ONE EVER MISTOOK Harold Tragash for the archetypal corporate man. A soft-spoken individual with buttonlike eyes and an owlish mien, he always liked to traipse around with a pipe clasped between his teeth and his shirt pocket exploding with pens, all of them arranged in precise order. He invariably wore horn-rimmed glasses with a metal chain attached to them. Often as not, the glasses would be dangling around his neck from the chain. When he came sidling into a room, he had the look of someone who was anticipated. People who didn't know him must have wondered: what was the local librarian doing here?

Hal Tragash was very much an academic, and he could be rather pedantic at times. He was so slow and thoughtful that I would get impatient with him. I would almost rather read something he wrote than listen to him because I'd be done sooner. Perhaps for this reason, he was ill-suited for managing large numbers of people. But he was extraordinarily smart, with an incredible range and depth to his knowledge. And underneath his academic coating lay a quiet revolutionary. He was the type of person who would travel around Xerox planting seeds. He got things going, slowly at first, but it turned out that they were the sort of things we wanted.

Trained as an industrial psychologist, Tragash had been hired in 1965, straight out of graduate school, as a personnel research specialist up in Rochester. At the time, growth at the company was fast and chaotic. Soon after Tragash joined, one of his colleagues cautioned him, "Every six months there will be an organizational change, every year there will be a major organizational change, and every two years there will be a cataclysmic organizational change. So just keep your head down, you can't affect it."

The first dozen or so years with the company, Tragash functioned as a sort of utility problem-solver. It was the type of work that truly challenged him, and out of which he derived enormous pleasure. A contentedness glowed on his face when he was puzzling over a mystery. His very first project was to determine how often repairmen ought to visit customers to do preventive maintenance on the 914 copier. At the time, they were showing up after a customer had made fifty thousand copies. But some studies had suggested that they could wait until a hundred thousand copies. Tragash recommended that customers be sampled to find out at which point they felt copy quality had visibly deteriorated. The conclusion was that most people couldn't tell the difference between the one-hundred-thousandth copy and the fifty-thousandth. So the preventive maintenance interval was changed to a hundred and twenty-five thousand copies, resulting in a huge savings to Xerox.

Tragash also got involved in an array of employee testing issues. For example, he worked on a means to screen hard-core unemployable people to see if we could identify those individuals who would bother to wake up in the morning and come to work. In time, Tragash was appointed the manager of personnel research and he immersed himself in studying employee attitudes almost full-time.

Meanwhile, Peter McColough had been making some trips to Japan in order to better understand the Japanese style of management. Some time during a meeting in 1976, Peter turned to our vice president of personnel and said, "I've been to Japan and I've seen what they do there with employee participation. The workers really have a lot of say in how the company operates. Get me some of that."

Such ideas were very much like Peter. He always thought the business was too darned complicated. He would complain about lengthy documents that thudded on his desk and that he dreaded reading. He felt we had an abundance of clever employees, and so we ought to take off their shackles and let them go. Let them come up with ideas and inform management. For whatever reasons, several years lapsed and personnel didn't succeed in getting him any of "that." Then, early in 1979, Peter went to see Doug Reid, who had recently become the head of personnel, and repeated his request: "We need to get our employees participating and involved—let's get moving."

In short order, a task force was set up to study the quality circles that had become the rage at many companies, and it was decided to appoint someone as the full-time manager of employee involvement. The person approached for the task was Hal Tragash.

When the job was offered to him, Tragash didn't have the first clue as to what employee involvement even meant, though he wisely kept his shortage of knowledge to himself. But he had concluded that if his career was going to advance he badly needed to get on the corporate staff in Stamford. It was August of 1979, and his wife told him that if he were sincerely planning on moving to Connecticut then he'd better hurry up and do it now before the kids resumed school. And so, having no idea what he was getting into, Tragash took the assignment.

For the next several years, Hal Tragash became a barefoot prophet wandering through the company's fields. I doubt he sensed how thankless his task would be.

He began by visiting places like General Motors and Lockheed to learn about their experiences with quality circles, and he took in a dozen-odd conferences on employee participation. One of the other early things Tragash did was recruit Professor David Nadler to do some consulting on the project. At the time, Nadler was a faculty member at Columbia's Graduate School of Business and had been doing some interesting work on employee participation with AT&T. Tragash and Nadler started talking to lower-level managers to try to build a network of people who had an interest in this concept. It did not exactly engender wide support. Tragash and Nadler held a meeting at the Holiday Inn at the Rochester airport, in which they tried to include everyone in the company who was curious about the subject. The turnout was on the sparse side. All of seventeen people showed up. I guess you had to start somewhere.

Sensing the mood of the place, Nadler recommended to me that it might be best if we not try to start a big corporate program because not enough people were ready for that. Instead, he urged me to begin a grass-roots effort.

In his brushes with various levels of employees, Nadler had come away with some rather pointed conclusions about Xerox. From his conversations, Nadler felt that a lot of people seemed to think that Xerox was an adolescent that didn't know what it wanted to do when it grew up. He also said that he felt that people at Xerox were overly consumed by superficial concerns. For instance, almost everyone thought you had to look a certain way. You had to look "crisp." There was a distinctive panache and style to the place. But he said that he thought aesthetics sometimes tended to override substance. People didn't seem to recognize that Xerox wasn't as great a company as it looked.

In particular, Nadler felt that there was a powerful conviction in the company that mere imitation of style got you somewhere, and to some extent he was right. It was astounding how far some people could take this notion. Once I had been elevated to the top executive ranks, I suddenly became one of the models to be imitated. It wasn't long before the "cloth-belt syndrome" emerged. I have always worn cloth belts with my suits, and some other high-aspiration executives suddenly looped cloth belts through their pants. I found this all pretty preposterous. I had never yet heard of a businessman getting promoted because of his belt.

It got so bad that other executives began teasing one of our operations managers who couldn't help but mimic me. He actually looked like me. And not just a little bit. In fact, one day one of my daughters happened to spot him at the local dry cleaners, and she turned to my wife and said, "Mommy, what is Daddy doing at the dry cleaners?" This manager not only began to wear cloth belts; he began copying other habits of mine. I have a sort of stoop-shouldered walk, and he soon had a stoop-shouldered walk. I have always had a stand-up desk in my office. He got one. I don't pretend to flatter myself that this imitation business had anything personally to do with me. It was my position. I know that, because the man eventually was transferred to England to work in the Rank Xerox organization. One of his bosses there had a disfigured finger from a war injury. Believe me, it was not an attractive sight to look at. It wasn't long before the story went the rounds of the company: "Did you hear what happened to our friend? He was found in his basement trying to disfigure his finger."

For months, Nadler and Tragash wandered around the company trying to drum up interest in employee involvement. Even though quality cir-

cles were so popular throughout corporate America, Tragash was cynical about the concept. In fairly short order, he set up his own idea of
quality circles, what we called employee problem-solving teams. He
hoped these small efforts would ricochet through the corporation. But
most people couldn't be bothered and were noncompliant. It was the
foreign body syndrome. Organizations long used to doing things one
way don't readily accept a new direction.

At one point, Tragash paid a visit to the new Cummins Engine
plant in Jamestown, New York, which made engine blocks for trucks. It
represented one of the first socio-technological facilities in the country.
It was a bold experiment in self-management, what was expected to be
a forerunner of plants of the future. Teams of workers basically ran the
place. The teams fixed the work schedules. There was a pay-for-
knowledge system, a safety management team. Tragash was mightily
impressed. He wanted to see another enlightened operation that Procter
and Gamble had, but the soap people were more protective of their
ideas and wouldn't let him in.

Once he had inspected the Cummins plant, Tragash began goading
Xerox managers to come along with him and experience the future,
too. By now, he knew that the only way to convince most managers of
a new way was to allow them to witness it with their own eyes. Talking
to them about it didn't do the trick. In fact, Tragash was reminded of
studies of shell-shocked soldiers in World War I. Because of the damage done to their brains, they were left unable to reason abstractly and
could operate only in the present moment. This condition was labeled
concrete-brained. As his own private joke, Tragash began referring to
Xerox managers as cement-brained. He used to even pass the joke
along to his colleagues, knowing, of course, that they were the most
cement-brained of all.

Gradually, Tragash did manage to penetrate some cement, but a lot
remained in the way. He wrote a series of little booklets about
employee involvement and waves of them would go out to managers
around the company. They defined benchmarking, a reward system, the
role of the manager. He called them his "Ayatollah Cassette Program,"
alluding to the fact that when the Ayatollah was in exile in France he
kept in touch with his believers by sending around cassettes of his

gospel. People at Xerox had been saying, "This is Greek. This is Chinese. What is this employee involvement?" So he tried to start as simplistically as possible. He also conducted a fair number of seminars. He created quality facilitators. But except in the manufacturing area of the company, the concept didn't catch on.

In fact, some of the very top executives thought that Tragash was more than just a goofy guy who puffed on a pipe. To them, what he was doing was burningly controversial. I remember one of them at a cocktail party saying that Tragash was essentially promulgating communism. He complained that his ideas were tantamount to the worker councils in Germany, and they would get us into a lot of trouble. We had actually had serious problems with our Germany subsidiary and had basically lost control of it. But Tragash wasn't thinking about anything like worker councils and he was a long way from being a communist.

Part of the problem was this was not a high-priority item at the time with top management. We were fixated on our costs and the Japanese. Although I wasn't opposed to employee involvement, I clearly didn't see it as a vehicle to turn around the business. To me, it was something on the level of a suggestion program. It was nice to have, but it wasn't going to solve the company's central ills.

And by this time things had already started to cascade down on us like Niagara Falls. Kodak was coming on strong. IBM was faltering somewhat in copiers, but it was still a powerful presence. It was obvious to me that we had service problems and had never addressed them.

Meanwhile, high inflation was battering just about everybody and we were unable to fully price for it because of the ferocious competition. We had a customer base that wasn't especially pleased with us because we hadn't been servicing them that well. And we were extremely vulnerable because most of our machines were still being rented. It was the easiest thing in the world for a customer to hear about a new copier from somebody else and say, "Hey, I'll give it a try." All he had to do was just rip up our contract and tell us to pick up our machine. People were terminating a lot of rental agreements because they weren't happy with them. The more I thought about this, the more I felt as if a deadly octopus was wrapping its tentacles around us.

* * *

The deeper we studied what was going on in our industry, the worse things looked. One day, Frank Pipp, who had now become the head of worldwide manufacturing, and I were talking with Tony Kobayashi of Fuji Xerox. Kobayashi wasn't overly happy. He was complaining about how far ahead of him Canon and the other Japanese competitors were; they were just murdering him in the marketplace. Frank and I had been concerned and this was the catalyst. It became clear that if we were going to counteract this we needed to find out exactly how Fuji Xerox stood vis-à-vis the other Japanese copier makers. At the same time, that would give us a clue as to how Xerox itself stood against the Japanese.

To do the spadework, we dispatched a team of people to Japan. It included plant managers, financial analysts, engineers, and manufacturing specialists. We were fairly confident that we knew what we were going to find. For some time, our suspicion had been that the Japanese were making copiers somewhat cheaper than we were, though we didn't think the gap was enormous. After all, we were doing pretty well at improving productivity compared to other big companies in the United States. Whereas most American corporations were advancing 2 or 3 percent a year, we were achieving gains of 7 or 8 percent. But despite these gains, the Japanese continued to price their product substantially below us. We kept wondering: how were they doing it?

Our team went over everything in a thorough manner. It examined all the ingredients of cost: turnover, design time, engineering changes, manufacturing defects, overhead ratios, inventory, how many people worked for a foreman, and so forth. When it got done with its calibrations, we were in for quite a shock. Frank Pipp remembers the results as being "absolutely nauseating. It wasn't a case of being out in left field. We weren't even playing the same game."

We learned that the Japanese were able to carry six to eight times less inventory than we were, they were so efficient in getting their products out. The quality of incoming parts at Xerox was 95 percent; at the Japanese firms, it was 99.5 percent, a significant gap. Our overhead was twice theirs. We found out that for every direct worker who put together a copier, painted it, or packed it into a box, there were 1.3

overhead workers who were clerks or managers. In Japanese firms, there was .6 of an overhead worker for every direct worker. We were clearly overloaded with managers. In category after category, the difference wasn't 50 percent better or anything like that; it was almost always over 100 percent!

The unit manufacturing cost—in other words, the cost to get a machine to the dock for shipping—of the Japanese companies was about two-thirds of ours. That statistic was absolutely astonishing. When we understood that, we were terrified. We had no idea they were making machines that much cheaper. That was no gap. That was a chasm.

Just like that, we realized that the progress we had been making was totally inadequate. We had to establish productivity gains of something like 18 or 19 percent a year for five years just to catch up to the Japanese. And that was if the Japanese continued to improve by about 6 percent a year, what we thought at the time was a reasonable assumption. We would later learn it was nothing of the sort. The Japanese firms managed to improve at a rate of around 12 percent a year. Japan proved to be one of the fastest-moving targets anyone has ever tried to shoot at.

For a long time, we had been getting engineering reports on the Japanese cost structure and now we realized that they had been hopelessly wrong. And I was buying them. Was it bad analysis? I doubt that it was a case of the information not being available. I think it was purely a matter of denial. To a large extent, it was arrogance. I never thought of myself as arrogant, but that's what it was.

Faced with this extremely disconcerting news, we conceived the idea of business effectiveness, a strategy to improve the basic competitiveness of the company. It embraced two underpinning thoughts: employee involvement and benchmarking. We knew we had to reduce costs significantly. We had done a lot of belt-tightening and laid off a lot of people, and we didn't want cost-cutting to dominate the company thinking, so we chose business effectiveness to describe our effort.

What we were going to do was establish benchmarks for different aspects of our business and then attempt to match or beat them. We defined the approach as the "continuous process of measuring our products, services, and practices against our toughest competitors or those companies renowned as leaders. Our goal is superiority in all areas—quality, product reliability, and cost." For example, we would identify which company was the best at distribution and use it as the standard to shoot for. The same would go for manufacturing, engineering, marketing, and so forth. We began in 1979 in manufacturing and slowly, over a period of several years, we adapted the concept to the rest of the company.

This meant a new way of viewing the world. The monopoly environment that Xerox thrived in encouraged internal competition, but not external. We would measure the quality of a new Xerox machine according to the specifications of older Xerox copiers. Those specifications didn't mean very much if other companies were producing something altogether better. We also needed to adapt to a whole new way of setting budgets. Up until then, an area would look at what it had spent during the current year, then tack on some negotiated improvement factor and enough to offset inflation, usually 5 or 10 percent, and presto, there was next year's budget. With benchmarking, budgets were set by looking at the best of the competition and industry leaders. Benchmarking was one of the first concrete things we did to get Xerox on its feet and moving again.

In July 1980, I asked Dwight Ryan, one of our most talented young executives, to take charge of business effectiveness. He spent some time groping for direction, for the task of arriving at the benchmark companies took a considerable amount of digging. Early on, we turned up L.L. Bean in distribution. John Deere became our benchmark in data processing. Other companies we used were IBM, Texas Instruments, Motorola, and Burroughs. We actually studied these companies before adopting them as our models, and we learned a great deal.

At the same time, I personally continued to get an education from the Japanese—often in the most startling ways. One Saturday in late 1980, I boarded a plane for another of my periodic trips to Japan. Along the way, I flipped through a copy of a recent issue of *Forbes* magazine and stopped at an article entitled "GM's Chance of a Lifetime?" It concerned General Motors' decision to overhaul its plants and improve quality by spending a whopping $3 billion. The writers of the article, however, were highly skeptical that the plan would pan out and gave the impression that GM was pretty much pouring the $3 billion down the sewer. I doubt that other American automakers put much credence in the strategy, either.

And yet before my trip was over I learned from Frank Pipp that one of the Japanese automakers had copies of this article pasted on the walls all over its plants. Far from laughing about it, the Japanese were making the assumption that GM would accomplish exactly what it had set out to do, and, accordingly, it was resetting all its objectives for cost, quality, and reliability to offset those projected gains. Meanwhile, we in the United States were being doubting Thomases.

When I got on my plane for the trip home, a commercial flight out of Tokyo, I was faced with a two-hour delay. The plane just sat there inert on the ramp. By now, whenever I boarded a plane back from Japan, I was never sure which emotion was going to overtake me—deathly fear or invigoration. Was I going to be frightened to death by what I had seen of the Japanese? Or was I going to be pumped up to try to beat what they were doing?

This time, fear had the upper hand. The way I overcame any anxiety was to write things down. I'm an inveterate scribbler, and with plenty of time on my hands, I began scribbling in earnest. I took out a ledger pad and started writing down a list of reasons why the Japanese business leaders were taking us American business leaders to the cleaners. Some of my notations were the usual stuff that had been talked to death—the fact that they were educating their kids better than we were, their planned economy, their monolithic society. There was not much I could do about those things. Then I tried to figure out what I could do, and I thought about the reactions to that *Forbes* article. That really jogged my brain and I fixated on the word "expectations." That, to me, was the key. The Japanese managers expected so much more than their American counterparts did.

As I chewed this over in my mind, I realized that we were fine-tuning a bad product—the bad product being our management system—and by doing nothing more than fine-tuning it, we were not going to change anything at all.

When I finally returned to the office, I drafted a little speech about expectations. The following week, in return for a favor, I had agreed to give an address at the New Canaan YMCA men's group, an organization for men who were at least sixty years old, and I decided to try this expectations notion out on the gathering. To my delight, it seemed to strike a nerve. After that, I began talking incessantly about expectation levels inside and outside of Xerox. "We have to raise our expectation levels," I kept saying. "We don't expect enough of ourselves."

Getting that message to sink in, however, was going to be tough. By 1981 Hal Tragash was working his employee involvement assignment hard, but the successes were modest ones. The one truly auspicious accomplishment that gave employee involvement an important early lift was a deal we struck with our principal union. The union relationship at Xerox was instrumental in the future progress we would make at the company. In 1980, during contract renewal talks with the Amalgamated Clothing and Textile Workers Union, the union that represented Xerox plant employees, the union bargainers were pressing Xerox for guaranteed employment. They wanted the company to assure them a set number of jobs—namely four thousand positions in Monroe County. I wouldn't do that. But I got to thinking about the request. While the last thing we wanted to do was to guarantee a specific number of jobs, I found the idea of guaranteeing specific people their jobs appealing. In other words, we'll guarantee that Jones has a job. Smith has a job. Roberts has a job. If Roberts retires or leaves or is promoted, that's the end of that guarantee. Frank Pipp was my key adviser on this, and we both thought it made good sense. Through intense bargaining, this type of guarantee was agreed upon. Both Xerox and the Amalgamated employees have benefited from the agreement and it has become a model idea. The feeling was that we couldn't hope to achieve employee involvement if the company was writing workers out of a job. And so this gave the whole employee involvement movement a big lift.

Not long afterward, another difficult decision was made that was to set the stage for employee involvement's first meaty test. In our continuing quest to carve fat out of our manufacturing costs, we decided we would have to close a Webster, New York, facility that made wire harnesses. Closing plants is not something anyone finds fun to do, but there didn't seem to be any alternative. Wire harness was a basic commodity—a plastic device that held the nest of wires together inside a copier, the very spinal cords of machines—and it was being made appreciably cheaper in Mexico, Taiwan, and other offshore points. We had concluded that we could save $3 million by eliminating that work from our Webster plant.

Despairing of losing their jobs, the employees at the wire harness department said that if employee involvement meant anything at Xerox, then they would like a shot at figuring out a plan that would both accomplish the needed savings and yet keep their department in Webster open. So an employee-involvement team was organized, and after a period of some weeks managed to come up with $2.3 million in savings. It was quite an accomplishment, yet it still left them a good $700,000 short.

Tragash wanted to get involved in the effort, and a meeting was arranged that he was to attend as a sympathetic ear from corporate headquarters. The business effectiveness people, however, wanted someone there as well as a counterbalance. So they dispatched a financial type from their ranks by the name of Norm Rickard.

Rickard's presence there was one of those quirks of destiny that was to have a far-reaching impact on Xerox. For Rickard was another maverick of a totally different stripe from Tragash who had been prowling around the company, and his footsteps were starting to be heard. He had a knack for getting things done, but he was often short of fully realized ideas. He needed someone to educate him. The best man to do it was the funny guy with the glasses dangling from a chain who was sitting across from him.

Both Tragash and Rickard pretty much followed the expected script at that meeting. Tragash graciously complimented the team members and told them that the savings they had come up with were impressive indeed. Rickard, using a cold financial eye, said it was not enough and the harness plant was still a goner.

Subsequently, Tragash called me and made a plea that if the employee team were able to wring out some more savings and come anywhere near the three-million-dollar target, then I ought to accept the proposal and keep the department open. If I didn't, he said, it would be such a devastating blow to the concept of employee participation that it would probably kill it.

Shortly thereafter, the team presented a new plan that it figured would save $2.9 million. I approved it and the wire harness operation was rescued. This success by an employee participation team attracted widespread notice, both inside and outside Xerox, and, as Tragash would put it, it began to convince other plant managers that "there was gold in these hills."

With the wire harness episode behind him, Tragash returned to his lonely efforts. But he had not forgotten his chance meeting with Norm Rickard, someone who ranked several steps higher in the corporation than he did and who was dealing with matters central to the future of the company. One day Tragash called Rickard. "Look," he said, "if you're involved in business effectiveness and I'm involved in employee involvement, we could help each other. You could be the problem identifier and I could be the problem-solver. We ought to work together."

Rickard was at once receptive to the overture, which would come as no surprise to anyone who knew him even faintly. Rickard was the last person to ever brush aside free offers of help.

Norm Rickard is a tall, lanky, spirited man, born in Rochester, the oldest of four boys. He taught for a while at NYU before he realized he needed a little more money in his pocket if he were going to live decently. The academic world wasn't likely to provide it. He landed a job with Oxford Paper in Rumsford, Maine, where he headed up capital spending and special projects. After a spell, he returned to Oxford's New York headquarters and one day, in the course of a career talk, he was advised that after a year or so of good behavior he might well be able to run a mill for the company in someplace wonderful like West Carlton, Ohio. That mightily underwhelmed him. Almost immediately upon leaving that meeting, Rickard began circulating his credentials, which led to a job at Xerox in June 1966 as a business analyst. He would prove to be one of the best hires Xerox ever made.

Rickard defines high-intensity. His energy level surpasses hyperac-tive. His secretaries have to resign themselves to the fact that he has no prescribed hours. He has a near-photographic mind and little tolerance for the shortcomings of others. When he wants to share some exciting news with someone else, he gets so worked up that he nearly needs a plunger to force the words out.

At times, Rickard could get a bit tiresome. He would tell stories over and over again. And he would use the exact same words. You would have heard a story a million times, but you'd run into Rickard and hear it for the millionth and first time, and not even a preposition would be different. That's why a list of rules were instituted for meet-ings. One of them was, "Limit war stories." Rickard, and Rickard alone, was responsible for that rule. To this day, that code of behavior for meetings adorns conference rooms throughout Xerox.

Then there were Rickard's lists. He liked to work on graph paper, and before he met with someone, he invariably drew up a list of points he wanted to mention and put bullets beside them. Each point would have attachments. When he brought up a point, he would then present the exhibits, as if he were a lawyer arguing a case. During the course of the meeting, Rickard would constantly consult his list and cross off points as they were made. He would never have less than fifteen points for a meeting. He might have fifty. And he would not position them in any order of importance. They would go down as they popped into his head. Number twenty-seven might be the only truly important point Rickard needed to make in a meeting, but he would slog through the preceding twenty-six before he announced it.

Another distinctive trait of Rickard's was his obsession about his future. As a result, he would never pass up an opportunity to ask those above him in the organization what his chances for advancement were. I used to dread sitting next to Rickard on plane flights, and would do everything short of switching to a Greyhound bus to avoid that happen-ing. I knew that before the flight was over, Rickard would pepper me about his career. I never knew when he would bring up the subject, but it would invariably happen. All through a plane ride next to him, I would be wondering whenever the topic of conversation would change because I'd think that I would hear that magic question, "Now, what am I going to be doing next?"

But there were also evident contradictions about Rickard. Despite his insecurity about his career, he was fiercely devoted to the company and brutally frank. He could not help but tell you straightaway if something was nonsense, even though doing so might well jeopardize his career progress. He could rub people the wrong way.

And yet there was no denying Rickard's bullish determination and tenacity. He was unexcelled at getting things accomplished. When he got a bone in his mouth, you couldn't shake it loose. He had a steely commitment to his work and volcanic energy. He took care of the unremitting little details that are essential to pushing things through a big organization. And by hook or crook, if not coercion, he got people to go into the fire for him.

For there was little doubt that Rickard was the ultimate student of Xerox politics. He even thought up his own fanciful way of describing the players at the corporation. The top management, meaning the dozen or so members of the Corporate Management Committee (myself included), were known as the kings. All of us had our offices in what was referred to in Xerox shorthand as 3-1, meaning the first bay area on the third floor of headquarters. Beneath us were the younger management guys who were destined to inherit the mantle from us some day. Rickard called them the princes. They lived in 3-2, the second bay on the third floor, or were running the major subsidiaries. If he had his way, some day he hoped to join them.

Rickard floated around the company for a number of years, including a stint of several years over in Europe. When he returned in 1978, he went to work for Frank Pipp and got involved in economic evaluations and helping with the cost-cutting measures in the business effectiveness group.

Tragash and Rickard made for a curious combination. Rickard would speak about princes and knights and how to get through the minefields of the place. Tragash would discourse on human dignity and the estimable values of Joe Wilson. I sometimes wasn't sure what either of them was talking about. Neither, though, ever thought of himself as working for who he worked for. They were entirely their own men. And perhaps for that reason alone many executives at Xerox felt the two of them were extremely loose cannons.

But it was fitting, I suppose, that Tragash and Rickard joined forces, because their own peculiar strengths actually complemented each other magnificently. Tragash knew nothing about how to get something done, but he sure knew what that something was. Rickard knew precisely how to get it done, but he wasn't always entirely sure what he was getting done. It was Tragash who knew all the dance steps, but it was Rickard who was the one who could dance.

They themselves came to look frankly upon their relationship as parasitic. They would say as much to each other. And as Tragash would later remember, "Both of us looked each other in the eyes and said, 'We don't care what happens with our careers, this is important so let's do it.' Though Norm might not have believed the career part quite as much as I did."

And despite their radically different temperaments and personalities, Tragash and Rickard genuinely came to like each other after a while. They went out to dinner together. They played golf together. (Even at this, Rickard was better at getting things done. He would cruise around the course in the low nineties, while Tragash would stumble in with a hundred and ten.) Tragash began to tolerate the excruciatingly long diatribes when he met with Rickard, though some days he still felt like jumping out of his skin. "Norm was like an enormous data dumping ground," Tragash once said. "You'd meet with him and he'd tell you everything and anything that had happened to him during the last twenty-four hours, down to what time he brushed his teeth and what his wife wore that day." Yet the two grew comfortable enough with one another that Tragash would even tease Rickard to his face that he was a "social klutz," and Rickard would just chuckle. Tragash nearly got used to Rickard's annoying habit of overreacting to humor. Over and over again, someone would tell a joke that nobody else thought all that funny and Rickard would dissolve into peals of high-pitched laughter.

With Tragash hooked up with Rickard, I decided that our business effectiveness effort ought to be relaunched with a focus on both competitive benchmarking and employee involvement. In September 1981, I announced this intention at a meeting of the company's fifty top managers. Dwight Ryan had already moved on to something else, and so we installed Rickard as the head of the new business effectiveness office. My hope was that these principles would begin to trickle through the organization and boost our competitiveness. Shortly after his appointment, Rickard held the first formal meeting of his people. It was hardly what he—or I—had hoped for. It was so downbeat that one of the guys wanted to bail out right that day.

8. Pushing a Wet Noodle

MY OWN ORDERLY PROGRESSION up the ladder at Xerox was continuing pretty much on schedule. Early in 1982, Peter McColough's long-term plan to retire at age sixty took effect and I was elevated to chief executive officer. The night before our annual meeting, Peter threw a glorious party for me at the Twenty-one Club in Manhattan. All the directors and their spouses came and some of my close friends showed up as well. My parents flew down from Rochester for the occasion and it was all very joyous and touching. Peter was an ardent sailor, and, as a farewell gift, we gave him a beautiful model of his boat. Needless to say, I felt terrific.

I got tons of letters from people congratulating me. Some of the nicest ones came from previous associates of mine at IBM. Gerry Roche, who ran the executive search firm Heidrick & Struggles, wrote to offer his best wishes and to say that I was one of the first business people who was outspoken against the Vietnam War and that fact always stayed with him. I had been convinced that the war in Vietnam was getting in the way of solving a whole array of domestic issues and had spoken against it with other businessmen. It was funny that he combined these two thoughts.

The promotion was the fulfillment of a long-standing aspiration of mine. For some time, I had had confidence that I could run a big company and I wanted to have my opportunity to see what I could do. All the same, I couldn't help but wonder: what am I going to do with this? It was a big leap from being second in command.

When you become CEO, the magnitude of what you have to do quickly sinks in. You find yourself thinking about the business twenty-four hours a day, seven days a week. You realize that everything ultimately teeters on your shoulders. If something flops, it's your fault. And so I found myself overtaken by two overriding feelings: on the one hand, a great sense of pride and accomplishment, and, on the other hand, a sense of "Oh, my God, I've got to make this thing work."

I was bent on immediately getting the rest of my team fired up. I called a meeting of the senior management on the first Monday in May to tell them that this was the first meeting of our future and that the destiny of the company was ours.

Heady as all this was, in the weeks and months that followed I found myself far from jubilant. I knew I had just crossed an important bridge. As I thought hard about the company, I came to the conclusion that the trends affecting Xerox were so ominous that if something revolutionary weren't done the company would surely go out of business. The institution was more than threatened; it was terminally ill. Clearly, from everything I could see in the marketplace, the scales had tilted against us. It was a depressing thought, to say the least. I made sure I kept it to myself and continued to put on a confident face, because I didn't want to create a scare. It would be like a bank president announcing to depositors that the vaults were bare. But I became obsessed with trying to come up with a plan of action to save the company.

We were drifting into highly dangerous waters, and it became evident that only drastic measures would work. The Japanese kept pounding away at us. And while we had taken dramatic actions, our profits were cratering. There's no other way to describe it. The research and development engine just sputtered. There were wars raging between the engineering and marketing people. Quality was seen as unimportant. We were selling off the old rental base to customers. While the numbers still looked good, eventually the piper would have to be paid.

There was truly no viable product out there from Xerox. All we had was old stuff that was prone to break down. One of the Japanese manufacturers was running an advertising campaign around this time that hit very close to the truth. The ad showed a closet with a copier repairman inhabiting it. It went on to comment that the repairman had to actually live with you because your machine broke down so much. Nobody was named, but it was pretty clear to everyone in the business that the copier in question was Xerox's.

It's important to recognize that the copier is probably the most complicated piece of machinery in the office. After all, it's electronic, mechanical, and chemical. Without doubt, it's tough to make one that's highly reliable. While Xerox products were not bad, and we had some promising new machines in development, our cost structure was not competitive and we had not figured out how to design for low cost and high reliability. In fact, the initial Japanese products were not more reliable and generally their copy quality was worse, but we were charging our customers appreciably more to cover our inefficiencies.

I faulted myself for failing to immerse myself in the engineering side of the business back when I became president of the company. Instead, I relied totally on Jim O'Neill, one of the remaining Ford men. He didn't understand engineering, either, and he depended on a team of people who didn't take the Japanese seriously and were arrogant. Their attitude was: I do it best and my product is better than anyone else's. I should have been smart enough then to have seen through that self-deception. I should have been a driver of greater change and have adopted change as the central strategy of the company.

By now, competition of all stripes was growing in leaps and bounds. Between 1971 and 1978, seventy-seven different plain-paper copiers were introduced in the United States. From 1978 to 1980, another seventy came along. The first plain-paper copiers out of Japan to reach the marketplace—from Canon and from Konishiroku—were like the first Japanese small cars. They didn't work well. Konishiroku's machine caught fire. Canon's never even got to America. In 1980, however, Canon came up with a much-improved product—the NP-200, a twenty-copy-a-minute tabletop model. Canon spent a ton of money advertising it, and Canon executives talked of waging total war with Xerox in press articles. A few years later, Canon shrewdly hired Jack Klugman, star of "The Odd Couple" and "Quincy" TV series, as its spokesman. Minolta later retained Tony Randall, the other half of "The Odd Couple," as its spokesman.

From 1976 to 1982, Xerox's share of American copier installations dropped from an estimated 80 percent to 13 percent, a staggering decline. In 1970, Xerox held about 95 percent of the market. Japanese companies—especially Canon, Minolta, Ricoh, and Sharp—were mostly responsible for our plunge. The presence of the Japanese had reached alarming proportions. It's not unusual in the business world to have a new competitor spring up one day. What is odd is to have a throng of competitors surface virtually overnight and begin snatching away your customers. And that's what happened to us. Within the span of a few years, something like ten Japanese companies were suddenly active in the copier business, all armed with similar strategies of under-pricing us. We tended to refer to them collectively as Japan Inc. They included Canon, Ricoh, Sharp, Minolta, Konishiroku, Toshiba, and Mita. At one point, everyone down to the Tokyo Aircraft Corporation, an airplane maker, was selling copiers in America. Wayland Hicks, who eventually became our head of copier development and production, began to make ominous speeches inside the company talking about how Xerox was engaged in an economic war and the goal of the Japanese was "total obliteration of us." Ricoh eventually built up such a commanding share of Japan's coated-paper copier business that people said "Ricopy it" in the same way that Americans said "Xerox it."

In May 1982, I took a trip to Japan to help Fuji Xerox celebrate its twentieth anniversary, an important milestone for that venture. I learned some interesting things over there and they stuck with me. On the plane ride back, as usual, I doodled. The thing I kept writing down was the Japanese commitment to quality, something that had come to be labeled Total Quality Control.

Tragash and Rickard were meeting with me on a monthly basis to report what was going right and what was going wrong. I had even spent some time with them touring all the operating units of Xerox and reviewing the business effectiveness plans with the top executives of the units. Some of this was symbolic, because my being there enabled my shadow to fall on the effort and to signal the seriousness with which I regarded business effectiveness.

Nevertheless, most of the units were slow to come around. Tragash and Rickard often expressed a fair degree of exasperation. At one of the regular sessions I had with them, Tragash even said to me, "I feel like a pioneer on the prairie with the wagons circled and the Indians shooting at me and trying to burn me up. It sure is hard doing this from the grass-roots level."

"Yes," I told him, "it's a lot easier for the chief executive to just tell everybody to do it or else. But that doesn't work, either."

Soon after that trip to Japan, I had a meeting with the two of them. I asked them what they knew about Total Quality Control. Rickard told me that he thought it was the next step in business effectiveness. On the spur of the moment, Tragash blurted out, "David, would you like Norm and me to go away for thirty days and come up with a strategy to create a quality company Western-style?"

I didn't know what they had in mind, but how could I say no. So I told them, "Sure, go ahead."

Tragash didn't really know what he had in mind, either. And Rickard didn't even know Tragash was going to make that offer. As Tragash would later express it, "I liked to think of it this way: Here was a guy who owned a piece of land and we were architects who were going to come back with some rendering of a house to put on that land. It wasn't going to be a New England colonial. It wasn't going to be a ranch house. It was going to be a Japanese modern. But we were not designing the bathroom or the color of the tiles. Norm in his compulsiveness did want to put in the color of the tiles, but I said that was too much. We were going to offer a starting point and then worry about the many details later before the people moved in."

The thirty days grew to more like sixty before they met with me again and handed me a thirty-page booklet. In broad strokes, it outlined a program that they called Commitment to Excellence. It involved making a dedication to quality the guiding philosophy of the company and called for the retraining of every one of our hundred thousand employees. The proposal was long on airy goals but short on specifics. So much of it was hazy that, when they tried to explain it to me, I didn't entirely grasp what they were talking about. I felt they were talking in riddles and abstractions. I was supportive. But with a shallow understanding I did not offer any specific suggestions. The conclusion of the report was that, if the strategy caught on, Xerox would become synonymous with quality in the same way that Mercedes-Benz and

Bang and Olufsen already were. As I well knew, that wasn't even remotely true of us then. I frankly wasn't sure if I would ever see it come to pass.

Nevertheless, I told them to push ahead and try to flesh out their plan. At this point, I was basically groping in the dark. To meet the high expectations I knew were necessary, a new management process, attitude, and environment was required. The chore was to find it and develop it fast.

While Norm Rickard and Hal Tragash sorted out and crystallized their thoughts about bringing total quality to Xerox, they also decided to determine how much of top management at the company was really into this quality idea. Nothing gets very far in a big corporation without a constituency of support in the right places. "The right places" means people in power. Rickard, the astute student of political life in the corporate world, knew the concept didn't stand a prayer of a chance unless there was a network of support beneath me.

They started out with the six kings—the most senior managers—and found that, outside of myself and Frank Pipp, interest was at best lukewarm. Then they paid visits to the eight princes—the group next in line—and were gratified to find that seven out of eight were supporters. The exception was no fence-straddler. He had no self-doubt about the worthiness of a quality program. He told Rickard, "This is the stupidest thing I've ever heard of. It's going to cost millions of dollars. We should spend that money on refurbishing equipment, not something this idiotic."

From these visits, Rickard knew that if the quality program, so amorphous to many managers, was going to get anyplace in the organization he would have to play on the support of the princes and, for the time being, to dance past the kings.

Rickard and Tragash queried the princes on who they thought might be good people to help get a quality program off the ground. They were looking for imaginative, hard-working individuals who were not afraid to step on some toes. People were identified, approached, and signed up. In all, eleven individuals were eventually recruited. They were a loose group of ebullient characters drawn from throughout the company. They became known as the Gang of Eleven. They were the plotters.

The first thing the Gang of Eleven tried to do was to learn what quality really was. It was one of the most talked about yet most misunderstood concepts in the business world. A lot of companies thought they had it and didn't. Others did have it and yet didn't know it.

When you talk to someone about quality, their eyes glaze over. It's abstract. It's tough to get a handle on. What it really is is a management process to run the business. But we didn't understand that at first. Rickard didn't. I didn't.

Once they finished with a tentative but still sketchy model, the Gang brought it to me. I made a few modifications, but nothing of real substance, and approved it at the end of July. The name we gave to the project was Commitment to Excellence.

On September 28, 1982, Rickard came and gave a presentation of the plan to the Corporate Management Committee. We told him that he'd better "crisp it up" for the future. Xerox is the only place I know of where "crisp" is used as a verb. It means to make it shorter and more understandable, to add more sound bites. But the CMC agreed we ought to try to implement Rickard and Tragash's plan. In actuality, I doubt the members had any idea what they had just approved.

Many of our executives, in fact, didn't think this quality push was any more than some sort of top-management fantasy. An amazing amount of people thought this was a crummy idea or that I and the others supporting it were silly. But once I had begun to believe that Xerox was on its way out of business, I was ready to go hammer and tongs after quality.

On the crest of the decision to plow ahead with the quality program, I made another decision that would have far-reaching impact on the company. It would also be stingingly controversial. As I considered the sagging state of the business, I realized that something else shorter-term had to be done to prop up the company. The chilly truth was that it was unlikely that the woes of the copier business were going to vanish anytime soon, and thus my strategic assessment was that it was necessary to diversify into another area that could be a source of reliable profits. In short, we needed to be able to buy some time while we saw if this quality concept was going to do the trick.

Thus two crucial decisions—to pursue the quality concept and to diversify—were born of the same concern: the extreme frailty of the company. We never said this to the outside world—why spook people unnecessarily?—but it was certainly the case.

And so we began a search for a new business. For a long time, there had been a restlessness in the company to diversify. During his years at the helm, Peter McColough spent a lot of time focusing on the long-term future of the business. He was always interested in acquisitions that were broadly connected to xerography or the world of communications. He did make a few acquisitions in the 1960s that had nothing at all to do with xerography but were related to education and publishing, including the *Weekly Reader* and Universal Microfilm, which worked out well. And of course, there was also the ill-fated SDS deal.

Western Union International became available and we bought that for a couple of hundred million dollars. I was president when it happened, and I was a little uneasy about the deal, because I wasn't convinced we had developed our strategy well enough, but I went along with it. It was opportunistic, so we did it. We later determined it was not a strategic fit and got out of Western Union, for what we had in it, by selling it to MCI.

So the willingness to do acquisitions was there even though the success rate was not all that good. The publishing acquisitions worked out well. Peter made the decision to get into them and I made the decision to get out of them at substantial profit. But the information and optical ones were not wildly successful. Yet we needed protection against the fear that the great xerographic process was going to go away one day. Growth had to come from new markets. In fact, we did need to look for a life beyond xerographic copiers and build a broader-based business strategy.

It was evident that Xerox could handle some diversification. For although the core business was not performing well at all, we had a strong enough balance sheet devoid of much debt. So the idea was to leverage the balance sheet by picking an industry that would be free of the hoary ills that afflicted copying. We had several key criteria that guided us in our hunt. The company could not be in manufacturing, because we had our hands full with the one we had. We desired a company that did the preponderance of its business in the United States, because we had been hammered by currency fluctuations in the late 1970s that played havoc with our profits. And we sure didn't want another company that competed against the Japanese. We weren't fools. And we also wanted something that wouldn't require us to fold the managements into one another but that could stand on its own feet.

One idea we gave some serious thought to was buying one of the television networks. Peter had a powerful interest in communications, and so we vaguely convinced ourselves that television and copiers were both in the field of communications, though I must admit that this struck me as quite a stretch. In any event, we actually went ahead and approached CBS. In early 1980 Peter and I went down to have lunch with Bill Paley, CBS's patron saint and then very much the boss, and John Bakke, the network's president. Paley was quite a cordial and fascinating guy. Though we never got around to actually talking about buying CBS, we did say that we thought we should chat further and trade strategies. Paley said he thought that was a splendid idea. Not long afterward, however, he called and said he had changed his mind and didn't see any point in further discussions. I don't know what happened to cool his interest, but we shrugged the rebuff off and figured there were other good fish out there.

Then we began to look into financial services. In this area, we had some experience. In 1980 we had started to finance our equipment sales because we were racking up a lot more sales. As we built the finance unit up in the early 1980s, we also began to do tax-based leasing and were doing very well. We started off by taking a broad look at the entire financial services market, including the brokerage houses, but never had any discussions with anyone. When we saw the sort of huge daily risks that these brokerage companies took, we realized that owning one would absorb too much of management's time. We were simply unwilling to take risks of those magnitudes.

Our corporate strategy group, working with Salomon Brothers and Goldman Sachs, had been huddling with the senior management team for some time on diversifying into the financial services market. We settled on the property and casualty industry. Peter, Mel Howard, who was our chief financial officer, the strategy group, and I spent a great deal of time talking to experts and learning about the industry. One evening Mel Howard and I had dinner at the Waldorf-Astoria in New York with Warren Buffett, the legendary Omaha investor who had had a spectacular record as a stock picker. Known as the Oracle of Omaha, he has been hailed by some as having had the most brilliant career in American investment history. What piqued our interest was the fact that he held a substantial stake in the big Geico insurance company.

Buffett was quite candid. He was far from kind about how the property and casualty business was managed; he felt there was great unrealized potential in a number of the companies. From his comments, it was also clear that he thought the value of Geico was substantially above what we thought and what the current market had calculated. Just as Buffett predicted, Geico would go on to perform very well indeed.

I was taken by Buffett and had a productive evening. How could you not like the man? He was no nonsense, bright, and highly focused. Here he was a billionaire, yet he wore suits off the rack and lived in a middle-class Omaha neighborhood in the house he bought in 1958 for $31,500. He collected model trains. He read the philosopher Bertrand Russell for relaxation. He had been tracking the stock market since he was nine and, while he was in high school, he impishly shorted AT&T because he knew all his teachers owned the stock and he wanted to torment them. So his conviction that there was untapped value to be had in the insurance industry meant something to us.

Shortly afterward, we came around to identifying a likely candidate. Crum & Forster had begun as a three-man fire insurance agency in New York City in 1896. Now it was a large, well-regarded property and casualty insurance company, ranked tenth in its field. Property and casualty was performing well at the time and Crum & Forster itself was doing nicely. We were concerned about asbestos liability, which had become a grave issue, but from what we could tell the matter was under control.

So in September 1982 we signed an agreement to purchase Crum

& Forster for $1.6 billion in cash and stock, then one of the largest acquisitions in history. Today the price sounds like pocket change.

The buying of the company was the most overt indication that we had a confidence problem in the original business. That's not what we said publicly. But that's exactly what it was.

Wall Street reacted with views that ranged from amazement to outright derision. Most of the analysts who tracked us didn't like the price and they didn't like the strategy. On hearing the news, one large and disaffected institutional holder in Rochester dumped all half a million of its Xerox shares.

Mel Howard and I met with quite a number of analysts and institutional shareholders to try to get our view of this across, and some gave us a torturous time. I had never been roughed up and bloodied as much as I was during a few of those encounters. With some, we assuaged them. But with others, we had no impact at all. One day, Peter walked into my office and Mel and I were sitting there with this big institutional holder on the squawk box. He was really giving it to us with both barrels. Peter was awestruck at the fiery language and the ferocity of the onslaught. Like others, he wound up unloading his shares and our stock price tumbled.

Internally, the deal was equally controversial. While senior management was utterly supportive of it, the rank and file felt differently. Many employees took this as a sign that we had given up on the copier business or that we were going to curtail our investment in it. That was hardly the case. For one thing, our problem in office products wasn't a lack of investment, but rather our inefficiencies. We had calculated that our research and development expenditures were perfectly adequate. The problem was how the money was being used. So it wasn't that we were taking anything away from the core business. Nevertheless, it was easy to see the reason for the hue and cry. We had had substantial layoffs, we had trimmed benefits, and we had been saying that we needed to wring more costs out of the business. And then, in the next breath, we announced that we were spending $1.6 billion to buy an insurance company. It just didn't jibe in many minds.

As we had with the Wall Street crowd, Mel Howard and I went out and conducted meetings with groups of employees to pacify them and explain our intentions. We didn't get quite the tongue-lashing we did from investors, but we met a lot of disgruntled people. All the sessions helped, but I know we didn't come close to convincing everybody.

People asked us what we thought the relative contributions to our profits would be between office products and financial services. We told them two-thirds would flow from office products and one-third from financial services. Fairly quickly, Crum & Forster performed better than we anticipated while office products fared worse and the ratio became fifty-fifty. That sent further waves of alarm through the office products ranks.

In the ensuing months and years, we would add other companies to our financial services group, though Crum & Forster remained the linchpin. We started Xerox Life. We bought two investment banking businesses, Furman Selz and Van Kampen Merritt. We acquired a minority stake in VMS Partners, a full-service real estate investment firm.

Our move into financial services would get close scrutiny in the years to come, and much later many would come to question whether we ever should have made the move at all. While Peter was involved, it was truly my decision, and yet I too would agonize over that very question.

As the months marched on, though, nothing much seemed to be happening on any front. I was beginning to feel a vise tightening around me.

We had done a lot of things, including laying off twelve thousand people in 1980–81 to cut costs. Within a year, it became evident that this was an inadequate amount. I had commissioned a major study of Xerox by the McKinsey people, which led to the announcement in July 1981 of a broad restructuring of the business into strategic business units. Too much was being done at corporate headquarters, down to the color of every new product that came out, and I wanted to do away with a lot of this centralization and reduce corporate overhead. This proved to be a good management decision and the new organization was working.

But despite all we were doing, we were still being eaten alive. Interest rates were way up. All the cutting we did wasn't close to being enough. We had done all the enlightened management things, even the unthinkable like the massive layoffs. We changed some senior managers. And the business stubbornly wouldn't respond.

Some time before, I had started a custom of having Monday morning breakfast meetings in the ground-level cafeteria with the half-dozen most senior executives in the company. It afforded an informal opportunity to air any concerns we had about the business or to put forth new brainstorms. At one of these breakfast sessions in October 1982, which would much later become famous around Xerox as the Wet Noodle Meeting, I was feeling particularly somber and frustrated. I told the others that for all the talk there had been about change and turning around the business, I didn't think we had made much progress whatsoever. To my mind, we had stirred nothing up. "I really believe that I'm pushing around a wet noodle," I said. "I'm pushing and nothing is happening, no momentum at all."

The others were mute, except for my old friend Bill Glavin, now one of the executive vice presidents. Once I had finished, he aggressively disagreed with me. I didn't understand what was going on, he snapped, his voice rising as he talked. He insisted that we really were making clear-cut strides. Since he was in charge of the staff, he took my complaint as a direct swipe at him and I guess he felt compelled to defend himself.

But Glavin's arguments left me unconvinced. I returned to my office, persuaded that we were doing a lot of talking but in fact very little real change was taking place. As far as I could see, if Xerox were going to make it, we had to firm up the wet noodle.

Meanwhile, as Norm Rickard and Hal Tragash continued looking for answers, Tony Kobayashi of Fuji Xerox offered them some valuable input. He would be in the States every six weeks or so and would spend a couple of hours with members of the Gang of Eleven discussing Total Quality Control as he understood it. He hammered home the idea that it was important to have an outsider involved, someone with no political agenda and no career aspirations at Xerox. That person could look at the company with a clearer perspective, and he would be able to look me in the eye and tell me when I was wrong without being mortified about the effect on his livelihood. Rickard and Tragash agreed. They needed another prophet.

9. Another Prophet

BURLINGTON, MASSACHUSETTS, was cool and clear, with a battering breeze, but the weather made no difference to David Nadler on this October afternoon. He was conducting a workshop for Honeywell executives at the Holiday Inn. There was a rusty glow on the hotel façade and the trees outside had begun to be stripped of leaves. While the attendees were immersed in some group work, Nadler strolled down the hall to a pay phone and called his office to see if there were any messages. By now, he had left his teaching job at Columbia and had formed his own consulting firm, which he would eventually name the Delta Consulting Group. His secretary told him there was one urgent call from Hal Tragash. Nadler found that odd. He hadn't heard from Tragash in months. What could he want? Nadler dialed Tragash, who picked up and said, without preamble, "We finally got it."

"Got what?" Nadler said, mystified. He had no idea what he was talking about.

"Our quality thing," Tragash said.

"What quality thing?" Nadler said.

During the months Tragash and Rickard had been traipsing around preaching quality, Tragash assumed Nadler knew all about their activities when, in fact, he was totally out of touch with what they had been doing. Bubbling over with glee, Tragash said, "They bought this concept of Commitment to Excellence, and they approved the idea of getting a consultant. Guess what—we want you. I want you to come here as soon as you can and meet a guy named Norm Rickard."

On October 9, 1982, Nadler arrived for his first meeting with Tragash and Rickard, who proceeded to brief him on all that had been going on. Nadler quickly realized the circumstances: Xerox was in grave pain and had decided it had to do something. That something was to instill a quality mentality throughout the corporation. Nadler was quite taken by his two collaborators—Tragash and Rickard. As he would put it, "They were mavericks and outlaws in the organization. They had been working in the vineyards and knew what was going on. They were revolutionaries trying to make something happen. It was guerrilla warfare. And they had signed up the king to participate in the revolution. Best of all, they had little to lose. They were not running for high corporate office."

A few weeks later, Nadler met with me and I expressed my extreme frustration and gave him my wet noodle spiel. "I'm trying to get a hundred thousand people to act and think differently toward the product, the customer, and each other every hour of every day," I told him. "All of my senior managers say they agree with me. But I feel that if I leave the company for a couple of days, they will go right back to doing what they were doing. I'm pushing a wet noodle."

I also told him, "One thing I wrote down on the plane coming back from California the other day was that if Norm Rickard went away or got hit by a car, then quality at Xerox would stop. So I'm going to have to become more active in this." I pointed out that quality simply wasn't getting enough senior management attention. "We need to concentrate on the customer," I said. "We need a commitment from the organization. There has to be unity, and that means a cultural change."

Nadler told me that he could help me, but pointed out that the core problem that I was facing was how to manage a massive change in organizational behavior. He also said that if I were really serious about bringing about such extensive upheaval, I would probably have to shoot someone along the way. Unless people get rewarded and punished for how they behave, he said, no one will really believe that this is anything more than lip service. This made me slightly uncomfortable. Firing people was never something that I or most people have much taste for, but I agreed with him. Then he told me that I would have to furnish symbols and signals and create a TDY, and old army term meaning a temporary duty team, and I would have to lead it.

I had met Nadler on several previous occasions, but at this meeting his tough-minded and intellectual approach to what Xerox needed to do attracted me, and I agreed to move ahead.

At that time, Nadler himself didn't know all that much about quality. But he felt he knew how to implement change in an organization. And for this particular battle—one that could be to the death against the Japanese—he was a most ironic warrior.

Nadler's father, Leonard Nadler, worked for the government, and in 1959, when Nadler was eleven, his father took a job as a foreign service worker in the U.S. State Department. He was dispatched to Japan, where the family lived for three and a half years. As it turned out, he became the last American foreign aid officer to Japan.

This was at the tail end of the U.S. Occupation, and it was a pretty turbulent time. The country rocked with riots and demonstrations by hundreds of thousands of students. President Eisenhower was scheduled to come over, the first American president to visit the country, but the trip had to be canceled because it was felt that his safety couldn't be guaranteed. All the same, there was tremendous curiosity on the part of the Japanese about everything American.

Nadler's family lived in Tokyo in one of the homes built for the U.S. Embassy staff. The Americans had constructed American-style ranch houses to show the Japanese how to make better houses, and Nadler's family was assigned one of those ranches. (When he returned to Tokyo in 1981, the houses had been torn down and replaced with modern white stucco Japanese-style houses.) Living there was a profoundly altering experience. In essence, he lived much as a consultant does—in the system but not of it.

At that time, the United States wasn't giving the Japanese any money but was trying to improve their managerial ability. With that in mind, Nadler's father worked with the newly formed Japan Productivity Center. Its purpose was to send teams of Japanese middle managers to the United States to learn about modern technology and quality—the very things that Japan would go on to better us at and that Nadler would spend his career trying to teach American companies. One of the principal places the Japanese visited was River Rouge to see the fabled car industry. When a team was put together, which occurred about once every couple of weeks, Nadler's father would invite the members over to his house for an American-style dinner to get them ready for their new experience.

After Japan, Nadler's father was assigned to Ethiopia. As Nadler remembered it, "I found Japan very different from America, but Ethiopia was something else again. There had just been an attempted coup on the emperor, Haile Selassie, which was put down with some American help. I'll never forget our introduction to the country. We landed at the airport and loaded into a Land Rover. There was a sign saying 'Fly Ethiopian Airlines.' The sign was in the shape of an airplane and from the nose someone had been hanged. When we got to the hotel, there were bullet holes all over. At night you heard the hyenas howling. In school, I was one of sixteen students and the principal wore a holster with two sharp-shooters buckled to his waist."

After two and a half years in Ethiopia, Nadler's family returned to the States and settled in College Park, Maryland. His father worked for the Job Corps as part of the War on Poverty. He had a high work ethic, and felt Nadler ought to work during the summers. So Nadler found a job in the Department of Public Welfare. This was 1965, and it marked the first time he had ever seen a Xerox machine. The department had a 914. "Most of the time I typed reports on stencils, but if something was really important, you were allowed to copy it on the Xerox machine," Nadler recalled. "It was kept in a glassed-in room near the director's office. You had to sign in to use it. Most of the time when I got permission to use it, there was a line of people waiting. It seemed to me a fascinating machine. You just put something in there and you quickly had that copy. I thought, Wow, this is pretty super stuff."

Nadler went on to study international affairs at George Washington University, and while he was there he landed a summer job at IBM, in Rockville, Maryland. It was an intoxicating experience, where he got to rub noses with some senior IBM managers, and worked under a true model manager named Don Osgood. Once back in school, Nadler went to the placement office one day and discovered that the Civil Service Administration was recruiting college students. He signed up and was put in the pension benefits division. There had been changes in the benefit law, and so all the files had to be updated. Nadler would open a file and copy the benefit and then multiply and divide by hand to calculate the new benefit. As he did his arithmetic, he realized that his reward for getting things done faster was getting more files to do. There was no incentive to be productive. Thus he devised a little program for calculating benefits (since he was taking computer programming). He took this to his supervisor, who told him, "When I want your advice I'll ask for it." He wound up being assigned to a room where he was handed a box of punch cards and told to refile them and put them in order. After two days, he quit. Here he had been at IBM where there were intelligent managers and concern for employees, and he got stuck in this environment. It boggled his mind.

Nadler's next job was in the Manpower Administration, which administered programs for job training. It became evident after a while that they didn't have any work for him to do. He'd go to his boss and he would say to Nadler with a big grin, "Have I told you how wonderful it is to have you? It's great for a young person to be in government." As he looked around, Nadler realized that many of the people there had nothing to do. As Nadler put it, "I was seeing the classic dysfunctions of bureaucracy. It was bizarre. I felt I had entered some sort of 'Addams Family' world. People were writing books, drawing cartoons, going bananas. But nobody was doing any work."

Next, Nadler enrolled in the Harvard Business School, where he decided he wanted to do something in organizational behavior. In his second year, he took Harry Levinson's seminar on psychoanalytic theory and organizations. As part of it, a group of the students studied a chronic disease hospital in Cambridge and wrote a three-hundred-page paper on it. After they finished the report, they sat down with management to spell out their recommendations. Management totally ignored them. The experience taught Nadler that just knowing what is wrong and what the solutions are didn't necessarily lead to anything.

Levinson advised Nadler to continue on at the University of Michigan, and he went there and entered the organizational psychology program. This was a time when the country was starting to think about work, and it was a very exciting time to be at Michigan. Nadler got a job at the Institute for Social Research, which had begun a study called the National Survey of Working Conditions. Remember, it was a radically different time then. The Japanese had not appeared. Workers in Michigan had more overtime than they could keep up with. The auto industry was booming.

Another person who had a big influence on Nadler as a teacher, colleague, and friend was Ed Lawler, who was an industrial psychologist and had started to think about change. He taught Nadler a lot about individual behavior. Lawler and Nadler worked on a project in which they studied the impact of participation and rewards at a company called Donnelly Mirrors in Holland, Michigan. They controlled 80 percent of the market for inside rearview mirrors for cars. It was a company that was very much run for the well-being of employees and allowed major decisions to be made by them. Nadler found that when you increase participation, the people at the bottom feel better but the people at the next level feel threatened.

Lawler went on to start something called the Quality of Life Work Program, in which he tried to come up with new ways of changing organizations and improving worklife. He rounded up some Ford Foundation and government money and went out to talk to the auto companies. Nadler remembered once going to Ford to advise them that they had this money that would allow the company to collaborate with its unions to improve worklife. The Ford managers looked at them and said, "Why would we want to do that?" So the group ended up working with some strange places: auto parts companies, a coal mine, the Tennessee Valley Authority, Mt. Sinai Hospital in New York.

Nadler continued to wonder why management would receive feedback about its problems and still do nothing to eradicate them. So he did his dissertation on a bank now called Banc One, an innovative company that was interested in conducting research. He and some others worked in the branch system that was run at that time by a young man named John B. McCoy, now Banc One's chief executive officer. They studied the effect of feedback on bank branches. They built a monthly feedback system under which ten branches got feedback on their performance and ten didn't. They followed them for fourteen months. At first the two sets looked alike, but at branches where managers held meetings and did problem-solving there was tremendous improvement in performance and customer service. This led to further research on participation and a book that continues to be used to this day.

After Michigan, Nadler decided that he wanted to go back into the business school environment, and so in 1975 he went to Columbia and taught M.B.A. candidates for a while. This was just after the Vietnam period, and most of the students were interested only in getting a job. Nevertheless, Nadler was keen to have them understand organizational behavior. In Michigan he used to teach at night at Wayne State University—mostly basic management to auto company managers. He wanted to figure out ways to show how organizations worked. He took some ideas he had seen and tried to meld them with some systems concepts. As Nadler put it, "I was looking for a way to help students understand organizations—the whole thing, the full catastrophe, as Zorba the Greek says about his life. If there were good and bad organizations, wasn't there a way to get the bad organizations to act more like the good organizations?"

For several years, Nadler was fairly focused on his academic work. Then, in 1977 and 1978, he got involved in two things that changed his life. Walter Wriston had appointed a new line person to try to change the way Citicorp managed the organization. The bank hired some consultants and Nadler wound up being recruited to teach Citibank people about managing people. At the same time, Nadler was hired to help AT&T. A man named Bob Maher was running a consulting group inside AT&T trying to instill change at the phone company. They would do studies of organizations and find all these problems. Then they put together a design team to work on the problems. By and large, they came up with a design that had gains of 16 to 20 percent. But most of the designs were never implemented. So Maher wanted Nadler to find out why some designs were successfully implemented and some weren't. Nadler started to write down some thoughts which led to a paper on organizational change. He was searching for lessons from successful companies that would help him arrive at prescriptions for managing change. In 1979 he took some of these change principles, applied them to Mountain Bell, and found the stuff worked dramatically. He had the sense that he had something—a model to create change in organizations.

In 1981 Nadler rethought his academic career, took a leave of absence from Columbia from which he never returned, and started a consulting firm. He originally called it Organizational Research and Consultation Inc., and later changed the name to the Delta Consulting Group.

Nadler poured himself into the firm. It did a lot of good work with companies like Westinghouse, Citibank, and Chesapeake and Potomac Telephone, but Nadler also made his share of mistakes. He hired some bad people whom he felt he could coach and teach to be better. But he couldn't. In early 1982, the firm had a near-death experience. So Nadler shrunk it back down to about three professionals from nine. He turned off the lights in half the office. He realized he had to do a much better job next time in hiring people. By the summer of 1982, the firm was securely on its feet again and ready to grow. And then, as Nadler put it, "I got the call from Hal Tragash. I immediately felt the Xerox problem was something I could tackle with a new purposiveness and vigor. I had finished my first stage of learning in my firm. So this came at the right time. Nothing could have pleased me more than a gigantic challenge."

Nadler began his assignment by doing some diagnostics. He roamed around the company paying visits to an array of people in order to take the temperature of the place, which happened to be at fever pitch. Nineteen eighty-two was one tough year for Xerox. Everything that everyone had been fearing came to the fore and showed up in late 1981. The piper was being paid for all the sins of the past, and it was no mean price.

Nadler fairly readily sensed the discomfort. He was particularly struck by a chat he had with one of our top financial people, who frankly confessed to Nadler that nobody had any clear idea of what made the place run. Then he related a parable. In an Arabian kingdom, a man was convicted of a nasty crime and sentenced to die. Mortified, the man went to the sheik who ruled the kingdom and begged him, "You can't kill me. It's not fair. Look, I'll tell you what I'll do. If you let me go, I will make your horses fly."

"Really?" the sheik said.

"Yes. I will do that."

"All right," the sheik replied. "Here is what I'm willing to do. If my horses fly tomorrow, I will let you go. But if they don't, then I will put you to death in a very painful way."

The man agreed and returned to his cell. Once he was locked up, he informed his cellmate of what he had done.

"Are you crazy?" the cellmate exclaimed. "You've just made it worse for yourself."

The man shrugged and said, "I look at it like this. The world could come to an end tonight and so what. Or nothing will happen and I'll get put to death anyway and so what. Or, just maybe, the horses will fly."

The financial officer said the story pretty much summed up Xerox. For a number of years, the horses flew. And so the management ran the company fully expecting the horses to keep flying. Until one day everyone looked and realized that the wings were gone.

Nadler went to Xerox Square in Rochester and took the elevator up to the twenty-ninth floor of the old headquarters building to see Dwight Ryan, now running all of U.S. Sales and Service. Nadler arrived with a bad head cold and a strep throat. He had taken some codeine and was pretty groggy. But his schedule was so tight that he felt he couldn't cancel anything. As Ryan talked on and on, Nadler fought mightily to stay awake.

As he would remember it, "Ryan was sitting with his back to the window and there was this depressing gray view. Ryan was going in circles, trying to decide as he went on whether he should even be talking to me. I was taking down notes, but my hand almost stopped writing, I was so tired. Then he mentioned something that really woke me up. He handed me a memo from his boss. He said in the memo that because of Ryan's difficulty in making projected numbers, he ought to 'take out' fifteen hundred tech reps, the guys who fix the machines. After I read it, Ryan said, 'I have a hard time thinking about quality when we're taking out fifteen hundred tech reps, which is going to make a lot of customers unhappy. And I don't like the way it's done. He doesn't talk to me or anything. I open up the mail and here's this letter. That's the way things get done around here.' I was blown away by this."

* * *

Next, Nadler went to take a tour of Building 200, part of the Webster manufacturing facilities. That was where they put machines together, and at the end of the long assembly line they tested them. As he roamed about, he spied a row of machines sitting at the end of the line that had failed to pass final inspection. Master craftsmen were busily taking them apart and trying to figure out what was wrong. It was clear to Nadler that Xerox had not learned to build in quality and therefore obviate the need even to have final inspection.

A high-energy middle manager with white hair told Nadler, "We're losing. And we're a company of winners. We would give a lot to win again. It hurts that we're not winning. And we have a lot of pride." Nadler realized that while there was great desire and pride, there was also tremendous despair and a sense that the employees had lost faith in their leadership. There was almost a feeling of betrayal.

Nadler had also gone to see one of our top-level managers, a sleek man with horn-rimmed glasses who was always impeccably dressed, almost to a fault. In the past, he had been an executive at a couple of the now-defunct car companies, including Willys, and whenever he was introduced to a new concept that didn't sit well with him, he would shake his head and say, "Well, that's not the way we did it at Willys." In his Stamford office, he had mounted on his wall an ax that someone had given him as a gift to celebrate his cost-cutting reputation. On his credenza was an autographed picture from Imelda and Ferdinand Marcos. You could quickly get a sense of the management style from those little mementos. There was a famous story about him that often got told, although I wonder if it was really true. He had a pretty short fuse, and whenever he heard about the sloth of a worker, he would immediately call for the man's dismissal. According to the story, the cost-cutter once visited a plant in Latin America and was told that they were having a lot of trouble with a paper handler (which the cost-cutter failed to realize was a component of a copier). "Fire the guy!" he boomed.

Chatting with Nadler, the man quickly made his view clear. He felt that workers really weren't that disciplined and it took too long to get their opinion on things. The best way to manage was to just tell them what to do. It was the old-line management philosophy. Involve every-one in a decision? That's not the way we did it at Willys.

Nadler had long been fascinated by how organizations get created and how collective behavior occurs. How is it that everyone comes to know what to do? From his work at Citibank and AT&T, he was particularly curious about how change takes place in organizations. He was fortu-nate in his timing. If he were interested in change in 1950, nobody else would have cared because nobody sensed any need to change. Corpora-tions were feeling no pain. The more he thought about this subject, the more a broad question nagged at him: can you in fact change a large organization?

If you were going to a physician to do surgery on you, you would hope he had some knowledge of how the organism worked. So if you're involved in change in a corporation, Nadler felt, you need to know something about how organizations work.

The way Nadler saw it, an organization is a system that takes input and does something with it to produce an output. What is the input? The environment. The resources it has access to (capital, technology, people, its reputation). Its history—meaning what events shaped it. Xerox, for instance, had deep history in the 914. People said it wouldn't work and yet the company went and did it. Nadler attended a meeting of new management and counted seven or eight times that the 914 got mentioned. Most of the people had not been at the company when the 914 was created, and yet they were still driven by it. A fourth kind of input is strategy—how we're going to use our resources in the context of the environment and our history.

On the output side, there are the total system, the units of the com-pany, and the individuals who make up the work force and manage-ment.

In the middle between the input and the output is the organization itself. Its function is to take a strategy and turn it into an output. The organization consists of work, people, formal organization arrange-ments, and the informal organization. The informal organization basi-cally refers to the way things get done—the culture and the operating style. One way to illustrate it is by using the example of alternate-side-of-the-street parking in New York City. If you park on the wrong side, you're supposed to get a ticket. But people have come to learn that they can leave slips of paper on their windshield saying where they are and escape without being ticketed. Unwritten understandings like that exist in profusion in corporations.

Clearly, if you can get a fit or match between work and people, you can get better performance. You need a fit as well with the informal organization. All together, there are six fits and relationships, and the better these fits the better the output.

In conceiving its strategy, Nadler felt, Xerox had to ask itself why somebody should buy from it. For a new competitor—the Japanese— had come along who said, "We don't have a big name or reputation but—guess what?—our machines don't break down and they're cheaper than yours."

For an organization to achieve quality, it was obvious to Nadler that it required change in all the elements of the organization. And he knew that companies don't change from the inside, they change from the outside. Rarely does someone on the inside say we have to change. Occasionally a visionary leader like Walter Wriston comes along and sees the need for change. But generally the external forces are the trigger. And that's what had come to bear at Xerox.

Nadler felt that there was a simple way to think about change. According to the nomenclature coined by Richard Beckhard of MIT, there is the current state, the transition state, and the future state. A company has to move from its current state through a tedious and time-consuming transition state in order to wind up in its future state. And when you're passing through that wrenching transition state, it's like a store being open for business while undergoing renovations. Needless to say, there are apt to be plenty of power, anxiety, and control concerns. It's not a fun time.

Nadler reviewed this theory with me in its earliest and most rudimentary form. Then he gave the pitch to the Gang of Eleven and told them that they needed to consider all this in their efforts to infuse Xerox with a quality mentality.

When Nadler first met with me and the Gang of Eleven, it struck him that all we had was a goal, someone who was committed to achieving it, and a date reserved on the calendar when we might hold a big meeting to talk about it. Therefore, he saw that we faced three major issues. While he saw that we wanted to do "it"—this quality thing—the "it" was poorly defined. The second matter was that I had little constituency of support. I was almost alone in this. And, finally, we had not thought through any transition plan of how we were going to get to "it." Those three issues became the underlying drivers of everything we would do for the next year. Nadler told me that I needed to focus on coauthoring a document to explain the effort, initiating a participatory process to get people on the bandwagon, and forming a transition team to do the planning.

For at this point, in October 1982, a stake had been put in the ground, but no one knew how to get there. We did know, however, that in the first year of this sort of long-range effort we had to furrow and seed.

Nadler himself began working two streams. He spent about a third of his time conferring with me and two-thirds of his time with the Gang of Eleven. As it got cracking on the initial planning to get the quality effort off the ground and flying, the Gang would convene almost every day for hours on end. We have these wonderful (some would say diabolical) conference rooms at Xerox that have no windows, and you would enter them, close the door, and lose total track of time. Time would dissolve. Working with a lack of windows was an interesting exercise in sensory deprivation. The rooms became isolation tanks. In one or another of these conference rooms, the meetings were held.

Early on, we decided that in February 1983 we wanted to have a big meeting over several days to get some sign-up for this program. Our idea was to invite the top twenty-five people in the company to our corporate training center in Leesburg, Virginia, and kick off the effort. I could have simply declared the project but then everyone would have grinned and nodded at me and that would have been it. We had to make it seem like this was everyone's process, not a Kearns mandate. But before we could get to that point, we had to define what our "future state" would be, because it was mighty fuzzy even to me.

As the Gang of Eleven set about trying to do some of the early planning work, it became clear that the meetings were less than efficient. Keeping things on track was not always easy. Norm Rickard seized every opportunity he could to tell war stories, which sent meetings off on tangents for long stretches. The trouble with Norm was that he was so full of information and so anxious to get it out for others to hear that he often lost track of where he was and would start talking about something totally unrelated. Finally, John Kelsch, the head of competitive benchmarking and one of the most industrious and thoughtful members of the Gang, wrote up a set of guidelines for the meetings that he hung on the wall in the conference room. They were entitled Gatekeeping Guidelines. They read as follows: Be open to and encourage ideas; look for merit in the ideas; strive for win-win situations; listen nondefensively; pay attention and avoid side conversations; limit war stories; look for facts; help to summarize; each member is responsible for the team's progress. Once those hints went up, meetings began to move a bit better.

Even so, in fairly short order the Gang of Eleven proved to be unworkable. The members were saddled with too many personal agendas, and if we had listened to them all, we would have wound up with an eight-humped camel. After having attended several meetings, Nadler said, "Let's declare victory and go home." Some members of the Gang were sent back to their units and others were assigned to smaller groups that seemed to function better. From then on, the fundamental work was done by a reconfigured Gang of Seven. Its principal members were Nadler, Rickard, and Tragash, with strong supporting help from John Kelsch; Ian Raisbeck, a training designer from Rank Xerox; Paula Fleming, an energetic woman who worked for Tragash in the personnel department; and a colleague of Nadler's named Ron Dukenski.

The Gang of Seven began its work by attempting to create two artifacts. There was the artifact of the "book" and the artifact of the "slide-and-tape show." A third artifact would be the meeting itself—the meeting as theater loaded with symbolism.

It was important that we clearly define a future state and transition plan for the company and get that definition on paper. This took its material form in a looseleaf book known as the Blue Book, because of its cover color, that was to form the basis for the meeting in Leesburg.

At the same time, the Gang of Seven knew there would be a problem building support, given that I didn't have an automatic constituency rooting for this program. No one else had any equity in it, and therefore the Gang would have to flush out a constituency. So it put together a slide-and-tape show, a thirty-five minute presentation that described why Xerox should care about quality. By showing this to people, we felt we would be able to figure out who was for the effort, who was against it, and who was neutral. We were never going to get anyplace until we had some grasp of where people stood. Quality is like motherhood. Everyone is ostensibly for it. But it was necessary to know who was genuinely for it and who wasn't.

One day Nadler and Rickard drew up a list of the members of the Corporate Management Committee and went down the names and made their own guesses about who would be a supporter and who wouldn't. Listening to them with some bemusement, Tragash said, "This is like an account list for a presidential campaign. We need to assign people to get the votes. A National Account Strategy."

"Exactly," Rickard agreed.

In the ensuing weeks, either Nadler, Rickard, or Tragash went out and talked to the top twenty-five people in the company and played the slide-and-tape show as their stalking-horse. They were like Fuller Brush salesmen hawking their wares to people who just wished they would go away so they could return to the soap operas. The slide show explained what we were doing and what quality was about. Once the show was over, the presenter asked the person how it should be changed. What was missing, what wasn't? It got people to feel they were involved. Also, you could tell from the responses who was really engaged and who was bored to tears.

The slide-and-tape show began with a capsule history of Xerox. It ran through the 1960s and the 914, then told how, as Xerox entered the decade of the 1980s, it became clear that the cost of doing business was too high and the quality of its products and services was not high enough to meet new competitive challenges. Accordingly, finances suffered. Other major multinational companies wanted a piece of the Xerox action. The tape went on to talk about how some parts of the company had implemented competitive benchmarking and employee involvement, but that more was needed. Finally, it said that if Xerox were to succeed in the future it had to become synonymous with quality in the eyes of the customer.

After observing people's reaction to the slide-and-tape show, the team created a "watch list" and divided people into three categories: "true believers," "in the middle," and "not with the program." At first, among the top managers, only Frank Pipp and myself were positioned as true believers.

To move people into the true-believers camp, we knew we had to use every bullet we could find. So we began to bombard them with education. Rickard was highly useful in this drill, for he loved to get his hands on books that pertained to what we were doing and send copies around to people. He did this in such profusion that we used to tease him about Norm's Book Emporium. He would find something he liked and order a hundred and fifty or two hundred copies and start circulating them through the company. Rickard had his own peculiar way of passing on books. He knew everyone was busy and would be disinclined to pick up anything extra to read, and so he would mark the important passages with Post-its and yellow highlighter pens. He'd say, "You've got to read this. You don't have to read it all. I've saved you time and marked up the key parts." The trouble was, by the time you went through all the highlighted passages, you'd find you had read the whole book.

As another way to develop true believers, the team arranged for some people to visit IBM and Westinghouse, two companies more advanced than most in improving quality, to inspect how they did things. Some members like John Kelsch had never been to Japan, and so he and a few others went over to attend Fuji Xerox's annual Quality Circle Convention and to tour some Japanese plants. Among those who went with Kelsch was the president of Xerox's Rochester union local. One of the places the contingent toured was the Juki Sewing Machine company, which was bigger in Japan than Singer was in America. They saw these amazing electronic sewing machines that were tossing off shirts at an unbelievable clip. When the union leader spied them, he turned to Kelsch and said, "You know, one of the reasons we won't fight automation is we saw how the Rochester clothing workers got wiped out. We know that if we're not competitive at Xerox, we'll lose all of our jobs." It was that sort of enlightened thinking that made the union a key supporter throughout our drive for quality.

We also spent a good deal of time hunting for quality gurus to guide us. After all, at this juncture, quality was a goal that all of us had to learn together. None of us really knew precisely what it was.

To increase our knowledge, one of the first people we spoke with was Phil Crosby, who had made quite a name for himself, and a lot of money, by teaching quality. Crosby popularized quality, and he did it at the right time. That was his master stroke. By now, Crosby had published his famous book, *Quality Is Free*. In actuality, it really isn't. It may be free eventually, but it costs money to get there. Crosby had sold his concept better than anyone else, but he did have some weaknesses. He tried to make achieving quality sound too easy. He wasn't tuned in to employee involvement. And he was very manufacturing-oriented. Manufacturing happened to be a large part of Xerox. But our biggest problems were in marketing and service, and Crosby didn't address those areas.

One day, we invited Crosby to have lunch with three members of the CMC, and they weren't too warm toward him. The thing he said that stood out was that our behavioral ideas were bad news. He said if you wanted people to act in a different way, all you had to do was tell them. "You tell 'em and they do it," he said.

Later on, Crosby spoke at a dinner of our top fifty managers. This was a formal year-end management meeting we always held where we talk about what we're doing and lay out the plans for the coming year. Here, he was fairly effective. The most important reason was because he spoke business-ese. He made an entertaining pitch about the cost of quality that energized me. But many others were not excited at this "simple notion" of how to achieve quality.

Crosby did have several provocative ideas that hit home. He gave a clear image of what quality is. It's not goodness. It's not that a Mercedes is better than a Honda. It's that a product conforms to requirements. And he made the startling point that it costs more to produce low-quality goods than to produce high-quality goods. Crosby said that the cost of bad quality is 20 percent of a company's revenues. It's the cost of scrap, the cost of repair, the warranty costs, the cost of customer complaint lines. That's a huge number, and I don't know how he got it. But we subsequently did some studies at Xerox and the 20 percent proved to be about right. Some studies of Japanese companies have also been done, and it's been found that the cost there is about 3 percent of revenues. Also, Crosby said that quality is management's job. You can in fact control it. So he cleared up three misconceptions. It's not an abstract goodness thing. It's not something that costs more to achieve. It's not something that is the workers' fault.

In January 1983, a bunch of senior Xerox managers, including Bill Glavin and Wayland Hicks, flew down to Winter Park, Florida, to take Crosby's two-and-a-half-day course on quality. Glavin in particular liked it and said he wanted me to come down and take an abbreviated version of it. I agreed to go, as did David Nadler and Frank Pipp. I must say, I enjoyed a lot of that course. Crosby regaled us with some good stories. Most quality guys are deadly dull. Crosby is an entertainer. And most quality guys beat up on you. They say, "You're doing everything wrong." Crosby didn't. He told anecdotes about companies. But when I pressed Crosby for more examples of how his training worked, he was evasive. He didn't respond well to questions. His answer to everything seemed to be: "You need to do training and you need to do my training."

Crosby made it clear to us that he wanted to do all our training. We would have liked him to, if he would have agreed to some modifications. Basically, we wanted him to unbundle his package, but he didn't want to. Crosby wanted to sell quality and sell it off the shelf. Maybe that was the right decision for him to make, but we didn't think it would work for us and we decided not to use him. Nevertheless, the exposure to Crosby got the top people at Xerox thinking along the right lines. To this day, in fact, I continue to be a Phil Crosby fan. The introduction to the subject I got from his book and his class got me going.

We also met with and read the work of the other famous quality guru, W. Edwards Deming. Deming, the former U.S. government statistician who gained fame for helping to bring quality to postwar Japan, is a quirky, often cantankerous man, such a stickler about precision that he dates the eggs in his refrigerator with a Magic Marker to make sure the older ones are eaten first. He knew that the only way to create quality was to build it into a product in the first place, not check for it after it was finished. And he believed in establishing statistical controls for every part to avoid variations in quality.

Deming had a nifty way to illustrate his beliefs. It's known as his bead trick. He fills a container with three thousand white beads and seven hundred and fifty red ones. Volunteers are then asked to reach in with a paddle and count out fifty beads. Every red bead represents a defective product. Unless a miracle occurs, every paddle is sure to contain a sprinkling of detested red beads. But you can't blame the workers. It's a faulty system. So management needs to establish some statistical parameters and then ask the workers to try to stay within them. In other words, quality control begins with management and the design engineers. Once they've done their part, then it becomes possible for workers to chip in. Bad management spells bad quality.

Deming delineated his philosophy into his "Fourteen Points," measures that he felt needed to be followed to achieve quality. We got from him that you must change the management process and not just tell employees what to do. By and large, we agreed with that. But it worried us that Deming didn't really address how you got there, and he didn't seem to consider the implications of the fact that these changes run counter to a culture.

At one point, we invited Deming to give a speech before some of our top people. He was his usual gruff and abrasive self. He really blasted management. He more or less told us that we were doing everything wrong and we had to change everything, but we probably wouldn't do it because we were all messed up.

Another leading quality guru who spent time with us was Joseph Juran. While less abrasive than Deming, he gave us the same message—change the way we thought about the business.

The more we examined the other quality gurus, the more convinced we became that it wouldn't do to just lift someone else's plan. It would never work to just follow their prescription. We needed to take pieces from all of them, stir in our own ideas, and create a soup that was totally unique. And we felt we had an opening in quality that nobody else had yet cracked—how to get it done. This confirmed our decision to work with Nadler and Delta. For the more we learned about quality together, the more we realized that none of the quality gurus seemed to know how to deal with organizational change. Having said that, we could not have done what we did without the help of Deming, Juran, and Crosby.

As it began to intensify its preparations for the Leesburg meeting, the Gang of Seven focused on how to engineer an engaging session that could cause people to own this concept. The Gang's principal focus became the Blue Book, our road map to what we were proposing to do.

Many people talk about how management is a spectator sport. At meetings, underlings give their overviews. Meanwhile, management sits there and watches the presentations and either gives a thumbs-up or thumbs-down. Nadler told me that for the Leesburg meeting we had to move the Xerox style from spectator to contact sport. The managers had to get all their fingers on this. We wanted a lot of hands to touch the book so they could all claim paternity.

The Blue Book would be coauthored by me and be a statement of the mission and the future state of Xerox. There would turn out to be four versions of it. Its aim was to spell out what quality was and what Xerox would look like once it had quality. If we had a video camera and were here ten years from now and taped Xerox, what would it look like? What would we see?

At the same time that the Gang of Seven wrestled with these questions, I met with Nadler once a week to discuss the Blue Book. These meetings were critical, because they allowed us to really hammer out our ideas about quality and change. Nadler would give me a sheet of paper with questions and blank spaces and I would fill in the spaces. Then he would sit with me and talk about these and write some more. Then the Gang would complete chapter drafts of my words and my thoughts and I would mark those up. In this way, I very much became a coauthor of the book.

Day after day, Nadler, Rickard, and Tragash would hold meetings of their own. In taking on the role of scheduling them, Rickard was relentless. He would ask, "When do you want to start?" One of the others would suggest eight-thirty. Rickard would retort, "Well, how about seven-thirty?" Then he'd add, "Why don't you come by at seven to catch up?" And everyone would wind up going until seven or eight at night. Nadler would leave his apartment before it was light out and when he would walk out of Xerox it would be dark. He would never see the sun. For all he knew, it had never come out.

At the beginning, everyone was feeling overwhelmed. In the middle of December and over Christmas there was a tremendous amount of work and real concern about whether it would come together. A couple of times the process almost came off the track. A few senior executives made it clear to me that they felt we didn't have to go to all this trouble but could just gather people in a room in Stamford for half a day and tell them what was going to happen. There was one executive who was deathly afraid of making a decision. He would always agree with the seniormost person. If two senior executives of equal rank were in a room together and disagreed, he would be in an absolute panic. How could he agree with both of them?

To relieve the pressure, the plotters had their fun, too. There were a couple of standing jokes that got repeated airing in their meetings. If any of the participants arranged for it in advance, fruit would be brought in for refreshment. A running joke was: "Is this going to be a fruitless meeting or not?" Most of the time it was fruitless and so someone would say, "Ah, another fruitless meeting."

Another standard diversion was to pretend that the group was casting *Xerox: The Movie*. This was Nadler's idea. He did it at other places, too, as a way to relieve tension. Some of the choices were Charlton Heston for Bill Glavin, Hugh O'Brian or Sam Shepard for me, and Ben Gazzara for Mel Howard. There was never any discussion of the plot of the movie, just the cast. Each day, someone new might be recommended to star in the film. As Tragash would say, "I often felt as if we were Mel Brooks and his guys sitting around writing *The History of the World, Part II*."

All of this was tied to the two o'clock syndrome. That was the time when everyone experienced a dip in energy and went off on tangents. If anyone said anything goofy early in the day, Rickard would bark,

"What, is it two o'clock already?" Then someone would say, "Well, it must be two o'clock somewhere."

Jokes were always being played on one or another of them. Rickard tried hard to avoid telling war stories, so he would come in and say, "Let me just ramble for about sixty seconds." Once he came in and said, "Let me just ramble for about sixty minutes." Nadler spoke up: "There's Freud when we need him."

Out of personal interest, Tragash read a lot of military history and he tended to salt-and-pepper his speech with military jargon. He might announce, "We've got to take this beachhead" or "We need to launch a strike here." In 1982 the army was not quite the paragon of a desirable organization that it is today. Nadler would point this out to Tragash. He would nod and keep on using his military terms.

Sometimes, particularly after a long, tiresome day, almost anything would cause the group to erupt in laughter. They would laugh till their sides ached. One day, someone knocked on the door and said, "Would you keep it down in there? You're making so much noise we can't work."

All this fooling around and digressive talk built an esprit d'corp. The freewheeling nature of these meetings served to ease the pressure of how much was at stake. For it was never very far from the core planners that we were embarking on a very big gamble. As Tragash said, "It was a lot of fun and there was a lot of creativity. If we treated it as serious business, we would not have been as bold. We realized we could change a whole company and were playing for high stakes. Yet we were not inhibited about how big this was."

A lot of work was done with flip charts. If you walked into the meeting room on any given afternoon, you would see all sorts of dirty dishes and books all over and taped on the wall would be all manner of flip charts. Flip charts were the consultant's tools of the 1960s and 1970s. This ensured that all the words that got spoken didn't disappear into the air. Afterward, someone would have to get the flip charts typed up.

Trying to focus on the conversations and the charts wore everyone out. People would get up and walk around, because they would get a headache sitting there all day. It's tough to be creative on demand. Nadler always had a particularly hard time sitting still. He would circle the room and often simply leave and go visit someone or take a walk down the hall. Usually, he would come back refreshed and with a new thought. Tragash and Rickard, on the other hand, had no trouble sitting in one place for hours on end, totally immersed.

Over time, the group developed the feel of a locker room. One member would go off and do a slide-and-tape show with someone, or another plotter would come by to see me. Then the others would wait to hear how it went. There would be a cheer when there was good news, gloom when there was bad. Victories and defeats were being absorbed in the windowless conference rooms.

The bulk of the writing of the actual words of the Blue Book was done by Nadler, Tragash, and Paula Fleming. To be sure, many of them were my words. Steadily, the book took shape. It was a lengthy document that laid out the basic philosophies of our quality strategy. It pointed out that quality improvement was the key priority for long-term business success, that quality was determined by the customer, either external or internal, and that quality improvement came from doing the right things and doing them well. The Blue Book went on to recommend that problem-solving and quality training be introduced throughout the company. It drove home the need of senior management to become a model for the new types of behavior we desired of our work force and managers. What's more, it urged that the reward system be revamped to recognize those who employed quality tools.

One of the things we inserted was a thirty-second elevator speech. The consensus was that if people were going to board this quality bandwagon then it had to be something that I could explain to anyone in the company during the course of an elevator ride. Since our headquarters had only three floors, the elevator rides were pretty speedy and thus we decided the explanation had to be condensed to a thirty-second spiel. That's a lot harder to do than you might think.

The final elevator speech went: "Leadership Through Quality is a comprehensive way of working which establishes quality as the basic guiding principle to enable all Xerox people to deliver innovative products and services which satisfy their customer's requirements in the most cost effective manner.

"Quality is meeting the customer's existing and latent requirements.

"Improving quality means understanding and working to satisfy the customer's requirements.

"Business Effectiveness, encompassing Competitive Benchmarking and Employee Involvement, continues to be an integral part of this process.

"All-pervasive quality—preventing errors, satisfying our external and internal customers in all our business activities, and continuously improving or innovating our work and products—is the key to maintaining and increasing our market leadership, and making our work life more satisfying."

While all this went on, I worried a good deal. Frank Pipp was constantly making the point of how difficult the task ahead was. Frank was one of the few senior people who really understood what we were trying to do and how important it was. But because he understood it so well he sensed the formidable obstacles ahead. He had a lot of wisdom and a lot of great sayings, many of which I appropriated. He once told me, "The chairman must be the leader. If you blink, by the time you get to the end of the line someone is standing there with his eyes closed all the time." He also said about our quality effort, "We have to put a sign outside the corporation saying, 'This company is open for business while under repair.'" I used to talk about the idea of trying to change a fan belt while the engine was running. As I thought about the complexities ahead of us, I found I was thinking about the task ahead almost twenty-four hours a day!

I began mentioning to people what I thought was an apt analogy. In 1935 the British realized that Germany had overtaken them in air power. So they went all out to build better airplanes and develop radar. By the time the war broke out, they had made great advances. But the British still did not know whether they were strong enough to beat the German advantage. In the end, the Royal Air Force narrowly won the

Battle of Britain, but they found they had been operating at the very thinnest margin of safety. American manufacturing was in the same position. The time to meet that challenge was short, but we didn't know how short. There is a point in every contest where, if you fall far enough behind, you can't catch up, no matter what you do. I believed we were competing dangerously close to the edge of the margin of safety—just like the RAF in the Battle of Britain.

But most of the top executives hadn't yet come to appreciate how dire our situation was and how badly we needed to change our ways. It's all too easy for those sitting in corporate headquarters to become isolated from the real world. So a seemingly innocuous program was begun that had some real effect in waking up people in a hurry.

Back in my days at IBM, I always tried to talk directly to at least two customers and two employees who called or wrote me every week to get a reading on how the business was faring. This seemed like a commonsense thing to do, though I found that many managers never bothered to speak to customers at all. At Xerox we had a department in Rochester where several people did nothing but respond to customer calls. Any time a customer dialed the chairman's office—as customers are wont to do when they've received no satisfaction on a problem and are ready to blow their stacks—those calls would eventually be routed to Rochester.

Someone came up with the idea that perhaps we ought to intercept some of them. So we began a formal program among our top two dozen executives. One day of the month, each one of us would be assigned a day in the tank, personally taking customer calls. I had my day too. If it were Norm Rickard's day, then all calls to the chairman's office from customers would be routed to Rickard with no screening. If he was in a meeting, he was to interrupt it for the call. Once he heard the problem, he was not allowed to delegate the solution. He had to fix the problem himself, and the idea was to locate the cause of it so that other customers with similar beefs would be satisfied.

Fairly quickly, the program had the effect of raising the sensitivity level among management to our inability to satisfy our customers. After hearing enough complaints, managers realized: we really mistreat customers. We also came to recognize how little freedom we gave our own employees in the branches to fix problems, even when the solutions were patently obvious.

The calls would be all over the lot—from the prosaic to the truly awesome. Some came from crochety people or from cranks. I remember one call from a guy who said we shipped a machine to him and it got lost. Some other guy told me that his machine burned up. But most were legitimate problems that no one was resolving. You found yourself getting angry. You were dealing with someone who was mistreated and you were incredulous. How did this happen? This was the visceral part of learning about the pain that the company was feeling and that you hadn't really understood. It brought down the wall between headquarters and the marketplace. After all, the senior managers did not regularly make a copy themselves on a copier, and if they did, it was on the very best machine we made and it was always kept in tip-top shape. That was not the real world, or anything close to it.

The other thing that increasingly caught the attention of our executives was the bad press we were getting. Our stock was doing terribly and securities analysts on Wall Street were beating up on us regularly. When their clients aren't making money off a stock, the analysts can be merciless. I became so disturbed about our image being irreparably tarnished that I went to see Gershon Kekst, the well-connected founder of Kekst & Co., the Wall Street public relations firm that had become famous for handling the press work in virtually all the major corporate takeovers.

When I spelled out my concern, Gershon looked at me and said, "Are the things that are being written true?" I said, "About half of them." And he replied, "I'll make a deal with you. You go fix the things that are true and I'll help you with the things that aren't true."

We did end up hiring Kekst, and we worked with him for a long time. Most of all, we found him extremely effective in helping to develop a corporate image strategy for a company with two disparate businesses in a time of major transition.

As the meeting in Leesburg, scheduled for February 7–9, 1983, drew closer, we sent the Blue Book around to the twenty-five people two weeks ahead of time. We also sent a list of thirty-four questions for them to think about and that were to be resolved at the meeting itself.

They included questions like: By what name should Xerox's total quality strategy be known? Is there agreement on the need to train all employees in the process? How should the units develop the cost of quality? With what level of precision? When should the system be in place and functioning? We wanted the participants to know that they would be coming down to Leesburg to participate, not to sit on their hands and watch some show. At Leesburg, we wanted thrust and parry.

By now, we felt we had a good plan. The design for the meeting seemed sound. But there were still plenty of things that could go wrong. I was a little nervous and apprehensive. I had a lot riding on this.

By no means was there widespread eagerness to attend. At the last minute, some of the executives mounted a ferocious attack on the quality plan, but I wasn't about to budge now. I could appreciate their distress. After all, we were running a nearly $9 billion business while all this was coming up. While we were making money, we were in a lot of trouble and so no one was thinking about just this. There wasn't much arrogance left among the managers. We were over that hump. A lot of people wondered why we should spend a lot of time and money on a quality program when there was so much to do. Quality was still a trade-off to about half the management team. They looked at it as at best an extra and at worst a complete waste of time. Some other people saw this as totally incompatible with all the cost-cutting we were engaged in. There were any number of attempts to get this whole exercise wiped off the calendar. "Why do we need this?" someone would ask. "Let's spend a half day in Stamford and that'll do it. We'll go nuts spending two and a half days in Leesburg! The weather isn't even any good." As Frank Pipp remarked to me, "It sure is hard to focus on long-term programs when the business is so bad. When you're in a swamp fighting alligators it's hard to remember that you're there to drain the swamp."

In 1981 Xerox achieved operating profits of nearly $1.15 billion, the best it had ever done. Some of that, of course, was inflated by an increasing preponderance of sales of copiers as opposed to leases. In actuality, more and more of the marketplace was coming to realize the inferiority of our products. In 1982 the market voted in a big way with its dollars. Our earnings plummeted almost in half to $614 million, which had a terribly dispiriting impact on our employees, not to mention our shareholders. Everyone in the company wondered if we would ever earn a billion dollars again. So did I.

10. The Meeting in Virginia

THE XEROX TRAINING CENTER sat among groves of trees on 2,265 acres of rolling land along the Potomac in Leesburg, Virginia, thirty miles west of Washington. It was a gorgeous part of the country, steeped in history. The town of Leesburg was established way back in 1757 and played a central role in the Civil War. Built in the early 1970s, the Xerox center was an essential part of Peter McColough's vision of creating a formidable sales and service force. There was a series of buildings that, ironically enough, mimicked a Japanese warlord's palace and then there was one colossal central structure. Passageways snaked from one building to another. As you drove up and soaked it all in, it was quite a wondrous sight.

Designed to house seven hundred and fifty trainees for as long as fifteen weeks at a stretch, the center was virtually unmatched in American business in the scope of its facilities. There were two hundred and twenty classrooms and laboratories. The place boasted studios and production equipment that a television station would have salivated over. In addition, there was an outdoor pool, jogging paths, a dance floor, and squash, tennis, and basketball courts. There was even a beauty parlor and a lounge area with a bar. Despite those trappings, though, "students" didn't have much time to luxuriate. Sales trainees would arrive at Leesburg and be all but drowned in education. Much of their time would be consumed by lengthy role-playing exercises. As their classmates looked on sternly, they would try to sell copiers to instructors posing as customers. Frequently, the pitches would not go over terribly well, and the trainees would be subjected to rather severe critiques. The hail of criticism that descended on a young, apple-cheeked salesman could be as rough as that in a top-flight acting course.

It used to be that no one but Xerox personnel were trained at Leesburg. At this point, however, Xerox training requirements had changed and space was being rented to outsiders, particularly to U.S. government agencies. It was a little disorienting to glimpse people buzzing around from the Marine Corps, the C.I.A, and—of all places—the Department of Justice.

The living quarters at Leesburg had the feeling of austere dormitory rooms. The decor was cold and monastic. Linoleum tiles and cinderblock walls were the prevailing decor. Everyone shared a bathroom with the next room. There was no television and only a small radio for entertainment, and no room service. You needed to dial something like fifteen digits to get an outside line on the phone. The place was designed for training sales and service representatives, not for highlevel management meetings. And so the arriving managers found themselves assigned to these concrete bunkers. There were four somewhat nicer rooms for customers, with carpeting and double beds, one of which I got, but they were still far shy of a decent Holiday Inn. No question about it, we weren't coming down here for a vacation.

And there was not going to be any sort of vacation schedule. During the three days our big meeting would cover, there was no play time allotted. Sessions would run morning, afternoon, and evening. Everyone would eat their dinner together and resume the grind. You don't launch revolutions with fun and games. I was excited, but at the same time I knew full well that if the quality project didn't fly here, it never would get in the air.

The state of the business certainly shadowed the mood of the managers who converged on Leesburg. Maybe they didn't have the dark forebodings that I did, but by now they were acutely familiar with the troubled condition of the company. They knew perfectly well the awesome strength of the Japanese. All of us had looked at charts that starkly demonstrated how swiftly American market share was being eaten up. Everyone was hearing about the whining of the American automakers, but we had one chart that pointed out that the Japanese market share of copiers was almost twice that of cars—more than 50 percent. The chart also depicted the sorry state of some other American products. The Japanese had a virtual lock on the entire videocassette recorder market. The story was pretty similar in CB radios and motor-cycles. With microwave ovens and sporting goods, I suppose there was still some hope. The Japanese cut was in the 30 percent range. We had another graph that we used to examine with shamefaced looks. It showed that our profit per employee had sunk by more than 20 percent since 1971. That was enough to give our managers second thoughts about our ability to turn things around.

We truly felt that we were being toyed with and taunted by the Japanese. In particular, the head of Canon, Ryuzaburo Kaku, was quoted again and again in newspaper and magazine stories about how Canon was immersed in "total war" against us. One day, Wayland Hicks picked up a copy of *Forbes* magazine and spotted an article with the headline, "AND THEN WE WILL ATTACK." It was a quote from Kaku about how he suspected that Xerox was taking its eye off its copier business and that this would mean an opportunity for Canon to launch an attack. The story really peeved Hicks, especially since he knew all too well that we were being bloodied in the marketplace. He carried the clipping around in his briefcase for about a week. Then he came up with a clever idea. He had a three-foot-by-four-foot blowup done of the article, including the picture of Kaku, had it framed, and then hung it on the wall of his office in Rochester. Next, he ordered a wooden plaque with a bronze face that was inscribed with the sentence, "When they do, they will lose." He hung that right next to the article.

There was considerable traffic in and out of Hicks' office, and the wall decorations became an energizing symbol throughout the corpora-tion. I know they got my juices flowing whenever I saw them. They even achieved some renown overseas, though they lost something in the translation. When Bill Glavin paid a visit on Kaku once, the Canon president told him that he had heard that one of Xerox's managers had a picture of him on his wall that he hurled darts at. Though he was mis-taken, the blowup did serve somewhat the same purpose as a dart board. Hicks later moved to corporate headquarters in Connecticut, but he wasn't about to dispose of the ornaments. He simply transferred them to the wall of the library in his house.

On top of everything else, with the massive wave of layoffs we had experienced, our employees, including the students checking into Leesburg, were uncomfortable and insecure. The other shoe always seemed to be dropping. Some managers were lamenting about how the company was being run as if it were Baskin-Robbins inventing its flavor of the month. One month the key word was growth. Another month it was cost-control. Another month it was quality. Nothing seemed to stick. The Baskin-Robbins analogy was a popular putdown batted around Xerox.

One thing was certain: there was no time to mope. Once we settled in, we immediately got down to business and set out to follow a feverish pace. Nadler had outlined a lot for us to do. To make sure people really got involved and worked out the answers to the questions we were to address in a collegial way, we had the participants spend the bulk of the meeting sessions split up into subgroups. Then the subgroups would report back to the larger group and we would bang out our differences collectively. In other words, people had to put on their shoulder pads and their helmets and play a physical contact sport. And this wasn't meant to be touch football. It was tackle.

We started off by telling the participants the obvious: that they weren't doing so well. The emperor's new clothes were pretty tattered. Probably the most dramatic piece of information we divulged was our conviction that lack of quality at Xerox was costing the company a whopping $1.4 billion a year. That number got everyone's attention in a hurry.

One of the interesting things we did for the meeting—though I must say some executives didn't end up thinking it was all that interesting—was to present findings from a special survey we had taken. Quite a number of the participants, in fact, tried hard at the last minute to dissuade me from circulating the results. The subordinates of each of the executives present had been asked to rank their bosses in a variety of categories. This was all done anonymously, of course, and then the results were averaged and a table created. Each boss had also been asked to score himself in these same categories. Then we gave out the results, with the subordinates' rankings printed adjacent to the executive's self-appraisal. There were quite a few stunning discrepancies. On a scale of one to seven, with seven being best, some executives had rated themselves a perfect seven in some areas, while their subordinates stuck them with a lowly one. Some of the managers responded well to their surveys; others responded somewhat less well. My own results were pretty good, but also pointed out some distinct shortcomings. Plainly, I had some self-examination ahead of me, too.

Despite the controversy this little exercise generated, I evinced no doubt that it was extremely important, because these two dozen executives were very much a part of our problem. Thus it was essential that they be an integral part of the solution. I wanted top management to start working hard on bettering itself and changing its behavior.

I told the group that the meeting was intended to address four major issues: why the quality strategy was being undertaken; what Commitment to Excellence was; how the effort would be implemented; and the role of senior management. I explained that in 1980 we had begun a major effort to improve the business effectiveness of the corporation through competitive benchmarking and employee involvement, but although both processes had become fairly widespread, employee involvement tended to occur lower down in the organization and competitive benchmarking tended to concentrate on costs. It had become obvious that to continue as a successful company, Xerox required a third effort that would become a unifying force. The time had come to build on the foundations of competitive benchmarking and employee involvement. We would do that by making quality the critical and overriding element in everything we did. It was imperative that we developed comprehensive ways of working that dramatically improved our quality.

I told them that Japanese companies had become phenomenally successful in world markets in large part because of a business discipline and management process embedded in total quality control. And I noted that Fuji Xerox had demonstrated the power of quality when it implemented the New Xerox Movement. That resulted in Fuji Xerox winning the coveted Deming Prize and accomplishing a remarkable turnaround in its business results. Its market share, revenues, and profits all rose in the most competitive market in the world.

I went on to spell out how our feelings about quality differed from the conventional view of quality in four senses. The traditional view of quality was that it meant "goodness" or "luxury," whereas we wanted to define it as "conformance to customer requirements." The conventional system of achieving quality was to inspect the product after it had been completed. We wanted to prevent errors altogether. The conventional performance standard for quality was some prescribed allowable level of defects. We wanted to strive for error-free output.

Nadler had thought up a simple way to explain what the overall effort was all about, and I showed that to the group. It involved three circles. One circle contained the quality principles, another management actions and behavior, and the third quality tools. All three, I said, had to converge if we were to be successful.

One of the points of the meeting was to get everyone to draft an overall quality policy for the company, a succinct dictum of our intentions that we would work to uphold. We played around with the wording, adding something here, subtracting something else. There was a highly spirited debate over the very first sentence that had been proposed: "We are a quality company." Some of the managers just shook their heads and grumbled, "How can we say this? We're really bad news. We're really awful." It was hard to disagree. But the point was, we wanted from this day forward to dedicate ourselves to quality and frankly didn't want to publicly say we were not a quality company.

The final wording of the policy was: "Xerox is a quality company. Quality is the basic business principle for Xerox. Quality means providing our external and internal customers with innovative products and services that fully satisfy their requirements. Quality improvement is the job of every Xerox employee." It sounded simple enough, but we knew that implementing it would be a tremendously arduous task.

I pointed out how the quality process meant we had to approach work differently. We needed to define measurable quality targets and set performance standards based on customer requirements. We had to review on a regular basis our progress toward our quality goals in the same rigorous way that financial targets were reviewed. We had to work as teams to solve problems and capture opportunities at all levels of the business. We needed to equip our problem-solving teams with a common, systematic problem-solving process. We had to take the internal competition out of our work lives. We had to prevent scrap, wasted effort, and errors, and we had to do the right thing for our customers the first time around. At the same time, we had to be constantly dissatisfied with the status quo and act on the conviction that quality can always be improved.

Then we laid out a disciplined problem-solving process whose use we felt was vital to the concept of total quality control. By following it, we felt, we would guarantee that the true causes of a problem were rooted out, and therefore we would have the best chance of arriving at a workable solution. The process broke down into six simple steps:

Identify a problem within the group's area of expertise and develop a clear understanding of it.

Analyze the problem by gathering data and applying the appropriate statistical tools.

Generate through brainstorming a number of potential solutions to solve the problem.

Select and plan the solution by evaluating all options and reach a consensus on the optimum solution.

Implement the solution by working with those who are directly or indirectly affected by it.

Evaluate the solution to determine the extent to which it solves the problem.

As the session moved on, the groups increasingly spent their time off on their own in their subgroups, each with its own facilitator, so they could address the thirty-four questions we had posed. The most recalcitrant managers—the ones who seemed furthest away from accepting any of this—were handed to Norm Rickard. His basic assignment was damage control. If he could neutralize them by the end of the meeting, that would be considered a success. We sorely wanted to avoid fratricidal wars.

A number of the assembled executives tackled the questions zealously, including Frank Pipp, Wayland Hicks, who was then the head of our mid-volume copier strategic business unit, and Paul Allaire, a highly promising executive who was at the helm of Rank Xerox. Interestingly enough, Paul came to sign on to the quality program entirely out of his immense frustration with the status quo. A bespectacled, auburn-haired man with a beguiling grin, Paul had a deep intelligence and scant patience for incompetence. For years, he had been bitterly complaining about how the company was not being run effectively. From the moment I became president, he would take every occasion he got to bend my ear about how I had to do things substantially different and to preach a new ethos. He once even wrote me a really cheeky letter spelling out a laundry list of things I ought to do. He was basically telling me how to run the company, and he later confessed to me that he always wondered why I didn't just give him a swift kick for having the nerve to send it. But I knew how talented Paul was and I could understand his anguish. The first time he got wind of the quality notion, Paul sensed hope. As he once told me, "I was a big advocate not because I was smart or because I fully understood it—I didn't—but because it was different. I could have been had for almost anything that was different."

As the Leesburg subgroups wrestled with their questions, some rather torturous debates arose. One of the most bruising skirmishes ensued over what to call this revolution we were mounting. There were a lot of names floating about but we couldn't seem to get everyone to settle on one of them. So I patched together a special group, which included Allaire, Pipp, and Hicks, and told it to go off to a room with Tragash and not to come out until it had come up with a name. If they didn't agree, they could sleep in the room. Out of the smoke, Leadership Through Quality won out. We could have called it ABC or Kearns' Crusade. I could have just picked a name myself. But we needed ownership.

During whatever idle moments I had down at Leesburg, I spent them with Nadler. As we wandered in and out of meetings, I asked him what he thought. One observation he made had a big impact on me. He said, "Your people don't work together very well. They don't listen, they don't build, they don't work collaboratively." When I thought about that, I realized he was absolutely right. Some of the younger executives like Paul Allaire stood out in that they did get involved. But the others were reticent. As Nadler and I talked some more about that, we concluded that we had to massage the executives to alter their habits. They had to get roughed up and get their uniforms dirty.

These conversations fostered a new sense of intimacy between Nadler and me. At one point, I sat down with him and he talked to me about my own rating by subordinates. He said I had to work on certain things, especially following through on policies and on discipline. He felt I ought to work especially hard on the quality of the management process.

Out of this, a routine developed. From 1983 on, Nadler would confer with me regularly, and once a year we did a personal performance review. We would meet during the week between Christmas and New Year's. Many people at the company took vacation time then, and the place was like a morgue. I liked that. I didn't have the press of appointments and the phone calls and could do some meaningful thinking. I would write my own assessment and then Nadler would go over with me his evaluation of what I did right and wrong and my strengths and weaknesses. I feel I'm pretty good at putting down the negatives about myself. How subjective I am, though, is probably open to some debate. Sometimes what I put down as a positive Nadler said was a negative. For instance, we created a task force on administrative practices. I felt that was a positive. But Nadler maintained that I knew of the need for it two years before I did it, so I was way late.

When I come to a decision, I act on it. That's one of my pluses. But Nadler told me that I may have waited too long on people matters. I was optimistic about people and hoped they would get better. I gave them too much time and I suppose some of the delay was pure procrastination over dealing with difficult situations regarding people I liked. For I never delegated firing. If someone had to go, I always broke the bad news myself.

A good example of my slowness to act was Jim O'Neill. I remember the time I finally had it out with him, because I have an annual Christmas lunch with Shirley each year the week between Christmas and New Year's. This was 1981, and she was waiting for me at the restaurant while I was having a real brouhaha with O'Neill, then executive vice president of manufacturing and development. I finally said, "Jim, it's time for you to go." I hadn't planned on taking such an action that day, but things had been building up and the kettle was ready to pop. I concluded that O'Neill was a very smart man who did very good things but had a narrow thought process. He went from one to two to three. Everything was done by numbers. He was rigid. If Jim was riding in a car with a tech rep and the rep told him a product didn't work, Jim would return to the office, look at a report, and if it said that the product worked that would be the end of it. He would close the book on it. I was the opposite. I would believe the tech rep.

As a person, I really liked Jim. He had a very quick wit. He was crusty, but I don't think he had a mean bone in his body. What Jim could do better than almost anyone else I knew was move from one subject to the next and shut off the previous topic as if it didn't exist (even if it had triggered a caustic debate). I enjoyed being with Jim socially and occasionally played tennis with him.

For some time, though, he was having a detrimental effect on the company. When I became president in 1977, I didn't get involved in engineering. I depended on Jim, who relied on a team of people who had the attitude that they did everything the best and that was misguided. Whenever we came out looking unfavorably in comparisons with the Japanese, they always found ways to rationalize the differences. I had been going to Japan, and I should have been smart enough to see through these deceptions. But Jim didn't help the situation, and I should have acted on him much sooner than I did.

I also talked with Nadler about why I hadn't brought change to the company earlier. There were a couple of reasons, I felt. One was the jolting impact on an organization and on people you like and care for. Second, you fear making changes that will disrupt the existing revenue streams. So you start to make more incremental, gradual changes. As a result, you do too little too late. Sometimes you need to introduce radical changes. Incrementalism can kill you. There happens to be a means to correct computer software by patching it with extra lines of code. If you keep doing that, however, eventually the software becomes "fragile." Then the fragility causes it to crack. The real problem was that the software itself needed to be replaced.

Sometimes incremental change is required and sometimes radical change is required. The difficulty is, it's not at all obvious which of the two is appropriate until well after the fact.

Without a doubt, I found the performance reviews with Nadler very helpful, and I suspect that most executives don't do them. In many respects, I imagine the relationship I had with Nadler was unique: an insider and an outsider working together. It was a process that, for someone just past fifty years of age, reinvigorated me to learn new things and change my management behavior.

As the Leesburg meeting wrapped up, I felt tremendously encouraged. Nobody argued against our concept, though some of the participants subsequently would prove to be at best halfhearted supporters. It was tough to openly argue against quality. But some of the managers really never did anything to try to implement the project.

At the end of the meeting I gave a closing statement, and a copy of it was handed out to everyone in the room. They were instructed to share that message with their people in order to bring them on board.

I proposed to the managers what we believed were the six elements necessary to become a total quality company: reward and recognition; training; standards and measures; communications; a transition team; and appropriate senior management behavior. I told the group: "This is a revolution in the company and we have to overthrow the old regime. The quality transition team is the junta in place to run things on a temporary basis. The standards and measures equate to the laws of the land and of the company. The reward and recognition system is the gaining of control of the banks and economic systems. The training is capturing control of the universities. Communications is the seizing of control of the press, and the senior management behavior is putting your own people in place to reflect the revolution. All of these elements are needed to change a culture. So let's go out and do just that, change the culture at Xerox to one of a total quality company!"

The meeting had been a succession of long hard days, but once it ended there was a feeling of euphoria. I went around the room and asked everyone how they felt. To a person, they said it was the best meeting they had ever been to at Xerox. I was ecstatic.

Tragash would later say, "Right after Leesburg, I remember a telling incident with John Kelsch. We lived near each other and shared a car home from the airport. The car dropped us at John's house with our wives. We looked at each other and wondered, What do we tell them? We told them that we had made significant history. We had gotten the management to make thirty-four decisions. I always had doubt we could get them to go there and make decisions. I understood now how powerful Norm's politics were and that the top really believed this. I was always looking over my shoulder up until then."

This was the high point so far. This was akin to laying tracks across the continent with a steam engine chugging along behind us. Now we had to keep laying more tracks.

In the wake of Leesburg, the top priority was appointing a corporate quality officer and assembling a quality implementation team, or QIT, whose task would be to figure out the means to lay those additional tracks. We were going to give the team a three-month deadline, so the implementation plan could be presented at a second Leesburg meeting in August. The team was to consist of fifteen people, six from corporate headquarters and nine culled from the operating units.

A decision that was to become controversial in its own right was the person selected to be the corporate quality officer, in other words the team leader who would be the number-one guy to drive this thing forward. Between February and mid-March, there was a lot of gossip about who would get the job. One possibility was Norm Rickard, and several key people pushed for his nomination, not the least of those being Rickard himself. He wanted the job desperately. He felt he had been like Moses taking the company to the verge of the promised land. Now that he was at the river, to deny him the chance to cross to the other side would have been devastating to him. But I and others felt Rickard was still a touch too weak in interpersonal skills to handle this delicate and important a job.

When Rickard learned he was not getting the job, he was mightily disappointed and peeved. I felt it was unfair to have him continue to work on the quality effort under someone else. Thus, although he was named to the QIT team, he mainly went off to resume work for Frank Pipp on a major project in the manufacturing side of the business. Nadler talked to Rickard about how the way he handled this blow would be important to his career. He urged him to assist the quality officer to the best of his abilities. To Rickard's credit, he did just that, and his actions would reward him later on.

The man who was chosen for the job was a manager named Fred Henderson, and he was nominated by the head of the U.S. Marketing Group in Rochester. The reason, as I subsequently found out, was not to serve the better needs of Xerox but because he didn't particularly like him. I approved Henderson for the quality job. When he was presented to me, I felt he was an able executive with an impressive track record who was possessed of strong drive, and to this day I think that some of the other key quality people and his managers failed in shaping him into the leader he might have become.

There was an interesting way to find out a bit about the makeup of Fred Henderson. He had become infamous among certain circles of businessmen as a result of starring in a videotape recorded by a college professor. John Kotter, a professor at the Harvard Business School, had shot videotapes of two Xerox managers to use in his classroom to teach future businessmen about differing management styles. He basically followed the two individuals around during their workdays. One man was Renn Zaphiropoulous, the head of our Versatec unit that was in the electrostatic plotter business. The other was Fred Henderson, who was one of the top managers running the domestic field force. The men didn't know it at the time, but I suspect Kotter's intention was to portray a hero and a goat. Henderson was to be the goat.

Nadler, Rickard, and Tragash knew next to nothing about Henderson, and so when they heard of his appointment, they got hold of the Kotter tape and played it for themselves in a Xerox conference room. Some troubling scenes came up.

From the tape, Henderson comes across as the prototypical bureaucrat, meant in the most pejorative sense of the word. At the beginning of the tape, the camera pans over his appointment book, which is choked with meetings from eight in the morning on. There is not one open slot, not even for lunch. But the scene that stands out the most starkly is one in which he is seen as being duplicitous.

He hosts a meeting with several underlings to review a theme movie to be shown to the sales force to pep them up for the next year.

Henderson starts off by saying, "First of all, I'd like to say I think it's super. I think it's excellent. I think the people are really going to get into it." He proceeds to raise a few fairly innocuous questions and then adjourns the meeting. Afterward, he ushers one of the men in the meeting down to a private office, closes the door, and says, "I just want to test you a little more." And he reveals that he actually thinks the movie is pretty miserable and wonders if there is time to change it.

The day plods on. Henderson is depicted as bland, uninspiring, uncharismatic. At the end of the tape, he is asked, "How do you feel about what happened today?"

"I feel pretty good," he says. "You very seldom feel you made much progress in the course of a day and I think today was similar. We tackled some real serious problems, some tough issues, and I believe we made a little progress. As long as you can inch this thing forward a little bit each day, I feel like I'm accomplishing my primary objectives."

Zaphiropoulous, on the other hand, is romanticized as the entrepreneur in the best sense of the word. You can't help but find him appealing. He speaks four or five languages. He plays the piano. He is a championship sailor. He is a master carpenter who builds exquisite violins and guitars. He is a superb cook. He is funny and intellectually stimulating. A real Renaissance man. You couldn't find a better dinner companion.

At the beginning of the tape, Zaphiropoulous confesses, "The only thing I have today is at three-thirty, when I meet some new people who come into the company and I talk to them about the company. The rest of the time is strictly up to me. I have nothing. That's my usual day. What I will do probably is go and meet different people in the company and establish some contact and get in some discussion about how shipments are doing, how some projects are doing, and so on."

He is fun-loving and good humored, not starchy like Henderson. He has a plaque in his office that reads in capital letters "BE BOLD." During the film, the camera follows him wandering around, clutching a Styrofoam coffee cup, smiling at people, poking his head into offices. Henderson's day seems stultifying. Zaphiropoulous's day seems like great fun.

In truth, he just chose to manage in a different way at Xerox than Henderson did. He would give these wonderfully uplifting speeches to his employees about how the company was not your parent and how you were an adult responsible for your own actions. And his employees loved him. But of all the people in the company, Zaphiropoulous was the most blind to the Japanese. He just never felt they would become a formidable force in his technology.

But used as a contrast to Henderson, Zaphiropoulous looks terrific. It was no wonder that, as he watched the tape, Tragash swiveled in his seat and said to Nadler, "This is our revolutionary?"

On paper, though, Henderson had been a very successful marketing manager. He clearly met the criteria we had established for the quality position. The person was to have credibility in the organization. He was to have line experience. He was to be young enough that he was still moving up the organizational ladder. And in being given up from one of the operating units, that was supposed to hurt. The unit was supposed to really feel the loss and wince a little.

The trouble with Henderson was that he was probably too political and probably more concerned than he should have been about what would be his next job. It was important to him that he controlled all the information that went into 3-1, the bay where the senior executives had their offices. That's not the spirit for a revolutionary. Yet, all the same, I must say that Henderson read the culture of the company right. He saw that Rickard was a bit abrasive and didn't get the job. So he thought that this was the style that management wanted. He failed to see that things were changing, or at least that we wanted them to change. He proved to be the sort of person who would never lay himself across the railroad tracks unless he was certain no trains were due that day. And we needed somebody to put his body there all the time.

When Henderson was picked, there was some disgruntlement right away. As Tragash put it: "I thought he had a long way to go to learn what this was about. He would pick our brains. It was sort of the coach sending in the players from the sidelines. You began to wonder if the players had the ability to implement the plays. We lost a lot of time with him. We used to say that he was a batch processor in a random access world. He could only do one thing at a time."

In formulating the QIT, we made some other mistakes. We had some first-rate people from corporate who joined the team, including Tragash, Rickard, the tireless John Kelsch, Joe Cahalan, from corporate communications, Hyman Elias, a quality assurance expert, and Ian Raisbeck from Rank Xerox. We had established explicit criteria for executives to nominate people from the operating units for the QIT. They were to be upwardly mobile leaders who had good credibility in the company. Many units did deliver their best people. But some of the executives didn't play straight with us. They ignored the criteria and offered up people who were certainly not going to get the job done. Some were simply too junior in experience to have any credibility. Others were senior burnouts, riding out their days until they could retire to an easier life in Florida. Undoubtedly, some units saw this team as a splendid opportunity to dump some seasoned deadwood that they didn't want anymore. One person who made the team actually had great difficulty completing a full sentence. No one could ever figure out what he was trying to say.

Units that didn't really believe in this effort were the ones that offered up discards deliberately. It was the old case of perfuming the pig. Suddenly this ill-suited person was just wonderful, couldn't be better for the job. I would estimate that roughly half of the members were wrong choices. We simply weren't rigorous enough in reviewing the people who were presented to us; if an operating unit said here was a perfect candidate, we took its word and initiated the person onto the team.

Because there was no homogeneity to the group, friction arose. Some of the perfectly qualified members of the team complained that they weren't comfortable with some of their colleagues, that they didn't fit in. When these people got around to dealing with their home units they proved risk-averse. They would come back to meetings and talk about all the problems their cohorts at home were raising. They didn't want to cross their own people, and as a result the status quo prevailed.

This proved terribly unfortunate, for these people were the true change agents, the ones who were going to bring about this metamorphosis or cause it to fail. Because some of the people were not up to the task, we spent far more time than we needed to. Looking back, we may have wasted months.

Without a doubt, the QIT team was not a blue-ribbon task force. And we knew that. We didn't have to go ahead with it; we could have reformulated it. But we didn't. Frankly, I was impatient and anxious to get going.

By early April, the team was assembled for its first meeting. Nadler, his colleague Ron Dukenski, and Tragash had now developed the curriculum they were to work from. After all, they were in roles brand-new to them. They needed some guidance. At that opening meeting, I kicked the program off by basically telling them, "I'm asking you to make a revolution. And I know it's a lonely job being a revolutionary and it's a perilous job, because revolutionaries often get shot. And the difficulty is we're going to have to continue to conduct business while we launch this revolution. But I'm your sponsor. I'm asking you to do it."

Meanwhile, we decided not to communicate with the employees about any of this until we had something credible to say. So while this was all going on, there was no mass announcement. This was all a management exercise.

Some executives didn't see the sense of this approach. One said, "Who needs this? Why don't we put up a bunch of posters announcing it and just go ahead and do it?" I told him, "We've tried that, it doesn't work. The quality idea ought to apply to the implementation process. You do it right the first time."

The immediate mission of Henderson and the QIT was to transform the Leesburg book into a final implementation plan. Most of their time was to be spent meeting among themselves. But every other week the members of the committee were to return to their home units and confer with the management teams there to share information and ideas with them. That was how additional thumbprints were put on the final plan.

The first month, however, was devoted to educating the team. Some knew a lot about quality and some knew absolutely nothing beyond how to spell the word. A number of them hadn't even seen the slide-and-tape show. To become indoctrinated, they went to Japan and did some personal benchmarking. They visited IBM and Hewlett-Packard and Westinghouse to hear about what they were doing. Nadler taught them about change management.

Already, though, Henderson began to present problems. He turned out to be a real authoritarian. He believed in the chain of command. He didn't brook any criticism or dissent, and could be very punitive and judgmental. As it happened, in one of the first sessions with the quality implementation team, there was some dissension and Henderson didn't deal with it at all well. A consultant who worked for Nadler was sitting in on the meeting and once it had ended he said, "Let's process it." That's consulting lingo meaning let's review the meeting and see what we think we've accomplished. So Henderson went around the room and invited comments from each of the participants. When this consultant's turn came, he offered some gentle criticism of Henderson, which he meant to be constructive. Henderson didn't say anything until the meeting broke up, when he turned to the consultant and said, "Come with me." They went to Henderson's office, where Henderson warned the consultant in no uncertain terms, "Don't you ever criticize me in front of the group again. And, to be sure you don't, I don't want you at our meetings anymore." This was hardly the climate we hoped to foster. The idea of quality was to provide an open environment in which disagreements could be aired.

Henderson wore ambition on his sleeve, and I thought that was a positive factor. I figured he sensed that he could make a big splash in this job and that would propel him upward. But it turned out to be a negative. Looking back, how could we have insured we had the right person for the job? There's a real dilemma in picking a change agent. You want someone who is credible but often someone is credible because he is successful in the culture you want to change. Henderson perfectly exemplified that. I think we would have been better if we'd searched for someone who had a high intellect and was able to understand processes but forgot about making sure it was a superstar. But you also have to be wary of putting in someone who has retired on the job. And there are a lot of people like that doing quality around the country. Companies say, "Hey, what do we do with old Joe? I've got it. Let's make him the head of quality."

Nadler told me again and again that Henderson wasn't working out, but I insisted they try to get along with him. I told him, "He's the best quality officer we've got. You make him successful." In hindsight, I may have made a mistake. Perhaps he should have been replaced sooner than he was.

While they served on the QIT, the members from the operating units stayed in a Stamford hotel, and they lived a somewhat schizophrenic existence. They had to worry about pleasing their local bosses, pleasing Henderson, and pleasing me. Because they lived in a hotel together and drank and ate together, these members had a rather different experience from the local people, who went home to their families at night. By living together, the out-of-towners became very tight and developed their own leadership separate from Henderson. Bob Trimper, who represented the Latin American group, busted out and made something of this and became one of the unofficial leaders. He was increasingly unhappy with Henderson. Trimper was not bothered by discord. He was someone people often didn't know what to do with. But if you wanted things done, you'd go to him. He was a professional expatriate. There are some of them in all multinational companies who like to work abroad more than anything else. At the time, he was the operations head for Latin America for us. He spoke Spanish, Portuguese, and Arabic, and nothing pleased him more than living on foreign soil.

The QIT's work went dreadfully slow, hindered by the unevenness of the group. Some rose to the occasion. Some never rose to anything. One guy was part crazy. He wouldn't sit still in a meeting. He lasted about three weeks before Henderson got rid of him. There was another man who could speak English but I'm not sure he could write a word of English. He lasted—barely.

Fortunately, there was a core of dedicated and talented members, including Bob Trimper, Doug Harper from Xerox Canada, Vic Muth from engineering, and Derek Hanley from headquarters. Together with some of the carryovers from the old Gang of Eleven—Tragash,

Rickard, Kelsch, Elias, and Cahalan—they put in the effort that ultimately made things happen. In time, the revised Blue Book got hammered out. It laid out an overall plan based on Nadler's change model
for the next five years, during which we hoped to fully implement
Leadership Through Quality. In it, we underscored the sweeping management process and cultural changes that were required. We said that
we needed to train managers and employees in the tools and skills to
work and manage continued quality improvement. We had to create
dissatisfaction with the existing culture. We had to have strong communications to support the quality effort, which was why we printed up
small business-size cards with the Xerox quality policy spelled out on
them that were handed out to everyone. To this day, I always carry
mine in my shirt pocket. Standards and measures had to be developed
so that quality performance could be used as a basis for management
decision-making. Finally, rewards and recognition needed to be established for quality-oriented performance. People are motivated to do
what they perceive will be rewarded.

The timetable that the QIT established called for 1983 to be a year
of start-up activities during which the guidelines to implement the
strategy would be finished. Then 1984 was to be a year of awareness
and understanding, during which some four thousand senior and middle managers would be trained. We expected them to begin using the
tools, and we hoped that customer-satisfaction indicators and
employee-attitude surveys would show some positive results. In 1985
we expected a year of transition and transformation, during which most
managers and about half of the workers would be trained. We felt people practicing quality improvement would begin to be rewarded and
promoted. We thought that quality improvement would become evident
in business results and in the morale of our employees. Then 1986 was
to be the year of significant results. All one hundred thousand Xerox
employees were to have completed their training. We envisioned our
products becoming the industry standard in the copier business, and we
felt we would see upward trends in our market share, revenues, profits,
and return on assets. Finally, 1987 would be the year of approaching
maturity. Implementation of Leadership Through Quality would be

completed, and the pursuit of quality improvement would have become a way of life at Xerox. Our products and services would be rated superior by our customers and industry analysts.

On paper, the plan seemed well-paced and eminently appealing. We would never come close to matching that timetable.

Meanwhile, we had embarked on a major product introduction that would prove crucial to our comeback: the 10 Series.

I never had to think twice whenever anyone asked me if we had a lot riding on the series. Did we ever! Had the 10 Series been a big flop, it would have tanked the company. There's no doubt in my mind about that. It was vital to our having any future at all.

The creation of the 10 Series functioned as something of a bridge between the old Xerox and the new Xerox I envisioned. When the 10 Series development began, we weren't involved in the quality process. But we did manage to intercept its development and apply some of the quality principles. Frank Pipp oversaw the series, and he made sure it was the first development project at Xerox to test employee involvement and benchmarking. And the ultimate success of the machines more fully ingrained the process in the company. To some extent, it was a pilot case of whether we were on the right track.

There were ultimately to be five machines in the series, introduced over a period of years, with the 1075 the linchpin. Up until now, the 9200, which we brought out in 1974, had been the biggest and most expensive undertaking in Xerox history. The 1075 was every bit as ambitious. The 9200 took on the order of eight years and cost somewhere between three hundred million and five hundred million dollars. The 10 Series ran even more, in excess of six hundred million dollars. People used to say that it was as expensive as a new jet fighter.

More than a thousand people worked on the 10 Series for upward of seven years. A great effort was made to dismantle the bureaucracy that strangled copier development in the past. Instead of engineering and manufacturing guarding their own territory, teams were set up with a common purpose. Known as product delivery teams, they were made as autonomous as possible, eliminating the need for top management to continually review stages to flash the go-ahead. The chief engineer was given certain boundary conditions. If he remained within the cost and schedule targets, then higher-ups didn't have to look over his shoulder and give their blessings. He was on his own. This system wasn't fully in place for the 1075 until near the end, but it was for the latter models in the 10 Series. The whole goal was to make better products faster with fewer people at lower cost. In fact, the 1090 was available throughout the country within two months of its announcement date. Never before had Xerox rolled out a product that speedily. It was heartening to witness.

The 10 Series machines represented the third generation of Xerox copiers and were intended to be far easier to use and much more reliable. The 1075 was a medium-sized copier that could make seventy copies a minute and was intended for businesses that made twenty-five thousand to a hundred thousand copies a month. In Paris we intended to introduce a somewhat smaller machine, the 1045, designed for four thousand to twenty-five thousand copies a month. The key to the new line was that a customer could buy the central processor, which did the basic copying, and then he had a choice of input and output features such as automatic collators or feeders. Previously, different features were provided by different machines.

One important aspect of the 10 Series machines was their sophisticated microprocessor brains that enabled them to work, tying together all the components and devices communicating with one another about what tasks needed to be done. The brains actually watched the copy quality and controlled the workings of the machines. In effect, they were invisible electronic managers barking orders to the copiers. If a bit more toner was needed, the electronic managers would have it automatically added. The machines pretty much worked like a self-focusing camera.

The 1075 also had a recirculating document handler and an organic photoreceptor. Although Kodak had shown that the recirculating document handler was possible, we had gone one step better by designing something that could mix all different stocks of paper. You could shuffle together regular paper, cardboard, and a photograph. To handle the paper, we came up with a vacuum corrugated feeder. It drew the bottom sheet in a stack of originals snugly against a vacuum roller, then sent the sheet along what is referred to as a racetrack configuration around an oblong shape. The paper paused for exposure and then proceeded on its journey before finally being coughed out on top of the stack. The organic photoreceptor was something that Kodak also had. It was a significant ingredient. For one thing, it dispensed with the need for a drum. Second, since it allowed more freedom in the paper path, it meant that you could assemble all the components in a much tighter package. The 1075 took up about a quarter less space than a Xerox 8200, no mean achievement.

Everyone was waiting for the 10 Series—and waiting. It should have been ready two years earlier than it was, but there were perpetual problems meeting the reliability targets. The delays were putting critical pressure on the company. And they incited the further sale of the rental base.

Thus everyone expressed enormous relief when the series was finally ready. They weren't shy about bragging a little about their accomplishments—and who could blame them? When the 1075 was unveiled in late September of 1982, a bunch of Xerox engineers leased themselves a plane and flew over Rochester dragging a sign reading "We did it." Outside the Webster manufacturing plant, trailer trucks bore mammoth banners that said "Happy Birthday 10 Series." Clearly, the mood was as upbeat as it had been in some time for our workers. When we announced the 1075 and the 1045, I stated that they represented "the most significant product announcements in Xerox history," and I meant it.

The 1075 was a spectacular machine, and the teamwork that went into it deserves much of the credit. When I asked Joe Marino, the chief engineer on the 1075, why the product was so successful, he replied, "Because nobody ran for their functional foxholes. The team decided to put the best product out."

A much-debated issue was the last-minute decision to change the name of the products. Originally, they were not supposed to be grouped as a series. In fact, the first two models were named the 8600 and the 3850. All the promotional and technical materials and announcement films had been made. But Bill Glavin and some of the others in marketing wanted the name to stand out. Wayland Hicks agreed. At the last minute, the machines were changed to the 1075 and 1045 and the whole family was dubbed the 10 Series. It surely sounded more impressive to be bringing out an entire series, the way IBM had come out with its spectacular 360 series years before. But as a result, we needed new name plates, new labels for supplies, new movies, new media materials, new ads, new brochures, new operating manuals. The cost of the name change added up to something like $1 million. But this was a good decision and was another case of Bill Glavin's instinct and tenacity winning out.

I agreed with the change, though some others most vehemently didn't. Rank Xerox, for instance, was determinedly against it, though we finally convinced them.

Unlike the auto companies, which used numbers to identify their products while they were developed and then gave the cars colorful names to sell them, we worked the opposite. We had lots of interesting code names for copiers in development: Banshee, Scrapper, Moses, Manhattan, Fortress, Columbia, Mohawk, Yardbird, Firebird. When we introduced them, they came out as 9020, 8200, 1075, and other bland-sounding sets of digits. We did it this way from the beginning so that customers were buying the Xerox brand. It was the Xerox 914, the Xerox 813. We didn't want another name competing with Xerox. But everyone found that the idea of a series injected new excitement into our familiar numbers.

In ads, we went on to refer to the series as "Marathon" copiers, the idea being that they run and run and don't break down. Improved reliability was one of the foremost features we wanted to harp on. The ads we ran depicted runners participating in a marathon. We also sponsored a lot of races around the country to further drive home the point. Incidentally, the marathon concept was not my idea. Everyone seemed to think it was, because they knew I was a runner, but actually I had nothing to do with it.

The 10 Series was the first salvo back at the Japanese, and even the Japanese applauded it. The 1075 wound up capturing a prestigious grand prize award for industrial design from the Japanese Ministry of International Trade and Industry. We were thrilled to know that this marked the first time an American-made product had been so honored.

By late 1985, the 1090 was receiving the highest customer satisfaction scores we had ever recorded. One of the most critical measures of reliability was defects per hundred machine drawings (DPHM). It's similar to the way the auto companies judge the quality of their cars. The 1040 was getting a DPHM score of 50, better than any copier we had previously made.

The machines really were user-friendly in the best sense of that phrase. People came to like them so much that some of them even gave them nicknames. We had one customer who took two test models of a 1075; fairly soon afterward, he began calling them E.T.1 and E.T.2, after the lovable extraterrestrial in the Steven Spielberg film.

Our pricing of the machines was one of the important decisions that was made, and it sparked another big debate among the senior executives. We decided to take a hit on prices and be bold, because market share was such a critical issue. We needed to get some share points back. Bill Glavin was the driver on the aggressive pricing idea. He took the lead, and I will be forever grateful to him. The truth is, we kept margins up too high for too long, and I was as much to blame as anyone. The aggressive pricing had its impact on the competition. IBM was compelled to cut prices on its Series III Model 60 copier, and Kodak hurried the introduction of its Ektaprint 200 and 225 models. At the same time, it lowered the prices of its earlier Ektaprint models. And, significantly, the Japanese didn't show up with competitive machines to the 1045 in America until 1984, when Ricoh introduced its 6080. Canon didn't respond until 1985 with its 7500. It was nice to see that the competition had to react to us again.

To be sure, we didn't think the 10 Series would flop. But the long delays and the reliability bugs gave all of us plenty of fitful nights. Once it was out, we were gratified by the market reception. From its introduction through the end of 1985, more than sixty thousand 1075s were placed with customers around the world. In time, it would come to account for more than a billion dollars in annual revenues. In 1983, for the first time in over a decade, we wrested back some market share in copiers, and that reestablished some of our credibility.

There were those in the outside world who thought the 10 Series represented such a triumph for us that the woes of the copier business were over. That was far from the case. The 10 Series was a highly significant step in our recovery, but this was no time to rest on any laurels. If we did nothing more but continue on with the 10 Series we would still be on our way out of business. The basic nature of the company had a long way to go before it was suitably changed to compete in the altered world we were in.

This was made clear to me one day some months after we introduced the 10 Series. We had been doing a lot of talking about customer satisfaction and its importance and felt we ought to address it in some of our advertising. Our corporate advertising people hatched the idea of using me in some ads, a notion which often suggests that it's the last gasp for the company. Nevertheless, I reluctantly agreed. I remember trying while I was running to memorize like mad the lines from the script I had been given. I said to myself, "When you buy a product from Xerox, it's got a string attached to it, and it goes right back to the company." And then I was supposed to reach out and grab a string, and talk about our customer support.

After we shot the commercial, we showed the script to our marketing people. They said with some amazement, "You can't run that." "Why not?" I asked. "Because we can't support what you're saying," they said. When I heard that, I became really annoyed. Not because we couldn't use the ad. But because we couldn't do those things. And I didn't think they were such grandiose promises.

In August 1983, our second meeting was held in Leesburg, attended by the twenty-five managers from the prior meeting plus the members of the QIT. Once again, we followed the format that Nadler had designed for the first meeting. Because of the degree of participation that had taken place since then, this meeting was a lot easier. The final Blue Book was presented to the managers and ratified by them. By this point, I counted up about a hundred and twenty-five people who had their thumbprints somewhere on that book.

Shortly afterward, it was necessary to publish the completed book for all of us to work from. Tragash called the print shop to find out what colors were available. They said they had a nice shade of green. Tragash thought that sounded fine and so the Blue Book became the Green Book, the bible for our quality strategy.

With the ratification of the Green Book, the work of the QIT in Stamford was completed. The team members could now go home to their operating units and begin the awesome task of getting the plan implemented in the broader culture.

Meanwhile, Nadler was still having his difficulties with Henderson. After the meeting, everyone was waiting outside the conference center to board vans to the airport. Nadler wandered over to Henderson, pumped his hand, and said, "I want to talk with you soon and see how I can help you." Henderson said, "I'm really looking forward to working with you." Then, out of Nadler's earshot, he went over to Tragash and said, "We've really got to get rid of these goddamned consultants."

That same evening, I remained and had dinner with the Quality Improvement Team. They asked for my commitment to staying the course and wanted me to assure them that I would devote whatever personal attention was required. I told them they could count on it, and it was the beginning of a major change for the company and for me personally.

It was now time to move forward. In launching the effort, we decided we would have three major objectives. One would be to improve profits, for we were doing no better than a measly 7.5 percent return on assets. The Standard & Poor average for the *Fortune* 500 was 15 percent. So we set a target of fifteen as a minimum to achieve by 1988. Second, we wanted to boost our market share. And, third, we wanted to improve customer satisfaction. We set yearly targets for each as we headed through the eighties.

Now the real test of our revolution would start. For the rest of the company, relatively little had gone on so far. The work force itself had barely heard the drumbeats. Who knew how they would respond.

11. Dining at the Quality Restaurant

NOW THAT WE HAD LAID some tracks, we had to get the steam locomotive fired up and roaring down those tracks. It was clear to me that no wholesale change at Xerox would occur without widespread and effective training. The Japanese like to say that quality starts with training and ends with training. I don't totally buy that philosophy, but there is no question that a quality initiative must embrace intensive training. And it's far from a matter of getting the great unwashed together in a room and telling them to do something. If it were that simple, a lot more companies would have succeeded at it.

We had no false aspirations that the process was going to be easy or quick. Our best estimates were that the training of the hundred thousand people who worked for Xerox would take four years, an unprecedented training effort. One of our statistical whizzes actually constructed a corporate model of how many classrooms and how much time would be needed to teach everyone. No one was to be exempt. You couldn't call in sick or bring in a doctor's note. Secretaries would be trained. Tech reps would be trained. Janitors would be trained. If you believed in total quality, then everyone had to start breathing it. After all, how well janitors cleaned work areas had an effect on the manner in which people went about their jobs.

Nadler and Tragash, in particular, concentrated on the training, and the two of them devised a novel framework for it. The shorthand for it was: learn it, use it, teach it, inspect it—or LUTI. The common approach to training was to teach people and then have them apply what they had learned. But a long history of research shows that training is unsuccessful if you hand people tools that are contrary to what they are accustomed to. In fact, studies in the 1950s indicated that within a few weeks the behavior would revert right back to what it had been, because the environment wouldn't support the tools. So we took an altogether different tack, and it proved to be one of the most important contributions Xerox made to research on how to instill quality in a company. We wanted to have a manager learn it, then use it, then teach it, and finally inspect it to see if it was being used by others. By adhering to this system, we felt we could be sure that the work environment embraced the new philosophy with open arms.

Another critical decision was to have the training start at the top of the organization and sweep downward. We would get the senior management trained and then the learning would cascade to the bottom. Also, we wanted to have everyone trained in family groups, in other words with the people they worked with every day. It's actually rare in any organization for people who work together to be educated together. The normal procedure is to have classes made up of students from different functions, groups, and geography. This approach has its purpose. But we felt we had to make quality training directly applicable to what was taking place and what we needed in the workplace.

Synchronizing the training in family groups enabled employees to apply their new tools to problems that they faced collectively. And when everyone returned to their jobs, the environment would be such that all of their coworkers were now thinking alike. I've seen training at other corporations where the learning technology is first-rate but the employees who go through it complain afterward, "The problem is, my boss should have been here, because he doesn't manage me this way." We were going to have the boss and his team in the classroom together, looking at the same blackboard and doing the same homework. Our idea was to bridge the gap between the real world people worked in and the artificial world of the training.

The family groups were also important in our case because so many managers and employees were cynical about this project. Few of them had accepted the idea that this was the flavor we were going to eat month after month.

In keeping with the LUTI model, we decided that everyone who went through the course would subsequently become a cotrainer. The beauty of this was that everyone passed through the training twice. You got trained, you prepared, and then you taught. The other nifty thing was that knowing you were going to have to teach this stuff made you a lot more attentive when you were learning it. Nadler used to tell me about how he took statistics in college and then again in graduate school, but he never really mastered the subject until he started to teach it. Speaking of statistics, I was not the world's best student either. When I received a promotion once, I got a letter from my roommate in college in which he said, "If you keep getting important jobs like this I am going to have to stop making cracks about burning the statistics lab down to get you through school."

In our planning, the only people who would not pass through the training twice were me and the people on the very bottom—the tech rep, the salesman, the guy on the manufacturing line. I was excused because I was to go through first with the group of managers who worked directly with me, and the bottom rung would have no one else to train.

A quality training task force had been put together to devise the training. Ian Raisbeck headed it, and Paula Fleming and Carl Hill, a member of the Delta staff, were key members of it. We had decided that outside training packages didn't fit Xerox and thus we needed to design our own. When the task force was initially assembled, David Nadler went to address it with one thing on his mind: what can you say to the trainees that will keep them from laughing? He knew that if we just threw out some uplifting song and dance about how terrific quality was, let's go get it, everyone would just snicker. That sort of rhetoric, though used all too often in business, didn't work. Tragash used to say he felt like they must have in the Manhattan Project. They knew the thing was going to blow up, but they weren't sure how to get it to blow up. We knew we had to train everyone, but we weren't sure how to train them. So Nadler elected to do things in bite-sized chunks.

The training we mapped out consisted of a half day of quality orientation and then five and a half days of schooling in quality and problem-solving. And we didn't just pretend. We gave everyone real quality problems to work on. All in all, it worked out to forty-eight hours of training. Since everyone went through twice, they got ninety-six hours of exposure. Which doesn't count the time it took each manager to prepare to teach the course.

Before the training was thrust upon the corporation and the cascading process put into motion, we wanted to try it out first on a pilot group to see how well it went over and to engineer any alterations that seemed appropriate. In other words, we wanted to open in Philadelphia before we came to Broadway.

As our guinea pigs, we picked the real estate group, which managed the buildings that Xerox inhabited. They seemed an apt choice because they were outside the mainstream business and so wouldn't disturb the cascade. Between January 16 and 20, 1984, this group became the first to be educated in quality. For the most part, the instruction went over as well as we had hoped. But we did learn some things which led us to fine-tune some of the examples we used. And we scrapped some things altogether. We had a little exercise in which we used marbles to demonstrate a statistical theory and it completely bombed. Nobody got it. And so the marbles got the boot.

On February 27, with the tuning of the training completed, my group paraded into the classroom at the Arrowwood Conference Center in Rye Brook, New York, as the first official students to be given the training. Nadler and Henderson were our principal teachers. And I learned more about quality during those hours than I ever had—and by this time I had visited a number of companies, been to Japan more than twenty-five times, attended the Crosby School, and met with and read Deming and Juran.

Everyone in the corporation had by now been given some sense of the quality program, for they had all been subjected to what we referred to as "quality awareness." This meant they had sat through an orientation that included a video of me talking about our effort, the trusty slide-and-tape show, and a remarkable documentary we had shot about one of our Denver tech reps.

We started off by discussing with each group of trainees the rationale for Leadership Through Quality. We acknowledged that we knew some of them were skeptical and might see it as another "program."

But we underscored that it wasn't, that it represented a strong desire and commitment to change the way we ran the business. We said we were convinced that the process would enable us to meet our objectives and stay ahead of our competition. It was to be a long-term undertaking. Today was just the first step.

We reemphasized the dedication to two key aspects of Leadership Through Quality—competitive benchmarking and employee involvement. And I told everyone, "The plan we approved may very well be the most significant strategy that Xerox has ever embarked on. It is aimed at fundamentally changing the culture of Xerox over the next several years.... Without your active endorsement and total commitment, it will fail. With your active endorsement and total commitment, it will be the powerful lever that helps us to accomplish our ambitious but achievable goals for the remainder of this decade and into the 1990s."

The orientation continued with the cinéma vérité film about a tech rep in the Denver branch. We told employees that it followed real people with no script and thus it might be the most candid and honest film they would ever see about Xerox. After viewing it, most agreed it was. It showed a small piece of Xerox replete with all its warts and all its potential. It was a stark demonstration that, as a company, we were doing things wrong, a series of vignettes of ineptitude. The focus was on tech reps because these were the men and women who came into repeated daily contact with customers, often when those customers were most in need of help from Xerox. Despite the narrow focus, the film harbored messages for all Xerox people.

The actual subject of the movie was a lanky, dark-haired, rather earnest man named Don Marchese. The movie starts off with a team meeting during which a chart is being discussed indicating that customer satisfaction in the region has been steadily going down. Then Don heads off on his first call of the day. When he arrives, the customer tells him, "There have been three complaints within the last five minutes about why the machine is down." He says he thought it would have been fixed yesterday. It has been broken for three days.

Talking to the camera, Don says, "I appreciate the situation a down machine puts them in. When I was growing up, my father had a bit of a production business and when he was down it meant that eighteen people were standing around doing nothing."

After he fixes the copier, Don clambers into his station wagon and drives to the next call. "I've been with Xerox for ten years now," he says, "and I felt I was out of step with what management wanted. They were looking for targets such as response time and to achieve it they were going at it by quickly fixing each call. We were just running. And I ran into some problems with that. I didn't believe in running. And now it seems that management in Xerox is listening to these facts. They're listening to the fact that customers demand quality. They demand having their machines working the major part of the time and producing good quality."

Then there is a fade to Don's manager. He admits that he thought he always had the best ideas about how to get things done and he's begun to realize that people out in the field sometimes have better ideas. He says that he's forty-two years old and he thinks he's going to be able to change, but he knows it's not going to be easy.

Another call. The owner tells Don, "I do know it's broken down an awful lot of the time and we're about ready to throw it out and get something that works in here. It's just that simple. Because it's broken more than it runs."

DON: "You haven't seen any improvement?"
OWNER: "It's gotten worse."

He says there are five to ten paper jams a day. Eventually, Don finds that the xerostatic wire shorted out, which causes random jams throughout the machine.

The film goes on to record a team meeting of Don's tech group as they study a survey of customer satisfaction statistics showing the numbers veering in the wrong direction.

DON: "We seem to be spending all of our time taking callback calls over again whereas if we had taken the time in the beginning to do them right we wouldn't be going back again. Why do we always find the time to do it again when we couldn't find the time in the beginning to do it right? And the customer sees this. The customer sees that he's there again Tuesday and again on Friday and what the hell's going on."

Another rep says, "Unpleasant as it is to say, there are a few individuals on this team who are simply not doing their damn job. Now I've waited a long time for somebody to say that. Nobody has said it. Well, by God, I'm going to say it."

Still another rep says, "I was taught and religiously told constantly, Okay, watch these numbers. You know, do this, reliability, so on and so forth, get them calls, get 'em down, run if you have to. Well, forget that."

> DON: "That was the problem I had with managers for a long time. You know, whose side was Xerox on, the customers or their own? I thought I was fighting Xerox at times more than the customers or the calls or whatever. Because they didn't want me to stay there and finish the job."
> THE MANAGER: "Don't you have the same thing with a football team?"

"Yeah," one guy pipes up, "it's the coach."

Later on, Don says that he felt the meeting was more outspoken than normal, but he is disappointed that no concrete changes were agreed upon. A few months later, he is happier because the 10 Series has been introduced and it's been well-received. "We now have the best box on the street," he says.

At the end, Don's manager tells him, "We made the mistake in the past of feeling good about ourselves through our internal measurements and telling customers you should be happy because we're happy."

With that orientation behind them, employees were ready to tackle the real training. The first phase of the package was known as the family group start-up. We felt that before anyone could understand the instruction, they needed to comprehend what their work was. It might sound naïve to suggest that employees didn't know their jobs, but they really didn't. So we asked groups: What do you do here? Who are your suppliers? Who are your customers? What quality opportunities do you have?

Some groups would say, "Well, we don't have any customers." We showed some of them that they actually did. Employees tend to think of the customer as being someone outside the company. We introduced them to the Japanese notion that there are both external and internal customers. The internal customer is the function you next have to pass your work off to. In other words, if I'm in manufacturing, then I have to hand off my work to distribution. Distribution is my internal customer. Distribution has to hand off to customer service to install. Customer service is his internal customer. This "next in line" concept was an important one to impress on everyone.

Of course, when some of our groups said they didn't have any customers, they were right. And therefore they had no reason for being. This was true of some of the staff groups. A few of them tried to weasel out of this by maintaining that they were their own customers. Then we pointed out that Rule Number One was that you can't be your own customer. For those who couldn't pinpoint any customers, we had them stop the work they were doing. There's a vast amount of useless work that goes on in a corporation, and it's tough to get a handle on it until you undertake an analysis of it. From this process, we identified all sorts of reports of dense data that were going all over the system that nobody wanted. We made sure they were eliminated.

We also began a new drill. Any time a meeting was scheduled, we made it a prerequisite that two questions be answered. Who is the customer for this meeting? And what are the customer requirements? We had realized that Xerox was very much a meeting-oriented company. Meetings clog the calendars of most businessmen, but the congestion had gotten truly awful at Xerox. Your whole life seemed to get dribbled away sitting around a table at a meeting. Once we started asking those questions, though, we discovered that there was no customer for many meetings. That being the case, there was no reason for that meeting to exist. Hence, all meetings that couldn't identify a customer were to be dissolved. Suddenly, people began finding time to do meaningful things. This drill is done to this day at Xerox.

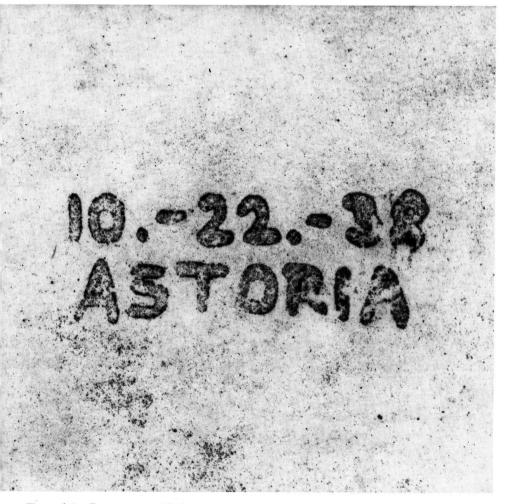

Text of the first xerographic image, created in a makeshift laboratory in Astoria, Queens, by Chester Carlson, the inventor of xerography.

Chester Carlson, the inventor of xerography, with his invention.

The first public demonstration of a xerographic printer, in Detroit, 1948. From left to right: John H. Dessauer, head of research and engineering, Chester Carlson, and Joseph C. Wilson Sr., father of the future Xerox CEO.

The Haloid Company, forerunner of Xerox, circa 1940s.

Joseph C. Wilson Jr., first CEO of the modern Xerox. He saw the promise of xerography and imbued the company with its early vision.

The first Xerox 914 comes off the assembly line in 1959. The first dry process automatic copier ever marketed, it's been called the most successful commercial product ever introduced.

C. Peter McColough, Joe Wilson's successor as Xerox's CEO. He transformed Xerox into an industrial giant.

Archie R. McCardell, Xerox's President from 1971–77. He was leader of the "Ford men" at Xerox.

The Xerox 9200 Duplicator, introduced in 1974, was a "bet the company" product that moved Xerox into new markets.

Xerox Square in Rochester, New York, opened in 1968 as the twenty-nine story corporate headquarters. Two years later headquarters moved to Stamford, Connecticut and Rochester became the base for U.S. marketing operations.

Xerox's sprawling research, engineering, and manufacturing complex in Webster, New York, a farming community just outside of Rochester.

The famous Xerox Palo Alto Research Center (PARC).

Xerox's state of the art training center in Leesburg, Virginia. This was the site of the two key management meetings that launched the quality revolution at Xerox.

Xerox current corporate headquarters in Stamford, Connecticut.

Norm Rickard, one of the original prophets of the Xerox quality revolution, who later became Corporate Quality Officer.

Hal Tragash, another of the original prophets, worked closely with Rickard in the early days.

David Kearns (in the middle of the couch), David Nadler (standing second from right), and a Xerox team, with Phil Crosby at his Quality College in Winter Park, Florida, January 1983.

Bill Glavin, who brought Kearns to Xerox, was an early instigator of quality and eventually became a Vice Chairman of the corporation.

Frank Pipp, a key manufacturing and development executive at Xerox, was the first executive in the company to recognize and understand the need for quality and major change.

Wayland Hicks, an early supporter of quality and an aggressive leader in the battle against the Japanese. He played a key role in the 10 Series development.

The Xerox 1075 Copier. The "10 Series" represented Xerox's first significant counterattack against the Japanese.

David Nadler (seated at left) meeting with some of his staff at Delta Consulting Group Inc., to discuss organizational change.

David Kearns speaking at one of the Xerox Teamwork Days, where quality improvement teams from across the corporation shared their accomplishments.

President George Bush presenting Kearns with the Malcolm Baldrige National Quality Award for Xerox. AP/Wide World Photos, Inc.

When Xerox received the Baldrige Award in 1989, it placed this ad to thank its customers, its suppliers, and its employees.

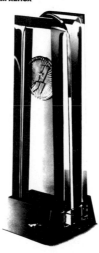
Xerox's ad for its total satisfaction guarantee, made possible by Leadership Through Quality.

Paul Allaire, another early supporter of Leadership Through Quality, and current Chairman and CEO of Xerox.

At the same time, we began to examine the participants at meetings and to question whether they all needed to be there. It was commonplace at Xerox to have a lot of huge meetings. By huge, I mean twenty to twenty-five people. It was an all too familiar scene to see people scrambling for chairs in a conference room and finding themselves unable to fit around the table because there were so many of them. Many of the people who were coming to these sessions, we discovered, were doing it simply because it was something of a status symbol to be at certain meetings attended by high-level people. Not only was this wasting people's time, but the size of the meetings was inhibiting progress. Considerable research on meeting dynamics indicates that if meetings get too large, then decision-making is retarded. There is also something known as "audience effect" that is created when too many participants are in a meeting. It causes people to perform and give speeches and think about who wins and who loses. The optimum size for a meeting in which a decision needs to be made is seven to nine people, and so we endeavored to limit our meetings to seven or eight people rather than the twenty or twenty-five. And we found it produced plenty of rewards.

If anyone wasn't aware of how much a lack of quality could hurt one's competitive edge, we included an article in the training manuals reprinted from a recent issue of the *Harvard Business Review* and written by David A. Garvin, then an assistant professor of business administration at the Harvard Business School. Entitled "Quality on the Line," the article reported the results of an intensive study Garvin had done of virtually every American and Japanese maker of room air conditioners. His startling findings were that the failure rates of air conditioners made by the highest-quality companies were between five hundred and a thousand times lower than the failure rates of air conditioners from the poorest companies. What's more, he found that Japanese companies far outstripped their American counterparts, with an assembly-line defect rate nearly seventy times lower and a first-year service call rate almost seventeen times better. The one piece of positive news to come out of his report was that the Japanese were so much better not because of any cultural differences but because of better management practices more effectively applied. American companies, in other words, could match those superior numbers if they rethought their approach to product quality.

The second phase of the training centered a great deal on problem-solving. This was the core of what we were trying to teach everyone. A day and a half was devoted to learning a wheel of six steps to solve problems. It showed you how to take a problem, work back and find causes, and then come up with a solution. For many of the participants, it was a strange exercise. From my standpoint, this was the most vocational part of the training. I really learned from it. I don't have the most disciplined mind, and I found the systematic process amazingly helpful.

When they are confronted with a problem, American managers typically want it fixed fast—by yesterday. And this can be a deadly disease. I was very much the epitome of that school of thought. I felt I was decisive and impatient, and so I wanted problems solved as quickly as possible. But I didn't think enough about root causes. Rarely would I ask, "What is the reason we are having this problem?" Now I think a lot about causes.

We also showed people how to employ various statistical tools to figure out solutions. We introduced them to such things as a force-field analysis, a concept developed by the social psychologist Kurt Lewin that isolates those forces that help and hinder you from moving from where you are now to where you want to be. We showed them a histogram, a specialized type of bar chart that depicts the distribution of a characteristic. We introduced them to a Pareto analysis, named for the nineteenth-century economist Vilfredo Pareto, which is a technique that separates the "vital few" from the "trivial many" and therefore points out inequalities.

Then a set of eleven interactive skills was introduced, some of which might have appeared commonsensical, but few people really gave much thought to what they were doing during meetings. We had these skills printed on small cards, of the sort you would find in board games: building, proposing, disagreeing, seeking information, attacking, testing, and so on. Then we played a little card game. A topic was chosen for discussion, typically a business subject in which action was to be considered, and each participant was handed a set of cards. One person was to begin by placing a "proposing" card on the table and making a proposal. If the others agreed that a true proposal had been made, then the card was discarded and play proceeded to the person to the left. Each player was to put a card from his hand facedown on the table and contribute something demonstrating that behavior. The rest of the group had to identify what he was doing. If the group agreed that it was an accurate representation, the card got discarded. Otherwise, the player had to revise his contribution. The round continued until one player had gotten rid of all of his cards.

Inevitably, some of these interactive skills became running jokes. A lot of people had fun with the concept of building on someone else's idea. They would be sitting in a session and say, "Let me build on that idea. You're wrong, turkey." Or someone would say, "That was a very good idea, let me build on it." Which meant the idea was horrible and you were going to fix it.

We also taught employees about how some comments that got made in meetings constituted an "attack." So you would hear people say, "Hey, that's an attack, cut it out." Once someone said to me, "Kearns, that's an attack." And I shot back, "You bet it's an attack."

Time was spent showing people how to code behavior. Employees were to watch videotapes and characterize the actions of the people appearing in them. We knew that even experts in interactive skills couldn't recognize what people were doing and saying all the time. We very much wanted to steer people away from attacking and defending and more toward listening, asking, testing, building, and understanding. Everyone had been making speeches at one another. We wanted to make people more disciplined.

Next, we spelled out for the students a nine-step quality improvement process that we wanted the entire company to follow. The steps were:

1. Identification of the output.
2. Identification of the customers for that work.
3. Identification of the customer's requirements.
4. Translation of the customer's requirements into objectives and specifications in order to meet them.

5. Identification of steps in the work process to meet customer requirements.
6. Selection of measurements for the critical steps in the process.
7. Determination of the capability of the process to deliver the expected outcome.
8. Evaluation of the results and identification of steps for improving the process.
9. Recycling for continuing improvement.

As the training went on, we would drill everyone in understanding and applying this process. We took some hypothetical cases and tried to solve them. One of them involved the New Era Telephone Company, an international company we made up that produced telephones for the general business and residential markets. The participants were supposed to be consultants hired by Sam Waterbury, president of New Era, to study the company and recommend actions that would enhance New Era's performance. We had prepared a video in which various purported employees spoke about their sense of the business and what problems they were experiencing.

The most popular case we used was the Quality Restaurant. We gravitated to this because we felt it was an example everyone could easily understand. Through the challenges of a simple restaurant, one could come to understand outputs, customer requirements, and specifications, the very guts of the quality process. We hired a film crew and some actors, and rented a quaint little restaurant in Ridgefield, Connecticut. Working between the hours of midnight and six in the morning, when the place was closed, we shot a little skit. We named the place the Quality Restaurant. Bernie Green ran it with his wife, Irene, who served as the waitress. Winslow was the cook. Despite having learned to cook in the army, his beef stew got good reviews.

We did a number of drills with the Quality Restaurant tape. For instance, we showed a customer named Ralph as he came in to eat his breakfast. Then we undertook a detailed analysis of that simple act. We drew a matrix to demonstrate how the staff of the restaurant had to produce a series of specific outputs if Ralph was going to satisfy his hunger. When Ralph gave his order, we explained, he was the customer and Irene was the supplier. This equated to sales. Next, we showed how the order itself became the output, and from that vantage point, Winslow was the customer and Irene was the supplier. Once the food was prepared, Irene became the customer and Winslow the supplier. This was manufacturing. Then came distribution as the meal was served by the supplier, Irene, to Ralph. We continued this analysis by dissecting the delivery of the check, the collection of the money, and the clearing of the table. The key point in all this was that an external customer like Ralph was always a customer, never a supplier.

Once we had finished the analysis, the students were asked to divide into groups and to each take one output in the restaurant, assume the role of customer, and decide what the customer requirements would be for that output. In other words, each was to put himself in the customer's shoes. You were expected to come up with things like a clean plate, a napkin, a full set of utensils, soup that is hot, pork that is cooked thoroughly. The upshot was, if you, as a supplier, understand what your output is, who your customers are, and what their requirements are, then your planning is complete.

Then participants were guided through an exercise to illustrate how you could decide what requirements were necessary to produce a quality product that conformed to customer requirements and what measurements would tell you if you had succeeded in achieving it. This was done with the elementary process of brewing coffee. The suppliers were Irene and the busboy who made the coffee. The likely customer requirements were: it had to be hot, quickly served, fresh (not bitter or too strong), rich, boasting a full taste (not too weak, no "off" flavors), and ought to cost no more than forty cents (this was not New York). Since Irene and the busboy didn't consider themselves arbiters of taste when it came to coffee, they solicited the advice of an expert, Winslow. His responses included: to be hot it should be brewed at 170 to 180 degrees, quick service meant within two minutes of the order, fresh meant brewed not more than an hour ago, rich full taste meant Colombian Blend, Grade AA commercial drip grind, a forty-cent price meant a bulk price of not more than two dollars and fifty cents a pound.

Then the goal was to identify the steps in the work process to prepare for improving quality. Every day you had to scrub pots and the urn with soap to clear the oil residue that could create stale taste. Everything had to be rinsed thoroughly to eliminate the soapy taste. Supplies—filters, coffee—had to be replenished. Every hour, the old grounds and filter had to be emptied, a new filter inserted, a basket filled with the right amount of coffee, an empty container put under the basket on a hot plate, and the start button pressed.

Once you had gone through all this, there was so much involved that you felt the need for a stiff drink, and not of coffee. But the understanding began to creep in that achieving quality in even the most taken-for-granted tasks was predicated on consistently following an orderly progression of steps.

We told the trainees that business was okay at the Quality Restaurant, but Bernie wanted to build it up. After a number of brainstorming meetings, he wondered if they could attract new customers by advertising that the restaurant would serve a customer breakfast in ten minutes or else give him the meal for free. Before actually offering the guarantee, Bernie and his team decided to time the service for a week from six-thirty to eight-thirty to see if the ten minutes was an achievable objective.

Here was where the trainees came in. We presented them with something like three hundred actual checks from the Quality Restaurant that they had to analyze to try to figure out if the ten-minute guarantee would work. As it turned out, it wouldn't. Too many orders exceeded the threshold.

The next step was to determine the cause. And that got tricky. There was no obvious answer. A quick perusal of the checks would not cause the problem to leap out. It took some analysis. In the end, the flaw turned out to be a faulty waffle iron. Orders that had waffles on them were consistently taking too long. So we asked participants to determine a solution. There were several paths to follow. You could get a new waffle iron, you could get several waffle irons, or you could stop offering waffles.

Once we were done with these hypothetical cases, we had the family groups pick a real problem that they needed to solve—and it had to be something that could be solved within sixty days so a result would be seen in the near future—and they were to begin work on it using their new tools.

My group picked operations reviews, the periodic rituals at Xerox in which senior management evaluated the performance of the various units. Top management was spending a lot of time on these report cards and they were clearly inefficient. Every unit was coming in for one of these reviews, sometimes monthly, and they would leave feeling unhappy and we would feel unhappy. After working on it, we totally restructured the reviews and changed who attended and what got covered, and they began to work much better. One thing we realized was that at these and other Xerox meetings huge stacks of slides often got shown. As a result, the meetings became worse than watching a relative's slides from his Hawaiian vacation. So we made a rule that all data for a meeting was to go out to the attendees ten days before the session. We would assume that everyone read it and thus very few slides—mostly those of a recap nature—would get shown at the actual meeting. If you hadn't bothered to read the data, that would be all right. Then you wouldn't be able to say anything at the meeting and it would end sooner.

The other thing that dawned on us in tackling these reviews was that the customer in these instances was not senior management but the operating unit management. Corporate management was actually the supplier. In other words, we needed to reverse the roles. We had to ask the units if we were doing things right and if they wanted any changes made in how they received their reviews. At the end of the operation reviews, the unit people basically reviewed how we did. That change proved to be a powerful symbol of how seriously we were going to apply the quality tools.

In the following months, each of the people in my own training session went ahead and cotrained his own group, which really helped drill the lessons into his own head, and the cascade through the company began. Nadler himself served as the principal trainer for four of the other senior teams. The feedback was encouraging. People seemed to enjoy the vivid and commonplace examples we used, like the Quality Restaurant, which helped soothe any pain some employees might be feeling about being returned to the classroom and finding themselves saddled with homework at the age of forty.

By the summer of 1984, the training cascade had begun in earnest. Each team that went through the training spawned six to ten additional groups that would then be educated as each team member became cotrainer of the family group that he or she led. By 1985, the cascade had become a virtual Niagara Falls of training, with literally hundreds of family groups being trained each month. As each one completed the training sequence, it turned its attention to the specific quality improvement project that it initiated during the training and worked it to completion.

As the months passed, we began to see progress—in very small ways at first, through improved meetings and more effective task forces—but then in larger doses as teams began to dig into some real meat. When we saw gains from these efforts, we made sure to trumpet them throughout the corporation to inspire and encourage others. We started to bring together sets of quality improvement teams once a year into events called Teamwork Days, at which the best teams from each location could share their innovations. I always found these days exhilarating. It really excited me to see the things our people were starting to do, and their enthusiasm about their work was infectious. We began these Teamwork Days in Rochester, moving over the years to larger buildings as the size of the event grew. We ultimately ended up holding three of them—one in the United Kingdom and one on the West Coast in addition to the Rochester event—all on the same day.

We also began to track our progress through fairly detailed surveys of employees to determine whether they felt their managers were behaving differently. Each manager who went through training was rated by his staff on whether he was managing and leading in a manner consistent with Leadership Through Quality. We also intensified our efforts to measure customer satisfaction, and we began to detect improvements.

During this time, Nadler and I met every other week to review in depth our progress. We worked together to examine the strides we were making, to find areas where we could do better, and to talk about my role as the leader of the quality revolution at Xerox. Nadler also served as my sounding board about other problems and challenges we were facing in the business. Our partnership and our friendship continued to grow.

As I watched the early groups pass through their training, I felt certain it was going to be effective. Still, I knew we all had to be patient. Scattered early gains meant nothing by themselves. This thing had no clear hill. It had no armies. It was guerrilla warfare. It would be a long time before everyone was conditioned to think differently, and it would doubtlessly take time before those who were trained truly got the knack of it. I kept having to remind everyone of something that Nadler had told me: "We have a long way to go. Xerox is clearly in a period of transition. We are no longer the company that we once were and not yet the company that we must be."

12. A Backward Step

On the second floor of Xerox, the corridors and offices stood empty and quiet. In a nearly bare, windowless conference room, David Nadler and Hal Tragash were deep in conversation, and the more they talked the more incensed they got. From what they could see, precious little of the quality effort was going right.

The problems found particular expression in a single product. Xerox had introduced a desktop laser printer called the 4045 in early 1985. It was a hybrid machine—part copier and part computer printer—all for something like fifteen thousand dollars. On paper, it sounded like a winner. Unfortunately, it was bombing in the marketplace. It was reliable enough, but the software simply wasn't right and it didn't do what customers expected of it. There had been inadequate effort made to find out what customers wanted, and so we failed miserably in meeting the needs of the segment we had targeted. One of the crucial mistakes was not realizing the importance of "connectivity" (the ability of the 4045 to work with other office equipment). Also, the cost base was way out of line and thus the product was initially priced far too high.

Quality, we knew, was not building a box that didn't break down. It was meeting customer expectations. It didn't do any good to think only about products. The customer buys an offering—the manual, the software, the peripherals, the expected effect on his business. He doesn't just buy a box.

To a large extent, we probably sold the 4045 to the wrong users. In any event, customers were mightily dissatisfied with it. In fact, of the machines that had been sold, not much more than a paltry 50 percent of them were what we classified as being satisfactorily installed, meaning that they were operating properly and the customers were pleased. Normally, you would expect close to a hundred percent of a product satisfactorily installed. In short, the product was a disaster. Some years later, we did an in-depth study of our handling of the 4045 to determine the lessons to be learned from the dismal experience. The report came to be known as the "Moose on the Table" report. This phrase referred to the fact that there are plenty of problems present at corporations as obvious as a moose standing on the conference table. You can't help but know that they're there, but you still neglect to do anything about them.

Nadler was intimately familiar with the shortcomings of the 4045. He bought one for his own office but, no matter what he did, he was never able to get it to satisfy the sophisticated needs he had. It was supposed to print out pages of exquisite quality, allowing the operator a choice of type styles and sizes. Yet all he got was pretty conventional typewriter-like text. Exasperated, he donated the thing to Columbia University.

Meanwhile, the various quality officers were meeting and saying that things were going splendidly because the units were meeting the training schedules. And they were given a good review by the corporate quality office because they were adhering to those schedules. This made Nadler and Tragash livid. They complained that the quality officer should have been arguing heatedly against the release of the 4045 and, if need be, sacrificing himself to prevent it from getting out into the field.

Fred Henderson, though, didn't want to hear any of this. He was more concerned about making sure he didn't embarrass the existing order. This was dramatically at variance with how we expected him to act.

It was dawning on us that, as we were trying to drill this new quality process into everyone, in many places the old Xerox culture was proving to be a finicky host. And we were continuing to battle some pretty forbidding business pressures. As the days seemed to get longer and longer, I was really getting anxious for results.

The difficult times actually began around the summer of 1984. Profit performance wasn't nearly up to what we expected it to be, and it

was affecting my mood in an unwelcome way. I was snappish at meetings and was severly critical of managers. In the best of times, I'm an
impatient person, and that summer I was worse than usual. To make
matters worse, my back was acting up. I had suffered back pain once
before, but I thought I was rid of the affliction. Boy, was I wrong. I
remember going out to a meeting in Cleveland when my back began to
act up again. I got home and was due to leave to attend the summer
Olympics in Los Angeles. As I was getting ready to go out the door of
my house, I picked up my briefcase and my jacket and my back just
totally gave out. I began sweating profusely and my shirt was soaked
through in a matter of minutes.

Because of my ailing back, I had to conduct a number of meetings
lying down at home. The pain also made for some arduous trips. I was
booked to go to Mexico with another senior executive for a plant visit
and then on to Brazil to meet with the president of the country. The
plane trip to Mexico was no joyride, and once we arrived there a van
was waiting to ferry us to the plant. The only way I was able to make
the trip was lying flat out like a corpse in the rear of the van. On the
plane flight to Brazil, I spent the time sprawled on a couch in the back
of the plane. Then we encountered serious engine troubles and the pilot
had to land prematurely in Panama City while another plane was dispatched to pick us up. We got to Brazil with one minute to spare to see
the president. And my back was a mess. I rode back lying on the floor
of the plane looking up at my associate as he talked about the business
for hours.

Nobody was giving me much compassion, either. One day Nadler
even said to me, "Did you ever consider that this back thing could be
psychosomatic?" That really annoyed me and I teased him that I didn't
hire him to become my personal psychologist. But he kept pulling my
chain about it. Several of my biweekly sessions with Nadler were held
in the upstairs bedroom of my house, with me lying flat on my back in
bed and Nadler sitting in an easy chair next to me. Almost every time
we met in these odd circumstances, I would get some ribbing.

The back did prompt some amusing moments. One day, it was acting up rather badly and I was home and had taken some medication. I
wanted to talk to Bill Souders, one of the senior executives, and so I

called him and asked him to come over to the house. He wouldn't do it. The next day I saw him at the office and said, "Why didn't you come over yesterday?" He said, "During this conversation on the phone you didn't make any sense. I don't know what kind of pills you were taking but I didn't want to come over and have a big debate with you when you were talking gibberish. So I just didn't come."

But not much was making me laugh. Bad news seemed to trip over bad news. It was right around this time that the strange letters incident occurred, certainly one of the low points of the year. Several anonymous letters, clearly written by someone knowledgeable inside the company and meant to represent the views of other Xerox employees, were sent to Peter McColough. Peter was still chairman, although he was not involved in day-to-day management, and he remained a figure of stature and respect to Xerox people. The letters were sharply critical of my performance. They suggested that I was getting too frustrated and was lashing out unnecessarily at the management team. They urged Peter to immerse himself in the business once again. For all I knew, the writer of the letters might have hoped that Peter would return and kick me out of the place.

Peter showed the letters to me and we talked about them in private. He took them seriously, and so did I. They were a surprise all right. Being put on the spot like this was hardly something I was accustomed to. I defended myself and told him that I was pushing people hard, but it was necessary given the state of the business. The letters, though, were a jolt, and I worried about them. But then, just as suddenly as they appeared, they abruptly ceased. Though I had my suspicions, I never found out who wrote them and didn't try to.

Larger issues harped away at us. For 1985, the copier group promised better results than they had achieved in 1984, and I thought they could pull it off. The revenue plan that was presented to me was ambitious. The key financial people warned me that in fact it was far too hopeful and they would never pull it off, but I told them we ought to wait and see. For much of the year, it seemed that the copier people wouldn't make the numbers. As the weeks droned by, they continued to lag well behind schedule and a big bubble remained in the final quarter of the year. Then they pulled out every trick in the bag—special pricing, added incentives for the sales force—and barely managed to hit the big forecast. To say the least, I was ecstatic that the numbers came in as promised and I praised the copier people to the hilt throughout the company.

Now the copier group was faced with what to do for an encore. All the last-minute scrambling had sucked a good deal of business out of 1986 and may have aggravated some of our customers. But the senior managers of the copier group didn't account for this in their 1986 forecast, when they predicted still more growth. I failed to challenge that plan sufficiently and accepted it. And it was clearly optimistic. It was unrealistic. It was what we wanted to happen rather than a reasonable outcome. I liked what they were telling me and failed to follow the quality process that we were trying so hard to implement. I had been pleased with the way 1985 had turned out and looked to another good year in 1986. I should have pushed, challenged, and questioned the copier people in detail about how they planned to capture those revenues. If I had, the optimism of some of their assumptions would have become evident. In the end, I neglected to acknowledge how much the old Xerox culture of "get the growth" was still fueling the company. And I continued to succumb to my own shortcoming of being overly optimistic about people and what they could accomplish.

Sure enough, 1986 proved to be a sorely disappointing year. I grimly referred to it as the year that the wheels came off. The copier group never managed to achieve its high hopes. At the same time, the systems group, whose sales force had been integrated with the copier sales force in the wake of the departure of Don Massaro, had introduced a bold collection of ten new office products. They had first been unveiled the previous April, during a flashy million-dollar show we threw at the Vivian Beaumont Theater in Lincoln Center. The curtain went up on a stage set up in a series of offices filled with Xerox equipment. More than a hundred and fifty reporters showed up, and they were pretty impressed. And they were impressive products, including a laser printer, a personal computer, and a workstation—but no one will ever know if they were the right stuff or not because of a string of miscues in the selling of them. For one thing, the copier sales force was never properly trained to sell them. Some of the products failed to come out on schedule, and the software lagged far behind and didn't perform up to customer expectations. Thus many of these products wound up doing poorly in the marketplace. It could have been that the products were wrong or it could have been that they simply weren't marketed suitably. Whatever the case, their weak performance contributed to the awful year. A snappish air permeated the company. If it hadn't been for our financial services business, which after a tough time in 1984 was contributing significantly to profits in 1985 and 1986, we might have really been in the soup.

Given the circumstances, Nadler began pushing me hard to appoint a president and chief operating officer—titles I also held. He told me one day, "David, you're a great chief executive officer but you are not driving the day-to-day business in enough detail to understand the product and market strategies, and they need attention." He also continued to push me to move more quickly in determining the future management team.

For several years now, Nadler and I had been having regular conversations about the senior management and my own succession. It all started one day back in 1983 when Nadler came in and said, out of the blue, "David, let me share something. I see your vision and all you want to do with quality and the company. But it's hard for me to see you getting where you want to go with your current management team."

I'm sure Nadler didn't know how I might respond. For all he knew, I could have grown irate and tossed him out on his ear right there. Instead, I said, "Wait a minute." I went and fetched a folder stuffed with sheets of yellow legal paper. On those pages were ideas I had about ways to change the management structure and team. I told Nadler I had been working on the exact same issues and fully agreed with him.

We talked right then about one of the big headaches we were having: the whole systems group out in California was continuing to have difficulty. I asked Nadler to go out to El Segundo and talk to people to find out what he could. When he returned, we agreed that some people just weren't providing the leadership we needed and ought to leave.

One of them I enjoyed working with and I was saved from what could have been a very difficult task by his coming into my office and telling me he was frustrated and unhappy and he thought it would be best for the company and himself if he left. I concurred.

Nadler and I had a lot of sessions devoted to constructing a different management structure. We talked about some upcoming executives whom I had my eye on, most notably Paul Allaire, who was running Rank Xerox very successfully. Shortly afterward, I brought him back and made him a senior executive and chief of staff.

Nadler felt that there was not enough intellectual firepower in the leadership ranks at Xerox, less than he saw at other companies he worked with. Few people, he said, were thinking profoundly about the company. I admitted that I wasn't bringing as much intellectual firepower as was required. I felt I was quick, quicker than most, and that was one of my main contributions. But I agreed we had to shore up the top ranks.

One top executive, for instance, suffered from a surfeit of ideas. He would have an idea one day and then two days later would have another idea. That drove people crazy, thinking he was changing his mind. When you get higher up in any organization, you have to be careful what you say out loud. You may have a thought while shaving and it may be a thoroughly rotten idea, but if you go ahead and mention it to someone he may think it's something to act on. You have to watch your tongue.

Xerox had a custom of its chief executive officer retiring at the age of sixty, and so I announced to the company that on August 11, 1990, when I turned sixty, I would step down as CEO as my predecessors had done. Nadler thought I had made a mistake doing that, because it touched off something like a presidential sweepstakes.

In pondering who should become president, I knew that whoever I picked would then be in line to succeed me. I truly feel that one of the single most important discrete decisions that a CEO makes is who will succeed him. One thing you always have stashed in the back of your mind is, Will it work? Will the guy behave under pressure? You make someone the CEO sometimes and the position overwhelms him and changes him. He becomes imperious or does zany things. Also, at many places, the chief executive doesn't think about his successor at all and then watches with horror as the person comes in and dismantles the system that he had painstakingly put in place.

Thus here was an important consideration: if this quality effort was going to take a long time, which it surely was, how did I make sure it lasted? The obvious answer was that we had to make certain it was organization-wide so the next team of management didn't just scrap it. In a corporation, you don't get too many brownie points for continuing what the old guy had done. So we made one of the critical criteria of a president the fact that he lived and breathed quality, too.

Three of us—David Nadler, personnel head Doug Reid, and myself—met regularly to wrestle with the issue. At many places, these decisions happen with little or no planning whatsoever. All too many executives believe that management at the upper reaches of a company is mysterious and defies any sort of worthwhile analysis. Nadler's personal theory is that the conventional way succession is decided is through what he likes to call the Tom Wolfe Approach based on the Right Stuff. At some point in a manager's career, he gets identified as being imbued with the Right Stuff. Exactly what that stuff is is rarely delineated. It usually boils down to fairly superficial characteristics. The person makes good presentations. He looks attractive. He carries himself with a certain aplomb. And unless he loses it, that person has the Right Stuff forever and gets moved up the ladder. It's wrong, and an often insidious approach.

Being deeply opposed to the Right Stuff theory, Nadler designed a rather thoughtful process of his own that we adopted. Called Strategic Selection, it is a systematic approach for matching people and jobs at the senior executive level. The concept was in large part based on conceptual work done by Dr. Marc Gerstein, a member of the Delta Consulting staff. In bare outline, the process requires that you make educated guesses about the business demands of a job. Then candidates are to be rated on how skilled they are in those areas. Finally, the ratings are put alongside the job to see how good a fit there is. By no means is this meant to make the selection process a purely mechanical one. Rather, it is a tool to structure the decision process.

A few years ago, we had done a significant reorganization of the company—which evolved from a big management meeting we held in Asheville, North Carolina—that allowed us to put the principal players in position so we could look at them and test them. The reorganization was also important in that it fulfilled my desire to greatly reduce the corporate role in decision-making for the organization. Virtually everything was being done at corporate, from pricing in Europe to the color of copiers. I wanted these things decentralized. In 1983, through another reorganization, we began to put a new team of senior players in place. As part of my goal to improve the quality of the management process, we then created a book of issues to discuss with each of them to let them know what they ought to be doing for their own careers and for the good of the organization. It's often thought, Well, these are big boys, they know what to do. Often, they don't.

Nadler, Reid, and myself began meeting roughly once a month for two hours to talk about the candidates. There were about six of them, though some would come and go as their performances ebbed and flowed. At the very first meeting, Nadler said, "We're all carrying some psychological baggage into the room. Rather than have the psychological stuff come out along the way, let's do a little exercise. If we had to pick a successor right now, who would we pick and why?" And we each named a candidate and gave our reasons. Each of us picked someone else. All the same, we concurred that there was a lot more we needed to know about these people before we could make a choice with any deep confidence. Before the process was over, we would have a total consensus.

Under the process Nadler had designed, we sat down and identified what the job requirements were and then we used a job-rating instrument to indicate how important each characteristic was for that position. We employed a scale of one to seven, with seven being the highest. Thus if "negotiation skills" was fundamental to the position and great strength in negotiation was required of a candidate, that would score a seven. If "self-motivation" was only fairly important, that could get a four. There were some thirty different traits we singled out for the president's job, and we also identified seven of them that were foremost in importance. Then we would use the same scale to score the candidates on these thirty items. On each requirement, a candidate would be given a one to seven rating. In effect, we were doing a Right Stuff approach, with an important twist. We were defining exactly what the Right Stuff was, and there was nothing superficial about it. And then we were measuring how much Right Stuff was in the candidates in an emphatically analytical way.

We did this analysis every year, and found that the scores bobbed up and down quite a bit and they fluctuated widely by candidates. There were some key elements such as commitment to an understanding of the quality process, integrity and forthrightness, decisiveness, ability to get things done, and performance. The ratings of candidates varied a lot on these. Some would be strong for a while and then flatten out and begin to lag behind the others. Serious doubt was sown about a few of them as time went by.

These meetings were usually held away from my office. One was at Nadler's home. Another one was on a plane. I was going down to Florida for a weekend, and since we badly needed time together, Nadler and Reid tagged along for the plane ride. During that trip, we hatched the idea of possibly having one of the candidates become a president for a period but not go on to become CEO, an idea we explored further and ultimately jettisoned. It was a productive meeting, nonetheless, though Reid and Nadler seemed less than thrilled that once I deplaned in sunny Florida they had to immediately head back to wintry Connecticut.

In the end, I recommended Paul Allaire to the board of directors, and on August 13, 1986, he was appointed president. As Nadler, Reid, and I worked this process, I had regularly met with the board to get their input on the key candidates. Paul had shown himself to have a crackerjack mind, and he could be tough as nails. He was now forty-eight years old, and had spent the bulk of his career at Xerox. He came from a background from which a top executive job would have seemed an inordinately ambitious goal. Paul grew up in the small, working-class town of Auburn, Massachusetts, not far from Boston's splendors. He was one of six children, whose parents made a modest living as vegetable farmers. The family squeezed into a house with a single bathroom. After the perfection of refrigerated trucks allowed California to drive many New England farmers out of business, his father went into a sand and gravel business. Paul put in many a day on the farm and in the sand pits.

After studying engineering at Worcester Polytechnic Institute—only the second member of the extended Allaire family to go to college—Paul worked for two years as an engineer at Univac in Philadelphia. But he couldn't save any money, so he took a job with General Electric as a systems engineer in Germany. The idea was to go out of the country and squirrel away some money through the lucrative compensation plans being paid Americans abroad. After two and a half years, Paul returned, got a master's degree in industrial administration at Carnegie-Mellon University, and joined Xerox as a financial analyst in 1966.

The question someone might ask is, Would I have picked Paul without this selection system? I don't know, but I do know that if I did I wouldn't have picked him with as much conviction. From the process and interactions with the board, I knew he was unquestionably the best man for the job.

Once the decision was made, I had the happy job of telling Paul the good news. I really looked forward to that, because I got a vicarious charge out of it myself, imagining how Paul would feel. I told him in the evening and then he and his wife, Kay, joined Shirley and me for a most pleasant celebratory dinner.

No sooner was I done spreading good cheer than I had the distasteful task of notifying the other leading candidates that they were not going to become president. The trick was to deliver the news without having them get mad and quit. Fortunately, that didn't happen. They were all disappointed but they all accepted the decision in an admirably civil way, or at least with pretty good feigned civility. The most uncomfortable chat was with a candidate on the West Coast. Naturally, I felt I had to go there and break the news in person. This was not the sort of thing you convey on the phone or through a fax. So I flew all the way out to the West Coast, where the man happened to be on vacation but in town. A car drove me to his house, a nice, modern affair with a breathtaking view. I came right out and said what I was there for, and he was reasonably cordial about it. Nevertheless, it wasn't the greatest conversation I'd ever had. It was obviously a little strained. But it was over in less than thirty minutes. I said good-bye and we agreed to meet in a few weeks to talk more about his future role. I walked up the drive to the road, where the car was supposed to be. Unfortunately, I had told the driver to be back in about an hour. I didn't imagine the conversation would conclude so quickly. So I found myself wandering up and down the street outside this guy's house, feeling foolish, until the car finally showed up. It seemed as if I was outside that house for a good two or three days.

By late 1986, doubts had really become widespread about our progress with Leadership Through Quality. We had worked so hard to get this launched, and yet sign after sign was appearing that it wasn't going so well. According to the timetable the QIT had established, many of the goals of the program were to have been met by the end of 1986. Everyone in the company was to have been trained, and quality was to be the guiding principle of the company and fully integrated into the daily work of the employees. By late 1986, it was evident that not only hadn't we met all those goals; we were not even on a trajectory where we would meet them anytime soon. We knew this anecdotally and we knew it from various quantitative measures we had, like the defect rate of our products and the change in production costs and the Teamwork Days we staged where quality teams presented quality tools they had come up with.

We began to sense that Leadership Through Quality was teetering on the brink. With a little shove, it could have gone over the precipice.

By now, Fred Henderson was eager to get out of the corporate quality job and into a line assignment, so we replaced him with Norm Rickard. He had done a great job on his manufacturing assignment and had shown a lot of maturity in how he dealt with his disappointment in not getting the quality job the first time around. What's more, Paul Allaire felt that what was needed in the position was a "hammer"— someone who would really bang away at people who weren't conforming—and he felt Rickard was a hammer. Rickard couldn't have been happier. For some weeks prior to the appointment, he knew he was being considered for the job, and of course he wanted it more than anything. He would become a corporate officer and get to move into bay 3-2. In his lingo, he would be knighted. He was constantly nagging David Nadler to find out if he had heard anything. The last week in January, Paul Allaire and Nadler went skiing in Vail, Colorado, for four days. They got there late on a Thursday night, after eleven-thirty, and Paul went to fetch the key to the condominium where they were staying. There was a phone message for David. Paul gave it to him and he ripped it open. It was from Norm. It said: "Any word yet?" David called him to calm him down and tell him to have a good weekend. The next day, Norm got the word.

With Paul and Norm in their new positions, it seemed the appropriate time to get a true reading of the state of the project. Paul was especially eager to have a good sense of where matters stood. Rickard had been asking around to the units about how things were going, and he wasn't hearing terribly encouraging news. And so we decided to conduct a thorough company-wide assessment to find out just where we stood and why we weren't further along. Rickard asked Delta to conduct the assessment. Two of Nadler's senior people, Jeff Heilpern and Terry Limpert, were chosen to head up an assessment team that included some of Rickard's staff.

The assessment was begun in March 1987 and was completed in June. Extensive interviews were done with a wide array of line managers and quality officers. Surveys were also distributed among a variety of employees to determine the degree to which the quality tools were being deployed. We also reviewed the ongoing Management Practices Survey, which was set up in 1983 and supplied information on how quality was being used and how it was perceived by key managers and subordinates.

The results were decidedly mixed. We found that people almost universally supported the strategy as being the right one for Xerox. This was nearly four years into the effort and it was fully endorsed. This wasn't a total surprise, but it was important to know and nothing to take for granted. There are a lot of efforts that get started in corporations and they don't catch on but slowly fizzle out. It's not an automatic assumption that a company would be four years into something and would enjoy total support.

When it got down to gauging the performance of the individual units, we found some pockets of excellence and some very inferior examples. The good news was that the pockets of excellence transcended cultures and job functions. They showed up in the United States, Argentina, Colombia, Spain, France, and Canada. So the results put to bed the persistent myth that we would always hear about how quality didn't work in someone's function, or it didn't work in South America because things were done differently there. Anyone could imbibe quality and like it.

Throughout the units, we saw that there was much improved teamwork and effectiveness at meetings, things that had been sorely needed. But, all in all, it was clear that quality had not been integrated into the daily life of the company. There was still a conflict between the drive for quality and the pressure to achieve financial results. Quality was not the basic principle of the corporation. The compulsion to get better profit numbers was.

At the same time, there was a lack of leadership and role modeling, as well as a dearth of inspection and coaching. You were supposed to pick up the quality spirit from your superior, but a lot of people were picking up nothing of the sort. What's more, there was inadequate support from the quality specialists, the people who had the deepest expertise in quality tools.

Of the pockets of excellence, France stood out. It was a mid-sized unit and it had managed to train all of its nearly five thousand employees. The top management of the unit really caught the quality fever and used symbolic gestures very effectively. Each year, the head of the unit sent a letter to every employee's home thanking him for what he had done. That was the only piece of communications that ever went to the employee's home, and so it held special significance. In 1984, to kick off Leadership Through Quality, the president of the unit mailed a message to everyone's home explaining the effort. And thus, right from the start, great weight was attached to it. To make something like this work, you have to use every symbol at your disposal.

Another thing about France: the quality officer was a key member of the management team and enjoyed real power and credibility. It became evident that the success of the program in a unit was closely tied to the dedication of the manager of the unit. As Tragash pointed out at the time, it was not enough for the generals to be on board. The colonels, who were actually leading the troops in the field, were critical to make quality happen.

Among the poor units, the domestic sales and service force was badly lagging. And the reason why truly shocked me. Because business had been so weak in 1986, the head of the unit ordered training in quality stopped cold. With sales sagging, he felt there was no way he was going to allow any of his people to spend their time being trained in quality. As a result, something like 30 percent of the force had been trained, a pitiful total. There was no doubt in my mind that stopping the training was a bad decision. For a group that was as large as the U.S. sales and service force and that had such extensive contact with our customers to be so poor in adopting this quality process was a significant lapse. We made sure that changed in a hurry. Among other things, we replaced the quality officer in the unit with someone who was more aggressive and dedicated to our mission.

The good units saw quality as a way to win, not as something to be done because of a corporate mandate. The poor units didn't get it at all. One manager acknowledged that he was trained but was not particularly interested in using the quality tools until Paul Allaire told him to use them for a project and to keep him abreast of the progress. Before that happened, he said, he was simply giving lip service to the idea.

One of the clear things we found lacking was managers not bothering to inspect work processes to confirm that the quality tools were being used correctly and were making a difference. Inspection was one of the fundamental aspects of the LUTI chain, and yet it broke down right away. We probably never should have used the word "inspect," because it implied looking at things only at the end and it had a military ring. As it happened, we never bothered to teach the art of inspecting during the training. For one thing, we thought it was fairly obvious. It would have seemed insulting to suggest to managers that they didn't know how to inspect the people under them.

One day, Paul Allaire said, "I don't think I know very well how to inspect." And that did it. We designed a four-hour workshop for the top three levels of management that taught inspection. We explained how you need to get continual feedback, not wait until the end. Managers had to become coaches by inspecting the steps used to accomplish the results. We showed videos that explained what managers should be asking when people came in for reviews. The idea was to understand whether the underlying causes of problems were identified. Soon afterward, inspection improved noticeably.

Another widespread problem that was singled out was that people said we were still promoting and rewarding employees who weren't true believers and users of the quality process. This was creating some noise in the system and sending mixed signals. Who gets promoted is a major sign to the organization of what the top management considers important. It had to stop. So we redefined the dimensions of who could be moved up. We established three categories: role model, competent (meaning you were on your way to becoming a role model), and needs work. To be promoted to one of the top fifty jobs in the company, you had to be nothing less than a role model and committed to the quality process. To get to be any lower-ranking manager, you had to be competent. Someone who needed work couldn't be promoted at all. In designing the criteria for being a role model, we made one of the most important factors one's belief in and implementation of Leadership Through Quality. This really put teeth in the program.

When the assessment came out in the late spring of 1987, it was a sobering document. I had an all-day meeting in one of the ground-floor conference rooms with Nadler, Allaire, Rickard, Heilpern, and Derek Hanley of Rickard's staff, and it was an agonizing meeting to sit through. Without question, the corporation was behind in its goals. Whereas we had hoped that the company would have reached a level of maturity in the quality drive, we now knew we were at least a couple of years behind schedule. We needed to redouble our dedication and our efforts.

It's like the missiles in Turkey during the Cuban missile crisis. I had told them to get those missiles out of Turkey and they were still there. I think missiles in Turkey happen all the time in corporations. People think senior management tells others to do things and they get done. They don't. The hardest thing in a big program is getting the action to happen. There is this chasm between hopes and expectable outcomes.

Quite a few people were grumbling that all the quality stuff was getting in the way of doing business, and that was really making me mad. I would tell them they had it all wrong. I would pull out my little card that had our quality policy on it and hold it up and say, "This is the way we accomplish this," and then show them in my other hand the card with our business objectives on it. The quality process was not in the way. It was the way we met the goals we had established.

One mistake we did make, and I believe I made it, occurred at the outset, in 1983. It was the idea of having three objectives equal in importance: improving return on assets, increasing market share, and bettering customer satisfaction. In other words, we had three things we were trying to fix. People used to press me to identify the most important objective. Going back to my IBM days, I used to say that learning to manage is the interaction of more than one thing. I refused to single out any one goal but told them to concentrate on the interaction. All were equal and we must succeed on all.

These three targets appeared in various forms, including the small laminated card that was given to every employee to carry. While all three goals were supposed to be equal, we behaved as if ROA was first. Market share and customer satisfaction were clearly runners-up in importance. This mind-set went back to Xerox's roots. How crucial was customer satisfaction when you were the only game? How important was market share when you owned it all? Everything had always been rewarded on return on assets and profit growth.

One day, I was walking in the halls with Wayland Hicks and I said, "We're not making the progress in improving customer satisfaction that we need."

Wayland agreed and said, "I have a suggestion. It may be hard for you, but I think you should say that customer satisfaction is the number-one goal. I don't think we can accomplish what we want to unless we make this decision and clearly communicate it to all employees."

Nadler did some informal research that supported Wayland's conviction. Managers were sensing too much of a tension among the goals.

I thought about this one night and decided we had to reorder the targets. From then on, we made customer satisfaction our focus, and I said it would drive market share and the combination would give us superior profits over time. To effect a cultural change, I realized, you needed to zero in on the customer above all else. So I feel it was an error to have had all three objectives equal. For one thing, no one believed it. Everyone knew improving profits was number one. This decision may seem inconsequential, but it was an important symbolic shift. It signified a fundamental turning point that reconfigured the trajectory of the program. It started the next chapter. Now I've changed my management philosophy totally. I really believe you have to train your attention on the ultimate user of your products and that will get the hard financial results. Had I done it the other way from the start, I feel we might have shaved at least a year and maybe two from this whole process.

Meanwhile, Paul Allaire and I, in conducting monthly operations reviews of our units, began placing a much stronger emphasis on Leadership Through Quality, so there was no sidestepping it. People were really taking note of that and it served as an invaluable catalyst to recapture our momentum. Not that people didn't try to weasel out of being reviewed on quality. The person running our international operations and the manager in charge of Rank Xerox were both somewhat hostile to quality. We had agreed that all operations reviews would include a segment on quality. In April 1987, one of these reviews was held for Rank Xerox, and the executives in charge fought including it on the agenda, to no avail. The review was conducted in person over eight hours, with a break for lunch. Leadership Through Quality, as it happened, was last on the agenda, and the executives were deliberately trying to drag out some of the other topics so they would never get to it. When the lunch break arrived, Allaire announced that he wanted to rejigger the agenda a bit. After lunch, they would begin with Leadership Through Quality. That touch of symbolism became famous throughout the company, and steadily we began to force the quality holdouts to come around if they expected to stay with the company.

As Norm Rickard put it one day: "The classic business literature talks about the mid-line manager being the bottleneck. I say it's really the upper-middle and lower-top manager because they've carved out a very nice way of life and they see that they're the most threatened. Say in Boston they banned baseball. Jim Rice, as good as they've got, complains: How can you do that, I'm a baseball player. No, he's told, you're an athlete. Go try out for the Celtics. He goes down and finds he's too short. Try out for football. He whines that he only weighs a hundred and eighty pounds. Go try out for the Bruins. He comes back and says he's got weak ankles and can't skate. In this radical change we made, we found we had a lot of managers who weren't tall enough, weren't big enough, and had weak ankles."

With each passing day, I felt I learned something more about the quality process and how to make it happen, and the lessons came from a wide array of sources. One of the things that David Nadler and I had been doing was working with other chief executives and high-ranking managers who were trying to wrestle with change—people like Jamie Houghton at Corning, Bob Allen at AT&T, and Paul O'Neil at Alcoa. I found this extremely helpful, because all of us were able to learn a lot by sharing our experiences—the pleasant and the painful.

In the wake of the assessment, Paul Allaire and I concentrated chiefly on two primary issues. We worked to improve the leadership being given by group and unit managers, and we zeroed in more on satisfying customer requirements. And thus began the push that would finally get us over the hump.

In pretty short order, the message started to sink in. In late 1987, Norm Rickard was traveling in Europe and bumped into a manager who mentioned that he had just gone through refresher training for himself and his team. Puzzled, Rickard asked him why he needed to do that. He replied, "Because I never paid much attention the first time through, since I thought this thing would be gone by now. I thought it was just another ice cream flavor. But I got scared when I saw that Allaire had picked it up with vigor. So we know we can't hide in the weeds anymore."

13. The Blooming of Quality

WHEN THE SEEDS OF THE quality effort were first planted, I had few illusions that I would see immediate crops, but I didn't imagine that the wait to notice something growing would be as long as it turned out to be. For someone as impatient as myself, it was agonizing. But with the changes and renewed push that evolved out of the 1987 assessment, not the least of which was Paul Allaire's stalwart dedication to our strategy, pleasant signs began to abound that Xerox was becoming a much different company.

We had come a long way since Hal Tragash and Norm Rickard started whispering about quality and I was groping in the dark for solutions to our problems. As each day and each week passed, we seemed able to sense real benefits from the massive project. By the end of 1988, all one hundred thousand Xerox employees worldwide had been trained in quality improvement tools. Xerox people were definitely beginning to work as teams. The quality of products and service, we would hear from more and more customers, was better. Revenues and profits began to increase. We continued to win back chunks of market share from the Japanese.

I began to see the change mainly in the acceptance of the 10 Series in the marketplace, which kept doing better and better. And our customer satisfaction measurements were showing notable improvements. Our internal meetings were getting better and more conclusive. The annual Teamwork Days we had instituted had become an ever more important vehicle for upper management to communicate with employees in an upbeat way. These quality fairs were now being attended by employees, customers, suppliers, community representatives, and academic and governmental leaders. With each year, they grew in popularity.

In May 1988, we had introduced the first major line of copiers since the 10 Series. Grouped together as the 50 Series, the new machines had more features and were of higher quality than anything we had produced. We were moving now toward sophisticated digital copiers that scanned, printed, copied, and bound pages, as well as connected to computers that incorporated graphics and various styles of type. In announcing the 50 Series, Paul Allaire declared, "We are setting the benchmark against which our competitors must be judged." Among the products was the 5090 duplicator, the fastest copier on the market, able to make a hundred and thirty-five copies a minute. The other models, aimed at the middle-price market, included the 5052, the 5046, the 5028, and the 5018. Development of the 50 Series had been going on for years, but the quality process was really imbued in it.

Benchmarking had spread like wildfire through the company. We were doing more of it than anybody. We were fast closing in on our goal of having every department in the company measuring its performance against similar operations at other companies—even lawyers and strategic planners. Significantly, we had expanded from benchmarking our direct competitors to benchmarking companies in altogether different industries. It was helpful to compare ourselves to Kodak, IBM, Canon, and Ricoh—for instance, when the competitive analysis lab had a problem with a Kodak machine, they called a Kodak serviceman and clocked him to see how long he took to respond and fix the problem—but they did things pretty much the way we did.

One day, Bob Camp, an inventory control analyst at Xerox who was instrumental in the whole benchmarking effort, read an article about L.L. Bean, the huge mail order distributor, and went up to visit the company in Maine. He toured their warehouse and found they could pick and pack goods three and a half times faster than we could our spare parts. L.L. Bean had developed a computerized system that alleviated the workloads of the pickers in the warehouse by calculating the distances the pickers had to walk to fill an order and then arranged the work by how the warehouse was stocked. Xerox had its own software created that mimicked the Bean approach. And so a Maine merchandiser became one of our benchmarks.

Bob Camp was clever. He went on to benchmark American Hospital Supply because they moved a lot of small things around the country fast and so did we. He benchmarked Caterpillar because they moved big things around the country fast and so did we.

To keep the effort going, we gave out a pamphlet on benchmarking to employees. It listed the rudiments of how to benchmark in plain English. As the pamphlet pointed out: "We must understand that Xerox does not, and cannot, always have the best answer to every problem we encounter."

American Express was another crucial company we turned to as a model. When you call up the credit card people, they're open twenty-four hours a day. One of the worst problems at Xerox was that customers got the runaround when they phoned us with a problem. Nobody seemed to have all the information to solve the matter. So we studied American Express and now our unit that answers phones can have the solution to someone's problem while the customer is still on the phone roughly 85 percent of the time. Before, the percentage was pretty close to zero. Our Canadian unit, trying to solve the same issue, benchmarked IBM and adopted a system that was so good that IBM came back to benchmark them.

There were certain ironies in some of the benchmarking tales. Our central data center in Webster, New York, wanted to do benchmarking and so the people there went to IBM salesmen and asked for the names of the best data centers in the United States. If anyone would know, it would be IBM. A particular company was suggested. As it turned out, the people there really did it right. They were significantly better than we were. But after a couple of years, we started to outperform that company, and the people there decided they didn't want to continue the information-sharing process. The gossip we heard was that they weren't looking as good anymore, and they didn't want to share that information with senior management and get beaten up.

Our electronics division, an internal supplier of Xerox, was always getting criticized for its low quality since it was, after all, a captive supplier. It jumped aboard the benchmarking bandwagon and examined companies in the Far East, America, and in Europe. The division got so good that it began bringing in business from the outside.

Our whole materials management had dramatically improved over the years. Some 70 to 80 percent of the added cost of our products was the cost of vendors, so there was a lot of money to squeeze out there. The key thing we did was make sure we were dealing with quality companies to begin with. As a result of studying Japanese inventory methods, we adopted what we called central commodity management. We managed to reduce the number of vendors we used for major materials from more than four thousand to less than four hundred. We cut our product cost throughout the world, after adjusting for inflation, by more than 50 percent. As a result of screening vendors better, we pretty much totally eliminated all inspections that we did. We used to have something like three hundred to four hundred people who inspected materials that came in from vendors. We got that down to less than fifty. Roughly 95 percent of the parts that come into Xerox today aren't inspected, because they don't need to be.

On a daily basis, we began giving assembly line workers at the copier plant in Webster a detailed report on all defects found in the previous day's production. The message was quality counted and everybody was involved.

The walls of all our plants were decorated with charts that showed the performance of various sections of the manufacturing process. That way, a machine could be adjusted before the parts it made began to fail to meet specifications. New products were designed to be simpler to assemble. Machine prototypes had historically cost Xerox about two hundred dollars a part. By 1989, that was reduced to seventy dollars a part, and we were shooting for forty dollars. And as much as possible, we tried for Japanese *kanban*, or just-in-time delivery of parts.

At the same time, we applied statistical methods developed by the Japanese engineer Genichi Taguchi to lessen the sensitivity of the manufacturing operations to disruption. For example, if the temperature in a plant cannot be adequately controlled, the Taguchi method suggested we develop a manufacturing process not affected by temperature. Virtually any materials and manufacturing processes could be tested for better performance through this statistical approach.

What's more, the Webster copier development people adopted the idea that each new Xerox product must contain at least one *dantotsu* feature. *Dantotsu* is a Japanese term that Tony Kobayashi popularized at Fuji Xerox. It means "the best of the best."

The littlest things began to change. One Xerox operation realized that its state-of-the-art computer system for processing customers' orders was hidden away in the back office. They reorganized the office and put the computers where they could be spotted. Customers were very impressed.

Several years ago, we used to congratulate ourselves because we could get a newly ordered copier shipped to a customer faster than the competition. We didn't realize that customers were less concerned about speed than in knowing precisely when that copier was arriving. And we couldn't tell them. At best, a salesman could tell a company that the order ought to be there in around two weeks, keep your fingers crossed. So Paul Allaire had a manager assemble a problem-solving team, which set up a system that follows every copier through the entire distribution process. Now salesmen can give the exact date that a copier will show up at someone's door.

Sometimes it took some real indoctrination, but people managed to shake bad habits. We had a refurbishing center in Oakbrook, Illinois, that was flush with problems. A new manager was installed, and the head of manufacturing told him that quality was the most important goal. "If you have to shut down the line to be sure we're turning out the right quality, shut it down," he said. Shutting down a line was pretty much anathema to a manufacturing man. In the past, you needed nothing short of a tornado or a declaration of a world war to do that. Sure enough, the day came when too many poor products were coming off the line and the manager saw no alternative but to shut it down. He called the head of manufacturing to advise him of his decision, fully expecting to get an earful of venom. "That's just fine," he was told. "That's exactly what you should be doing."

A major effort was made by the U.S. marketing group, which had come up so poorly in the 1987 assessment. In 1990 it decided to engage in a certification effort during which all of its hundred and fifty locations would be inspected in the most painstaking manner. Some managers didn't take too kindly to this at first. They felt we were spending more time on certification than we were on getting orders out. But the group stuck with it, and now the marketing group is among the leaders in the company in delivering quality after being virtually last on the totem pole in 1987.

There were innumerable examples of how teams used the quality tools to better serve our customers. One heartening instance was the Chicago Aces. This was a team of eleven sales people in the Chicago area who sold engineering products like large-document copiers. They had been setting no records in customer satisfaction. According to our surveys, they were lingering at about a 75 percent satisfaction rate. And so a core team of seven members was set up to find ways to bring customer satisfaction to 100 percent. In other words, every customer they encountered was going to be happy.

The team met regularly and went methodically through the quality problem-solving process. They contacted customers directly and asked them what they could do better. They found that sales people weren't following up on calls, that paperwork was being lost. Some large customers wanted special types of billing that didn't conform to conventional Xerox billing. We took those requirements and were able to bend the rules and accommodate them. Sales reps were on the road a lot, roaming through Illinois and Indiana, and customers weren't getting their calls returned promptly. At best, salesmen were checking in for messages twice a day, sometimes three times. The Aces made a new rule that salesmen were to call in four times a day for messages and return all customer calls immediately.

The engineering products that the Aces sold were immense, often requiring spaces of twelve by fifteen feet and special wiring. Although sales reps used to advise customers of what was necessary before delivery could be made, customers would frequently neglect to take care of the physical needs and so tech reps would show up with the product and be unable to install it. To eliminate these aborted calls, the Aces not only made sure salesmen spelled out exactly what needed to be done at the premises, but also instituted pre-site checks the day before a machine was scheduled to arrive. All this seems like common sense, but it wasn't being done and it was aggravating a lot of people.

As a result of these changes, customer satisfaction shot up significantly to nearly 86 percent. The Aces are still plugging away, trying to reach the elusive 100 percent mark.

Then there were the High Rockers. They were a group of service technicians based in Little Rock, Arkansas, who acquired their name because they worked on high-volume duplicators and printing equipment. They decided to become obsessed with pleasing their customers. From their surveys, the High Rockers knew that 83 percent of their customers in 1988 were satisfied with the service they were getting. Like the Aces, the High Rockers wanted that number to be 100 percent. So they embarked on a project called "Spoil the Customer."

The first thing the team did was go out and ask all of the customers what they felt was being done right and what was being done wrong. About 27 percent of the customers said that quick response time in emergency situations was important, and another 27 percent cited after-hours scheduled maintenance. It was decided to concentrate on response time first. The group returned to its customers to have them define what quick response time meant to them. From their comments, the High Rockers produced a set of supplier specifications. Priority one became an emergency call, and customers felt that we needed to respond to it within two hours. Priority two was a substandard machine that needed service but was not an emergency. An example would be a copier with an occasional paper jam. We agreed that response time for such a situation should be within four hours. Priority three was a machine that was operational with a minor problem like a squeak. Eight hours was to be our maximum response time.

Customers then agreed to tell the customer service support center what priority was involved when they called in a service request. The new set of response times went completely against the conventional Xerox method of response targets, which were tied to a machine's copy volume and not to its operability. Thus the same time target existed for a machine whether it had a minor problem or was completely down.

When the High Rockers first put the new approach into place in May 1989, they struggled to meet the new parameters. The first two months, the team didn't come close to hitting the two-hour limit for top-priority calls. Each day, a chart showing the response times was handed out to everybody on the team, and discussions were held at the weekly group meetings. Month by month, the results improved. Within four months, the High Rockers were in control and meeting the limits on all their calls.

And customers showed their pleasure. In 1989 the team's customer satisfaction rating shot up to 98.7 percent. In August 1990, it hit a perfect 100 percent, where it stayed. That's a pretty incredible achievement. To share their accomplishment, the High Rockers shot a videotape they entitled "16 Minutes," meant as a takeoff of "60 Minutes," that got shown throughout the company.

I can't tell you how gratifying it was to me to see these changes. We had moved from a business in which we had at best a feeble understanding of what customers wanted to a methodical approach to understanding and satisfying their requirements. We had gone from accepting a certain margin of error to striving to do things right the first time. We had moved from an environment in which problem-solving and decision-making were commonly done individually to one in which problems were tackled by teams and decisions were arrived at in a logical and consistent manner.

One of the best indicators I had that we were a different company was my own little secretive way of checking up on our products. Over the years, I regularly ordered Xerox products and had them delivered to my home. I used a pretty convoluted system so that there would be no tip-off that they were going to the head of the company. I wanted to get the same machines that any ordinary customer might receive. Once they arrived, I would install the products myself in the basement with the help of some of the kids. The cellar became my own version of the *Consumer Reports* test lab. I noticed plenty of problems in some of our earlier machines, but there were notable signs of improvement starting with the 10 Series. I ordered a couple of products from the 50 Series and they boasted clear-cut improvement, even in the manuals and instruction booklets. The instructions used to be hopelessly indecipherable. Shirley, who was a lot less versed in the intricacies of copiers than I was, even commented about how clear they had gotten.

Despite the great strides we had made by embarking on our expedition into quality, we still knew there should be no letting up. The quality process was like driving a car. You have to keep your foot on the accelerator or it will stop.

Meanwhile, we had continued to cut back and dismantle our systems businesses, which never came close to what we had hoped for them, and we got more realistic about what Xerox could become. We took a hard look at what we were best at and where we were likely to make our money. This self-examination led us to narrow our focus to the document itself. We no longer felt we needed to be in data processing and personal computers. Clearly, what we excelled at was selling machines that produced documents for the benefit of business users. But by narrowing our focus, we also realized that the opportunities to be mined were substantially bigger than we thought.

We wanted our employees and the outside world to think that we were more sophisticated than a copier company that converted one piece of paper into another piece of paper. Back in 1985, we started thinking about the future strategy for the company in depth, and I organized what was called Xerox '95, an effort by the corporate strategy office to devise what our niche ought to be in 1995. Nadler helped immensely by taking the quality and change principles and applying them to strategy. Out of this work, we started referring to ourselves as a document processing company, which was a sort of play on data processing. That didn't catch on too well, and so we redefined Xerox as simply "The Document Company."

The idea was to convey that we were focused on assisting business people to create, use, and transmit reports, memorandums, and data bases. We intended to transform our paper copiers into versatile equipment that could send documents and graphics to computers and over facsimile machines and could electronically link scores of workstations together.

The document notion wasn't immediately embraced by Xerox employees. Indeed, at first, Paul Allaire was almost alone in endorsing it. We had to wean people from thinking of documents as boring and full of negative connotations. To tutor employees, we began a communications program talking about the importance and elegance of documents and tracing their origin back to the hand imprinted on a cave wall. In the main floor hallway of our headquarters, we put up rows of photographs saluting documents. One showed a man studying his immigration papers. Another depicted a family merrily looking over the architectural drawings of a home they were building. Still another showed a newborn baby gazing at her birth footprints. As the months went by, people warmed to the idea.

As for economic measures, although we had not yet reached our financial objectives, our numbers were definitely on the upswing. Revenues from our core office equipment business increased from $8.7 billion in 1984 to $13.6 billion in 1990. Income rose from $348 million to $599 million. At the same time, our return on assets steadily improved. It went from 9 percent in 1987 to 10 in 1988 to 12 in 1989 and hit 14.6 in 1990. We were in shouting distance of our interim goal of 15 percent. It was continuing to be an elusive struggle to attain the 17 to 20 percent that seemed adequate, but it was getting within reach. Significantly, according to outside estimates we had regained a whopping seven percentage points of market share from the Japanese, moving to nearly 19 percent in overall share of installed machines from a low of 12 percent in 1984. Each point can be worth more than $200 million, nothing to sneeze at. Most important of all, customer satisfaction was up 38 percent in four years.

At the end of 1988, some of our senior management began to look a little enviously at the new Malcolm Baldrige National Quality Award. Various Xerox divisions had already won a bunch of quality awards. The Netherlands was honored in 1984, England picked up an award in 1985, and France won in 1987. But in America, the Baldrige was the coveted prize. It had been established by Congress in 1987 to honor American companies that had made achievements in improving quality. Named for the former secretary of commerce who was killed in a rodeo accident in 1987, the award was loosely modeled after Japan's Deming Award, which has been presented in Japan since 1951 and which Fuji Xerox had already captured.

There was no consensus among the management team over whether it made any sense to apply for the honor. We weren't sure we had accomplished enough yet to have a shot at winning, and thus a few of the executives wondered why we should bother if we didn't have reasonable odds of success. At the same time, some of the results from the quality strategy were flattening off a bit. We sensed that some people were already beginning to take quality for granted. As a result, there were discussions about a way to get the juices flowing again.

Paul Allaire decided that the application itself could serve as a motivator and a very broad benchmark of how good Xerox was. And so at a meeting in December at the Hyatt Hotel in Greenwich, Connecticut, the decision was made to go ahead and apply. I heartily approved. I would subsequently tell people that 10 percent of the reason for applying was to try to win the award; the other 90 percent was to do an objective appraisal of the company's quality efforts. We've since told other companies to make sure their motives are right. Don't set out to win the award, but try to make the company better. Frankly, I didn't think we had much of a chance of winning that year. I fully thought we would win eventually, but not on our first shot.

I know of nothing quite like the Baldrige application. It compels companies to go through a self-examination in seven categories: leadership, information and analysis, strategic quality planning, human resource utilization, quality assurance of products and services, quality results, and customer satisfaction.

It's not like any normal award for which you might have someone spend a couple of days filling out a five- or six-page application. For the Baldrige, applicants have to wrestle with a detailed questionnaire with thirty-three categories, each weighted with a certain number of points out of a total of a thousand—for example, "Employee involvement: Describe the means available for all employees to contribute effectively to the company's quality objectives; summarize trends in involvement." That is worth forty points.

The applications are reviewed by a board of examiners plucked largely from industry, but with a sprinkling of academics and consultants. Companies that pass muster on paper are visited by another group of examiners—this is known as a site visit—to make sure that what has been described is accurate. A nine-member panel of judges then delivers the final verdict. Although the award is public, most of the proceedings are conducted in secret. The applications are treated as confidential and an outside contractor is used to administer the program. The names of unsuccessful applicants are concealed.

To prepare the application, we created a Baldrige team. To head up the unit, we turned to Jim Sierk, who was running the Latin American manufacturing operations out of Rochester. He had joined Xerox straight out of graduate school, and had twenty-five years of experience in purchasing and manufacturing management. He was as able as they came. Sierk took the assignment only after receiving assurances that he would get a fair amount of time from the senior team, especially Paul and myself. He shrewdly knew the work would be thankless without that kind of input. He asked for four hours a week from the top people and we agreed to it. Under Sierk, we patched together a team of twenty people, mostly middle managers, from various parts of the organization. They were housed in a small building all to themselves, tucked away inconspicuously behind a bowling alley in Fairport, New York, a suburb of Rochester.

Once we had formed the team, I got keenly interested and spent a lot of time with Sierk and his group. I won't say the team was unduly optimistic, but the first time I visited its humble quarters, the team handed me hotel reservations in Washington during November 1989 so I could be on hand to accept our award at the Baldrige ceremony. Let them dream on, I thought.

The team was destined to remain in existence for a year, and during that year I learned more about the quality process than at any other time. I realized that it was a driver that could allow you to do almost anything.

To gather the information for the application, Sierk set up a group for each of the Baldrige categories. There were also steering committees. The first category, for instance, was leadership and I was put in charge of that. The human resources category was headed by our personnel chief. This was deliberately designed to get as many people as possible involved in the process. The steering committees went out and tramped through facilities to assemble mounds of data. There was an enormous amount that had to be put together.

Every last thing had to be quantified. You couldn't say, "Oh, we're pretty good at this, not so great at that." You needed hard facts, and a ton of them. We never put a claim in the award application that we didn't have backup data for. We were lucky in that we had been immersed in our quality strategy for a long time by now. The Baldrige people required three to five years of supporting data. In many instances, we had eight or nine years of it. We had been sending out our customer-satisfaction survey to fifty thousand customers a month for ten years.

Whenever a member of the team encountered a flaw that needed fixing, he wrote it down. These flaws came to be dubbed "warts." It was no idle choice. We wanted to call them something that wasn't obscene but that sounded ugly enough that it would get people's attention. No employee liked knowing he had warts in his branch. It was as if you had head lice. The wart work would prove to be a key turning point in the history of the company.

By the end of the process, there were five hundred and thirteen warts. That sounds like an overwhelming number, but we were a big company. Others our size who hadn't even begun to embrace quality doubtlessly could have counted up hundreds of thousands of warts. Some of the five hundred and thirteen were trivial: the halls needed painting in a facility. Others were major: there was difficulty transferring knowledge from one team to another. Some were problems and some were symptoms of problems.

At this point, the team couldn't do anything about the warts, and it wasn't supposed to. All it was charged with doing was identifying them. After the process was over, the team planned to go back and analyze the warts and come up with corrective action.

There was one truly bad flub that I worried might thwart our Baldrige chances. Soon after our 5046 mid-range copier came out, it became evident that it was a bad product. It was an important model, for it anchored the middle market for us. And yet it clearly didn't meet its requirements. Among other things, it operated off a cartridge that lasted far less than it should have, and it was plagued by any number of other reliability problems.

After we did some investigation, we learned that our people knew of the shortcomings before the machine was introduced and yet they were covered up, and at the highest levels. The product should not have been announced and shipped. Unlike the situation with some of our clunkers in the 1970s, we managed to shield the customer from a lot of the 5046's problems by quickly repairing them. By no means was it necessary to recall any of the machines.

But internally, we knew we had screwed up. And what caused me so much distress was that this had happened so far into the quality process. It was the sort of thing that the quality process was specifically intended to prevent. But the old culture of our people being afraid to deliver bad news was not yet rinsed from the company.

I was plenty mad about the episode, and people were removed from their jobs because of it. At our management meeting toward the end of 1988, I said that it was the most embarrassing thing that had happened to me in my business career. "Six years into the quality process," I said, "the quality process should have prevented this. It's appalling that it didn't."

The good news was that we had developed such a commitment to the customer that when the woes of the 5046 were revealed, we did whatever was necessary to placate our customers—including offering replacement machines. In some instances, we simply refused to ship the product and accepted lost sales.

The other bright note was that we later began what we called Presidential Reviews. Paul Allaire initiated them out of his interest in why companies repeat their mistakes. We would assign a team to fully investigate and report back on a product or process, normally something that worked out unfavorably. By examining it under a microscope, we felt we ought to learn enough to avoid making those blunders again. A Presidential Review was ordered on the 5046, and we gleaned a lot of valuable information that should ensure that a troubled product like that never gets out the door again.

We had to live with the 5046 incident and move forward. The Sierk team pushed ahead, working at a feverish pace. Sierk himself enjoyed just three Sundays off during the first six months of the process, and one of them wasn't Easter Sunday. The team worked virtually every night. For meals, it made a regular round of the restaurants in the Fairport area. A tremendous amount of pizza was consumed during the early months, until the team members got so sick of pizza that they issued a decree: no more pizza. Eating pizza became a wart. The team switched to Mexican food. Before long, cartons of Chinese food were the meal of choice. Then Chinese food became a wart.

There were a lot of surprises as the team made its rounds, but the overriding thing that stood out was that Xerox was pretty good. As Sierk would put it, "We felt, wow, we have been doing a good job. We're not so bad. I was a little amazed." Xerox was one of the few companies doing so much benchmarking. It was one of the few companies with executive bonuses tied to quality. People had been so focused on solving problems all the time that they hadn't reflected on all the things we were doing right.

By the rules of the award, the application itself could not exceed seventy-five pages. The first draft that the team wrote totaled an unwieldy three hundred and fifty pages and read like it had been written by a committee. It was rewritten three times before it was trimmed to the proper length and infused with more readability.

After the second draft, the team decided it needed to get a better sense than it could personally furnish of how Xerox stood, and so it hired some Baldrige-trained examiners to score it. This was the beginning of a cottage industry that has since sprung up of Baldrige coaches who nurse companies through the rigors of the application. The examiners evaluated the application and offered some helpful tips on where we were weak. Clearly, there were areas where we didn't know how to even answer the questions.

During the early part of April 1989, we got the feeling from the rumor mill that our application was going to be good enough to notch a site visit. That would mean we were sort of a semi-finalist. Up until then, we had been thinking we would be lucky if we even got a site visit. Winning, however, was distant from our thoughts. Members of the team had visited Westinghouse and Motorola to find out about the application process, and they knew those companies were really good. They also knew that Milliken was impressive, and it had been close the previous year. We figured that it was probably the front-runner to win this time around. All of these companies, as well as IBM, helped us a lot in our benchmarking effort. As we inched toward the deadline date, there was a lot of sharing among contestants.

We submitted our application on the first of May. We deliberately put it in three days before the deadline. We thought that getting it in a little early was evidence itself of a quality process. When I read through its seventy-five pages, I remarked, "This is the equivalent of earning a master's degree in business."

At this point, Nadler and Rickard felt that to prepare senior management for the home-stretch drive for the Baldrige, as well as to help us rethink future phases of the quality effort, it was necessary to scare the top managers a little. It was easy at this point to think things were going so well that we could all relax. And so, in June, Nadler and Rickard ushered Paul Allaire and his senior team, as well as myself, on a one-week trip to Japan. We toured a number of Japanese operations to inspect their quality efforts. Among other things, we saw how Matsushita put together a videocassette recorder. And, believe me, the Japanese were good. Nadler and Rickard wanted to scare us. We came back scared.

In July we were notified that we were getting a site visit. We announced that throughout the company, and there was widespread jubilation. That itself was a victory for us. Now that we knew about the visit, the team began preparing the branches for the examiners. We anticipated what sorts of questions might be asked and made sure the data to answer them were easily retrievable. People spruced up their offices. It was a little like getting ready to play in the Super Bowl. You could feel the spirit building day by day. On their own time, Xerox employees were boning up on quality as if readying themselves for the most important final exam of their lives. One day, following a meeting in Stamford, Nadler accompanied some Xerox executives to see *M. Butterfly* in New York and then to dinner. It was meant to be a long, soothing evening, but all the Xerox executives told Nadler they had to cut the outing short and get home. They needed to do some more studying.

In September the big moment came. Six examiners descended on Xerox. They met with the senior managers, including myself, in Rochester. They went to Denver. They paid a call on Los Angeles. In the space of just four days, they must have spoken to some four hundred to five hundred of our employees, at every level. They talked to clerks, secretaries, workers on the floor, engineers, salesmen. There was no way that all of them could have been fully prepared, and we didn't try to coach them all. But we had done our best to make it clear to as many people as possible what this was all about. They were questioned by the examiners about whether they were part of teams, what quality tools they used, on the quality policy of the company. And, I must say, they saw a lot of very spirited people. At first, there had been an attitude among some people of "Oh, the visit is that day. I'll make sure I'm on vacation." But once people learned more about the inspection, they wanted very much to be a part of it. Even people feeling sick dragged themselves to work.

Once the examiners were done, they gave us no feedback whatsoever. They simply thanked us for our time and went on to their next assignment. Around the Xerox offices, eagerness for news mounted daily.

The Sierk team took a well-deserved, albeit all too short, week's vacation from the rigors of their work and then returned to start wrestling with the mound of warts. It divided them up into categories and drafted recommendations of how to eliminate them. In essence, the removal of the warts would be the goal for the next five years of the quality process.

By now, we began to pick up rumors that we were among the handful of companies still in the stretch drive for the Baldrige. Everyone crossed his fingers. In early November, we got the fantastic news that we were winners. I felt this was overwhelming affirmation that everything we had been doing for the last seven years was beginning to pay off. Literally everyone in the company went nuts. It had been a long time since I had seen so many jubilant faces. There were parties galore and we even worked up a celebration videotape. Rallies were staged, and almost daily you could witness the sort of outpouring of wonderful emotions that you find in the streets of a city when its long-maligned team has won the Super Bowl for the first time. For months, good feelings about ourselves monopolized the company.

The Baldrige ceremony in Washington, where we would actually receive our award, was obviously a very big deal for us. I sincerely wished everyone at Xerox could have attended it, for I felt everyone was responsible for our winning the award. Unfortunately, we were restricted to twenty-six attendees. It would have been easy to just have our top executives go, but that seemed inappropriate. Accordingly, a cross-section of Xerox employees was picked, including some tech reps, union representatives, salesmen, and my personal hero, Frank Enos.

In December we threw a recognition banquet for our Baldrige team. The day before the dinner, I had to go to Germany to attend the funeral of one of our directors, but there was no way I was going to miss that banquet. I got on the first flight back I could, and after an eighteen-hour trip, arrived with barely enough time to get to the event. On the long plane ride, I read the final assessment report and recommendations to senior management from the quality award team, and at the banquet I told the team, "This report is worth millions of dollars to Xerox and far exceeded our expectations."

Shortly afterward, Xerox Canada won the Canadian national quality award. We formally decided that we were going to compete for quality awards in every country in which we did business, and in countries that had no awards, we were going to try to persuade the governments to establish them. Not for self-aggrandizement, but because we realized that competing for these awards furnished senior management with an external focus that is crucial in judging how the company is doing and in setting future goals.

But even before the exhilaration had a chance to wear off, we reminded ourselves that this was not the end. There were plenty of worrisome warts to fix. The Sierk team had whittled away at the five hundred and thirteen warts and came up with fifty key recommendations—virtually all of them managerial in nature—and handed them to Paul Allaire at the beginning of December. Most were adopted. With that, the team disbanded. Some of the members had gotten extremely close, and they all felt pleased that they had been part of that team. It had been awfully hard work, but it was one of the best experiences any of them had ever had.

As for the warts, they continue to be worked on to this day. Some are long-term and some require new systems being put into place. Others mandate cultural changes. These are not quick-and-easy fixes.

Allaire and Nadler organized those warts into six principles on which our intensification efforts for quality in the 1990s were to be based:

1. A customer defines our business.
2. Our success depends upon the involvement and empowerment of trained and highly motivated people.
3. Line management must lead quality improvement.
4. Management develops, articulates, and deploys clear direction and objectives.
5. Quality challenges are met and satisfied.
6. The business is managed and improved by using facts.

But while intensifying our efforts, our priorities remained the same: increased customer satisfaction, improved return on assets, and increased market share. Of these three, customer satisfaction continued to be paramount.

The process of applying for the Baldrige award taught me that Xerox was 20 percent of the way toward becoming the company it should be. For our ultimate goal was to be the best in every category that the Baldrige measures. But the facts that came out of the application were heartening indeed.

Product quality, as measured by defects per machine, improved despite increasingly stringent criteria. The Baldrige examination found that the number of defective parts was reduced from about ten thousand per million in 1980 to three hundred and twenty-five parts per million by the end of the 1980s. Machine performance during the first thirty days after installation showed an average 40 percent improvement from 1985 through 1988. Xerox copy quality was recognized as the best in the world.

Reliability, as measured by machine uptime, improved. The 10 Series was 5 to 20 percent more reliable than its predecessors. The 50 Series improved reliability an additional 25 percent.

Customer satisfaction increased 38 percent between 1984 and

1988. Labor overhead was trimmed by 50 percent. Materials overhead was reduced by 40 percent.

We had begun to build long-term relationships with our best vendors and to involve them in the very earliest phases of new product development. We began to treat our vendors as part of an extended family and to train them in the principles of Leadership Through Quality, as well as other quality processes such as statistical process control and just-in-time manufacturing.

When Congress created the Malcolm Baldrige National Quality Award, the intent was to elevate the quality of American products and thus make U.S. firms more competitive in world markets. Therefore, every company that received the Baldrige Award assumed an obligation to share its quality strategy and practices.

We did our best to try to spread the word on quality—and it wasn't easy. Within hours of our selection, we were flooded with requests for information and guidance. Interest was so great that we created a five-person team in Fairport to facilitate our responses. Within about a year, the team had arranged for more than four hundred and fifty formal presentations to over fifty thousand people. Beyond these, there were at least as many presentations arranged by districts, account teams, and others. We probably reached well over a hundred thousand people. In 1991 inquiries were streaming into the central Xerox quality office at the rate of about thirty calls a day.

Has the award meant new business? Nobody can quantify that, but our account representatives in the field have no doubt that it has. More and more companies are interested in offering quality themselves and that means they want to buy from companies who are committed to quality. When they come to Xerox, they've come to the right place.

14. The Race with No Finish Line

IN AUGUST 1990, when I turned sixty, I kept to my pledge to step aside as chief executive, and Paul Allaire was named to succeed me. Meanwhile, I opted to stay on as chairman.

I felt totally at peace and suffered no post-partum blues in passing on the top job to Paul, for I knew the company had made tremendous progress in negotiating some treacherous shoals. A lot of delightful things kept happening. In 1982 we didn't have a single machine rated as best in class by industry analysts. Now Xerox models were considered the leaders in all seven copier categories. We were the first major American company targeted by the Japanese to regain market share from them entirely on our own. We did it the hard way, without asking for government subsidies, trade barriers, or voluntary import quotas.

Maybe the factor that brought the deepest pleasure was being able to increase vastly the satisfaction of our customers. We did so well at this that in September 1990 we felt confident enough to offer a customer satisfaction guarantee, an extraordinary gesture, especially for a company guilty over the years of marketing so many unreliable products. We called it the Xerox Total Satisfaction Guarantee. It worked like this: if a customer was not happy with his Xerox equipment we would replace it without charge with an identical model or a machine boasting comparable features and capabilities. The guarantee was good for a full three years from the time of delivery. If the equipment happened to be financed by Xerox for more than three years, then the guarantee remained in effect for the duration of the financing arrangement. There wasn't much more customers could ask for than that. Xerox offers the guarantee to this day.

The month after we announced the program, Xerox introduced the

Docutech Production Publisher, the most versatile office machine ever—a $200,000 product that is able to receive electronic images of documents from remote computers, store them, allow them to be edited and shared over computer networks, and then create documents of print-shop quality at blazing speed. It's one behemoth of a machine, weighing in at a full two tons, about six times the weight of an old 914. You need to have some open space for it, because it's roughly the length of a car. We feel the Docutech will go a long way toward reducing the isolation of copiers from electronic office equipment, and we think it will revolutionize the way thousands of businesses produce everything from advertising brochures to bid proposals to contracts to newsletters. It's the wave of the future.

From our standpoint, the product also symbolizes teamwork at its best. Under the direction of Wayland Hicks, Xerox brought together engineers, manufacturing people, and marketers for monthly meetings so they could coordinate their work on the Docutech. Everybody was always up to speed on what the other disciplines were doing. Aptly enough, we called the team the Symphony Group, and it has since become a prototype for other major development programs in the company, including the drive to introduce color copying systems.

I wouldn't be forthright if I didn't admit that there have been some enduring bumps along the way to the reinvention of Xerox. There's no question that I was disappointed in the performance of Xerox stock. If this quality process was so terrific, I was often asked, why hadn't shareholders benefited? I even used to get mail from stockholders in which they would insert tearsheets of ads of our bragging about Xerox's improved customer satisfaction. The letter writers would circle those boasts and scribble underneath, "What about the shareholders?"

I could sympathize with their frustration, for I felt it myself. During the 1960s, Xerox stock used to be known as one of the "Nifty Fifty," because it was selling at such an astounding price-earnings ratio. Incredibly enough, the ratio once rocketed as high as eighty-eight to one in that breathtaking decade. However, during the time I was at the company, the stock clearly did not perform to levels I set in my mind. It had a big run-up shortly after I got to Xerox, but after that it was never an impressive performer for any sustained period. When I became chief executive, shares were selling for about twenty-seven dollars, and my goal was to boost the price to one hundred twenty dollars. I never announced that objective to the outside world, but I did share my aspiration with my management team. Not long before the stock market crash in 1987, the stock crept up to eighty-five dollars, and I fleetingly thought there was hope that we might make that number. But the crash sent it tumbling and I knew it would be extraordinarily difficult to meet my own objectives.

I do think that the stock will bounce back once Xerox's financial results improve sufficiently. Like everyone else, the company has been battling a weak economy as it implemented the quality strategy, and the financial services businesses have recently been a drag on earnings. But I have great faith that under Paul Allaire the results and the stock price will soar to new heights.

Another thing Paul must grapple with is our financial services operations. For a while, they had been a nice aspirin to relieve the pain of the office equipment tribulations. More recently, they became their own headache, and a splitting one. For several years, Crum & Forster performed better than we anticipated and it furnished significant profits when the company sorely needed them. In 1983, the first year we owned it, there was no dilution in our earnings and our stock bounced back nicely. At the same time, the office products business sagged worse than we had anticipated and sorely needed the earnings assistance. So the deal looked pretty good.

Then the insurance industry dove into a tailspin, a much deeper down cycle than anyone foresaw. People said it was the worst since the aftermath of the San Francisco earthquake in 1906. By now, Xerox Financial Services had made a minority investment in real estate, which we viewed as an expanding market. But the move backfired. First property and casualty collapsed, hit by intense competition, low policy prices, and unusually high claim levels brought about by a spate of harsh weather. Everyone was stung by staggering losses, unprecedented in modern times. Then the broader financial services followed down this doomed path. Next, real estate crumbled. There was trouble everywhere we looked.

Crum & Forster managed its portfolio well, better in fact than many of its competitors, but it fared worse in underwriting. One thing I observed was that, to a large extent, many managers in the property and casualty industry are what I call outcome managers. They look at things as a case of "That's the way it is, it's just cycles." You ask them something and they say, "You don't understand, that's the way it is." Still, some people did better than others during these times, and we were not at the top of the heap.

There were a couple of decisions we made that turned out poorly. For instance, the minority investment we made in VMS, a real estate partnership, did not work out. The idea at the time was to participate in real estate, a growing market. But we didn't predict the cratering of the market. In 1990 we took a write-off of VMS that amounted to three hundred and seventy-five million dollars. That really stung.

If I were asked in 1991 if I wished we hadn't gotten into financial services, the answer would be yes, given the current state of the industry. But that's a no-brainer. The tougher question is, Could I have been wise enough to have avoided getting into them back in 1982?

We bought Crum & Forster and expanded Xerox Financial Services for several reasons. We wanted to leverage a strong balance sheet by expanding in a growing market not involved with the Japanese. We did this at a time when the outlook for our office equipment business was far from sure.

One thing to remember is this: had we not bought Crum & Forster, we would have been a significantly weaker company in the early 1980s. I will leave it to others to answer the more difficult question.

Despite a few bad memories, I have nothing but proud feelings about the success of Leadership Through Quality. Which is not to say we didn't learn some hard lessons along the way. We did a lot of things right that allowed us to achieve the transformation that we did—and we also did some things wrong that I hope other companies can avoid.

What did we do wrong? Early on, we failed to focus adequately on core work processes and statistics. We didn't properly integrate the quality process as the business process, and we didn't work on the high service problems in an adequate way. We should have been willing to state clearly in 1983 that customer satisfaction was the number-one priority. As a result, for a long time we created a quality process that was somewhat hollow. For too long, quality was separated from the business. At the same time, we should have been more attuned to the embedded culture at Xerox, particularly the notion that complexity meant control. There was a pronounced feeling that if a report was one page, then two was better, and three was best of all. And there was a strong collusion atmosphere. Whether they agreed with a forecast or not, managers would collude and approve it. Paul Allaire used to joke about how, back when he ran Rank Xerox, he would feed corporate headquarters "popcorn." It took up a lot of space, it was airy and not hard to digest, and it didn't have many calories. Had we attacked this culture problem faster and with more gusto, I am certain we would have seen progress sooner than we did.

Without a doubt, we were clumsy in not picking more talented quality officers at the start, and I should have brought in Paul Allaire earlier to help out. We simply didn't push the operating units hard enough, and that allowed them to get away with doing training and little else. I think it would have been wiser to have had more follow-up education in quality, even to have set up a quality institute of some sort that employees could attend to polish their skills.

Finally, we forgot Leesburg too quickly. We should have kept reminding ourselves how symbolic those two Leesburg meetings were in getting managers committed to this effort. If we had, we would have staged further mini-Leesburgs as new managers moved up the ranks, because too many of them didn't feel they had gotten their fingerprints on the program. We sensed a lot of resistance from groups who had no connection to those first two meetings because they simply weren't around at the time.

But we did more things right than we did wrong. At the very beginning, we made the appropriate diagnosis of how to cure our ills. Quality was the key competitive problem we suffered from, and so a quality process was the right solution. Our timing was certainly good, for the company was feeling enough pain when we started the effort to make it stick. We had the commitment at the seniormost level, and we built a constituency in a very calculated and deliberate manner. The support of our union leadership was absolutely essential. Without the endorsement of the Amalgamated Clothing and Textile Workers Union, which has long understood the important role union workers have played in the success of Xerox, we would have never gotten very far.

But a change of this magnitude is like a conspiracy to cause a revolution. We needed people with a pulse on the company to get things started, and we had them in Norm Rickard and Hal Tragash. We created a highly effective and comprehensive change model, including an excellent training model. We provided every employee six full days of training. Add that up for a hundred thousand workers and it totaled one thousand six hundred and forty-four man-years. That was a big investment, but it was one of the best we ever made. It was important that we were patient and accepted the fact that results wouldn't come quickly. Without question, the successful implementation of a quality process requires continuous self-examination, and the 1987 assessment we did enabled us to move the strategy forward when it stalled. Finally, our pursuit of the Baldrige Award was instrumental as a reenergizing force for the company.

What everyone asks me now is, What next for Xerox? While I was there, I reminded Xerox employees over and over again that the pursuit of quality is a race with no finish line. Nothing ever stands still—not our competitors and not technology. Quality improvement must be a continuous and inexhaustible process. We learned that every time we improved, so did the competition. We also learned that every time we improved, customer expectations increased. And they should. And thus we were part of a never-ending spiral of increasing competition and customer expectations. No matter how good we got, we had to get better.

As I look at the 1990s, I know they will be harsher years than the 1980s. Clearly, there are three powers in the global arena: Japan, Europe, and the United States. Japan is stronger than ever. Europe, which was long thought of as the sick man, is becoming more vibrant than ever. Hence, our society and our very way of life are at stake. If we don't win this economic war we're immersed in, we are destined to end up a larger version of Brazil. I'm convinced the 1990s are going to be more competitive than the 1980s, because Japan will be stronger,

Europe will be stronger, and there are other Pacific Rim countries like Korea flexing their muscles. While American companies are certainly improving and are more competitive internationally than they were in 1980, I have great concerns that as a nation we have not set our expectations and standards nearly high enough. All of American industry must engage in reworking their organizations, personnel practices, and management behavior. We took seven years to reinvent ourselves. Others don't have seven years. They need to take the shortcut of learning from us and others who have gone through this transformation.

When I turned over the top job at the company to Paul Allaire, I wrote him a little note in which I urged him to do two things: "Trust your instincts because they're good, and change the company as fast as you can." I didn't mean change the quality process. That ought to always be there, just the way it was put into place. But he should use that process to make the company stronger than ever. I told him that of all the change we brought about in the last ten years, he needed to bring about even more in the next five. He has come to refer to this as 2X. He says he has to double the rate of change.

Paul is determined to make Xerox more market-driven. He is keenly attuned to the need to satisfy the customer. When he toiled in his father's quarry when he was a young man, his father taught Paul to toss in a few added shovels of gravel in every order. Paul found that customers always noticed the gesture and it helped keep them coming back. That little practice has colored his beliefs ever since.

Xerox remains in heated battle against a large number of potent competitors—Japanese companies like Canon, Ricoh, and Sharp, as well as American companies like Kodak and Hewlett-Packard. I'm convinced that quality alone won't be enough to prosper in an environment changing at an ever-faster rate. As we well know, the Japanese are exceedingly strong in quality themselves. It's doubtful that we can ever do better than to maintain parity with them. So while quality keeps American companies in the game, it doesn't give them the edge that ensures they'll score the most points.

Indeed, the very values embedded in the Japanese culture—traits like discipline, conformity, uniformity—are the values that are fundamental to total quality management. But where American workers shine is in entrepreneurism, diversity, and autonomy. The American response should not just mimic the Japanese. Our American character does not play to it. The American dream is to have your own piece of the action. So our challenge is to move beyond quality to take advantage of the novel strengths of the American worker. And we need to have high sight lines, because the Japanese are still learning new tricks, too.

Right now, Paul is assiduously rethinking the architecture of work and organizations. He foresees the day when Xerox and other big companies will be structured so differently that they will be almost unrecognizable. He wants to rip up the old hierarchical charts, get rid of the restrictive ways in which workers are managed, and start afresh. For jobs to become more meaningful, we need to throw away the old management handbooks and take some gambles. Paul has been promoting empowerment and self-management so that everyone has greater latitude and gets to do more than routine labor. He hopes to fashion groups, organized around natural units of work, that will evolve into self-contained work communities. No longer will there be the all-powerful bosses who bark orders to underlings. Instead, there will be coaches and players working for the common good. There will be new personnel evaluation systems that measure an employee's value rather than how many people he manages. None of this will happen tomorrow, and some people may have trouble adapting to a new environment, but Paul is resolved to seeing it come to fruition in timely fashion.

And so Xerox is revving up for another thrilling journey, and I'm off to a new and challenging assignment where I have set my expectation levels extraordinarily high. I will watch from afar as Xerox races along at 2X speed. And I just hope it never crosses the finish line.

LESSONS

The Lessons of Experience

WALTER WRISTON, who served as CEO of Citibank for many years, was frequently heard to say that "Good judgement comes from experience; experience comes from bad judgement." The gist of his message was the importance of learning, from both success and failure. We believe that the Xerox story is one that is pregnant with the potential for learning.

Up till now in this book, we've attempted to provide you with a sense of the Xerox story, starting with Chester Carlson and Joe Wilson, through the exciting experiences of the sixties, the painful problems of the seventies, and the severe struggles of the eighties when the company found itself under siege, and with Leadership Through Quality, beat back the onslaught that had threatened its very existence. We've also told the story of the two of us, Kearns and Nadler, and our efforts to do a tough job, and learn along the way.

You see, learning is what it is all about. The Xerox story is an interesting tale, but not much more than that if we cannot learn from the experience and draw some lessons for other organizations—corporations as well as other institutions. While we've pointed out some of that learning along the way, we feel that there is yet more to be learned.

During the past decade, Xerox was, of course, a central feature of both of our professional lives. At the same time, however, we were engaged with other companies facing similar challenges. Kearns, through his membership on a number of different corporate boards, was able to observe first hand the challenges of several different companies. Nadler, through his own consulting work and the work of his colleagues at Delta Consulting Group, was engaged directly or indirectly with more than fifty different client organizations during this period. Both of us were involved in numerous benchmarking trips to learn from other companies, both in the United States and abroad.

These experiences, combined with our work together at Xerox, have helped us to draw some lessons which we feel apply to the problems that many organizations are facing in these times. In the remaining chapters of this book, we seek to articulate and share some of the key lessons of our experience.

We will begin by discussing the causes of organizational decline. Xerox in the seventies provided an example of decline, but the actions of Xerox managers were not unique. In the second chapter we will discuss quality and address the question of what quality is and how we think about it. In the third of these chapters we will discuss how to manage organizational change and then discuss specifically some of the lessons concerning total quality management as one type of change. We then will talk about the role of the leader in the management of change, and in particular the requirement for dynamic and visible leadership as well as the requirement to move beyond the reliance on one dramatic leader. While we're thinking about leaders we also will share some views on why the CEO would want to make use of the consultant and build the type of relationship that we had for so many years. We then will talk about the future, and consider some of the directions for change that build on and go beyond quality. We believe that there are some unique characteristics of this country that could serve as a competitive advantage in global competition if we can figure out ways to harness our strengths. Finally, we will share some closing thoughts on how our institutions might begin to move from decline to competitiveness.

A Handbook for Decline

Once one has watched enough fabled corporations skid uncontrollably into decline, it's hard not to wonder: What happened? Did they grow arrogant? Did the times simply pass them by? Did they have a miserable streak of bad luck?

We think the answer is a little more complicated than that, and in our view the blame rests squarely with the corporations themselves. One of the fundamental things organizations instinctively do is institutionalize the things they did that made themselves fat and sassy. They sort of hardwire these behavior traits into the way they work. In reasonably stable environments, that's a perfectly good procedure to follow. What has worked well for me ought to continue to work well for me.

But environments rarely remain stable, and so what happens is that the sources of success in the past become the seeds of failure in the future. Over and over again, we've seen this pattern. As should be clear by now, that's exactly what happened at Xerox. We had lots of people at Xerox who were very proficient at selling copiers into an expanding marketplace in which there was virtually no competition. Once the environment changed, the old mind-set worked against the organization in a deadly way.

It's pretty easy to understand why this is allowed to happen. Large organizations tend to be well buffered from the outside environment. As a result, they are not apt to see and feel their failures. We are always struck by how you can stroll into a big company and, whether it happens to be experiencing good years or bad years, everything appears almost exactly the same, down to how healthy the ficus trees look. If you're a modern executive, you drive up in your car to the corporate headquarters and the grass is still clipped and the flowers are still blooming. You walk in and the receptionist says "Good morning" in a cheerful and possibly sincere voice. Life goes on. You see all the trappings that prove how successful the company has become and how successful you have become and what a big deal you are. This leads to your denying the data presented to you that show the company floundering. The trappings work against the actual situation and so you end up not believing it. After all, you don't see customers or hear from them. If the company were in sad shape, then the flowers ought to be dead.

To find out how companies can become much more effective, we think it might be useful and interesting to turn the matter around and pose the opposite question: What are the sources of competitive decline?

It's a question worth asking, because in virtually all of the industries in which we now suffer significant problems of competitiveness—consumer electronics, automobiles, office equipment, machine tools—not so many years ago American-based companies were overwhelmingly dominant. So how did we lose it?

To answer that, we've stitched together what we call a handbook for competitive decline, a succinct set of instructions to put your company out of business. There are ten chapters. Each describes a course of action to follow. If you follow them all, don't expect to be around much longer. See you at the graveyard.

Chapter One: Assume the Customer

This opening chapter instructs you to assume you own the customer, that you know what he wants better than he does and that he will remain loyal to you no matter how much you abuse him. The chapter also advises you not to waste your time measuring customer satisfaction and definitely not to pay attention to or respond to customer complaints. Who does that customer think he is anyway!

Chapter Two: Disinvest in Quality

This follows nicely from the first chapter. It assumes that the customer doesn't care one whit about quality and won't notice any differences in quality between one product and another. So don't even try to meet customer requirements. Do whatever you want. Don't bother investing in improving work processes and reducing error. Put the money into the corporate airplane and stock option plans.

Chapter Three: Ignore Design

This argues that you don't have to fret about industrial design and the aesthetics of your products and services. After all, design costs money. Why should customers care what anything looks like?

Chapter Four: Deemphasize Manufacturing

Don't pay too much attention to how the product is made, to improvements in the manufacturing process, or to the relationship among design, development, engineering, and production. Keep anyone with manufacturing experience well away from the executive suite. The true secret of success is to completely get out of the business of producing things yourself.

Chapter Five: Avoid the Low End

Listen, there's not much money to be made there, the margins are ludicrous, you have to spend so much time on process improvements just to save a few pennies, and the competition is brutal. Foreign competitors who jump into the low end don't have the capacity or skill to move into the bigger markets, so why worry.

Chapter Six: Do It Alone

We all know that real men don't eat quiche and real men don't do joint ventures. So if you're a real man and any good at what you do, steer clear of entangling alliances and confusing arrangements. Do it all yourself.

Chapter Seven: Underestimate Competition

Don't lose any sleep over your competitors. They're probably not any good anyway. Relax and assume that the competition is standing still and you can plan to compete tomorrow with what they have in the market today. Be comforted by the fact that competitors have been more lucky than good, and no one stays lucky forever.

Chapter Eight: Organize Traditionally

Nothing beats traditional organizational structures and processes, and in particular fractionated work, steep hierarchies, and large powerful staffs. Cut your costs by firing people or reducing levels, but make sure you maintain the same basic approaches to organizing. It got you this far.

Chapter Nine: Develop Talent Narrowly

Keep your people, especially your management, focused closely on their own special function, discipline, product, or geography. Why worry about the broad development of people over time?

Chapter Ten: Don't Question Success

Assume that the sources of success in the past will continue to be the seeds of triumph in the future. Don't spend time dwelling on failures or reflecting on mistakes. There are no lessons there. If it worked before, it will work again. If it ain't broke, don't even think about fixing it.

Sure, this seems like a ridiculous list. Who would possibly buy such a handbook, no matter how well-priced we made it, not to mention follow what it prescribes? The sad truth is that we see many companies that appear to be working straight from these ten chapters. Maybe they haven't mastered all ten of them, but they've come pretty close. It's fair to say Xerox did just fine with nine of the ten. We can't totally fault it on engaging in joint ventures, though it could have done more of them, especially in the systems area. Many big companies would score as badly, if not hit all ten.

We feel that decline feeds on itself and organizations get into almost defensive postures. So managers lay off people, thereby breaking their contract with employees and increasing disaffection. They cut costs, thereby decreasing the emphasis on quality. So you can pretty quickly get into a death spiral. You need a fairly dramatic breaking of the frame.

We're not saying it's easy to avoid these mistakes. We have both sat in a lot of meetings where managers lament, "What will the analysts say?" The credo of so many top managements is "Never surprise or disappoint the analysts." One of the key predictors of CEO turnover, outside of age and health, is results significantly different from the predictions of financial analysts.

For far too long, managers have been terrified of breaking out of their old molds. Well, they can't sit around much longer and watch their companies dissolve before their eyes. It's high time executives found a new handbook to study and stopped reading our dismal little offering.

What Is Quality Anyway?

THE SOLUTION THAT HALTED the decline of Xerox and richly rewarded it with a new vision was quality. By now, that magic word is on the minds of just about every corporate executive—or at least it ought to be. But for all that has been written and spoken about quality, more companies than not seem baffled about exactly what it is and why they should be thinking about it.

We have a very simple view of quality. We believe that the world is made up of customers and suppliers. The customer comes to the supplier with a set of requirements and expectations. The supplier provides customers with what we call an offering.

People commonly think that customers buy a physical product. They buy a CD player or a popcorn maker. They really don't. They buy a total experience—the nomenclature, the software, the instruction booklet, and so forth that come with the popcorn maker. When that total offering satisfies the requirements and expectations of customers, then you have a happy situation. You have achieved quality. If any part of the offering is wanting, then discontent results. You don't have quality.

The need to pursue quality is obvious. In the past, there often were monopolies and oligopolies, which didn't provide many offerings for customers to choose from. But that all changed with the entrance of new suppliers, most notably the Japanese. They came in and provided competitive offerings that meshed better with the requirements and expectations of customers. And so they captured a great deal of business.

As a result of this, customer expectations have been raised to new levels and fresh requirements have been established. Back in the 1960s and early 1970s, Americans bought cars that on average had twenty-three defects in them. In those days, car owners would keep a pad and pencil handy in the glove compartment to write down the defects that they spotted. Then they would take their lists to the car dealer and try to get the defects fixed, sometimes succeeding. None of this seemed to bother us all that much. We didn't know then that we really wanted to have cars with fewer defects, not to mention no defects at all. Then one day we were able to buy a Datsun and there was nothing to write down on the pad. Expectations were radically changed. Cars with twenty-three defects were now for losers.

As customers discover that they have choices, quality becomes a core competitive issue. Eventually, quality becomes a matter of survival, as it did at Xerox.

According to this perspective, the only reason to engage in quality is if you believe there is a marketplace—in other words, customers who have choices among different suppliers. If you believe your industry is on the brink of having new entrants—like consumer banking—you could be the one to change the rules yourself.

By our definition of quality—an offering that meets or exceeds customer requirements—what is quality one year is not necessarily quality the next year. It's not a constant. And so suppliers can be drivers of quality. Quality management therefore boils down to developing and operating work processes that are capable of consistently designing, producing, and delivering high-quality offerings.

What, then, is total quality management? This is the business process itself. It is not something that you lay on top of what you do. It is what you do. It is creating and implementing an architecture of organization that motivates, supports, and enables quality management in all the activities of the enterprise.

To help distinguish what we're talking about, we've identified six core concepts of quality, and they're worth listing.

1. The customer/supplier model. This has been derived from the work of W. Edwards Deming. Early on, he had the notion that the

world was composed of customer/supplier chains, and quality was created all along the chain. It used to be that one only looked for quality at the final output point. You fixed things there and tried to meet customer requirements. This was the U.S. approach to quality, and it was a brutally expensive way to accomplish it.

2. Process control and capability. This means you need to look at all the steps in the work process to ensure quality. This requires the use of quantitative tools like statistical process control. This was something we didn't focus on enough in the beginning at Xerox, and it was one of our worst mistakes.

3. Management by fact. You need to collect plenty of data from the chains if you're going to manage effectively. You can't do it through guesswork.

4. Problem-solving. You have to take that data you collected and use it to identify problems and come up with solutions.

5. The cost of quality. To figure out what quality costs you, you need to look at several elements. If you wait and inspect things once they're done and then try to fix problems, you incur a number of expenses. You are building things you can't use, called scrap, fixing things later on in the marketplace, called warranty costs, and making customers unnhappy who don't return to buy from you, called lost opportunity. One of the major lumber companies finds that customers paw through two-by-fours at lumberyards to pick out ones they like. Rejected strips get returned and scrapped. The lumber company says there is no such thing as a perfect two-by-four, but there is one that meets customer requirements. If the company could make it right the first time, it wouldn't have to throw all that product out. All of this is very expensive, though tough to quantify. The number, however, is huge. Essentially, the cost of quality is the cost of conformance plus the cost of nonconformance. Phil Crosby reckons that the cost is 20 percent of the revenues of a manufacturing company. Some say the Japanese cost is a mere 3 percent.

6. Teamwork and involvement. The notion here is moving from the idea of quality as a bunch of engineers sitting on the side to getting everyone involved. Employees want to work hard and are interested in

the future of the institution. It's management's job to create the appropriate environment to allow them to work well.

When you reflect on quality, it is also important to take note of what quality is not. It is not "everything"—the single answer to all your woes. There are any number of quality zealots around who think no matter what the problem, quality is the answer. Don't believe it.

It is not a substitute for "KKD"—a Japanese expression that translates into knowledge, experience, and guts. Tony Kobayashi of Fuji Xerox says that to run a company you need TQC and KKD. Without the KKD, you can't get the TQC.

Nor is quality a substitute for good strategic decison-making. Managers get paid to make decisions, and while quality will help them it won't guarantee that they make the right decisions.

By no means is quality a replacement for an effective organizational design.

And, finally, quality is not a substitute for selecting the right people. The wrong people can do much better with quality than without it, but you're unquestionably best off with the right people.

Once you've got a good feel for what quality is and what it isn't, you're a long way toward determining whether you need it and what it can do for you. We're strong believers in quality, but we're also strong believers in your understanding what it is.

Managing Organizational Change

YOU CAN TAKE IT FROM US that instilling quality in a corporation is no simple undertaking. There were easier ways to have spent seven years. Change sends chills down a company's spine, and any change keeps you pretty busy. But introducing quality really keeps you busy. All sorts of change occurs in a corporation: strategic, structural, cultural, technological, mergers, downsizing, growth. Introducing quality and making it stick is one of the most pervasive, for it embodies strategic, cultural, and usually technological elements. If you hope to be successful at it, you really need to start by comprehending the tricky subject of organizational change itself.

The concept we like is that to bring about change a corporation must pass from its current state to a future state. In between it moves through a transition state. And it's essential that there be a willingness in the corporation to think hard about this transition state, something managers often find repugnant. You can get managers to go off and dream about the future state. They love that. All the products are terrific and the profits are rolling in. It's like dreaming about a vacation on a tropical island. But they hate to reflect on the wrenching transition period. That state is flush with uncertainty, instability, and stress—but there's no avoiding it.

One of the shortcomings of American corporations is that they have focused far too much on good strategy and not nearly enough on good implementation. There's often plenty of strategizing but no hooking that strategy to what's do-able. That happened for a long time at Xerox. Not surprisingly, the Japanese behave differently. The Japanese actually relish thinking about how to get from here to there, and they love to map it all out on big charts. When they think about transition, they don't even wince.

So what constitutes successful change? Essentially, it happens when the organization manages to reach the future state and function as was planned. At the same time, the transition occurs without undue cost to the organization and to its employees. If you change a company and everyone in the place is morbidly depressed, we wouldn't consider that successful change. If the place ends up broke, that's not successful either.

Bringing about change, however, is more difficult than it might seem. It would be nice to think of a company as a big machine where parts can be replaced at will. But it is nothing of the sort. It is made up of people whose behavior is not altered very easily and without noticeable consequences. The good news is change infuses an organization with a challenge, excitement, and opportunity. But there are clear-cut problems.

Power struggles inevitably get triggered. All organizations are made up of political factions. During periods of stability, you can bet that there is far less political activity than there is during periods of instability.

There is also widespread anxiety. "We're going to change the company" are not words that make most employees giddy. They rarely inspire reverence. Not long ago, at an oil company, when change was discussed at a meeting of top management, one person spoke up and said, "There are nine questions on everybody's mind. The first three questions are, 'Me, me, me—what's going to happen to me?' The next three are, 'When, when, when?' And the final three are, 'Why, why, why?'" That's a pretty common reaction. In fact, anxiety gets so great during periods of change that employees don't even hear the messages they are being told and have to be told over and over again. We certainly found that out at Xerox.

The last problem of change is there is a loss of managerial control as the current state is disassembled and before the future state is put into place. This was a major thorn at Xerox. Everyone fears losing revenues while the company is torn apart, especially since the change normally takes place when the corporation is already in a troubled state that has left it weak and vulnerable.

What must be done to manage change effectively? First of all, it is necessary to shape the political dynamics and build support with key power groups. There are three types of people: the ones who make it happen, the ones who help it happen, and the ones who let it happen and get in the way. To deal with these various groups, there is an array of options: you can persuade, offer incentives, isolate, or, if nothing else works, fire people.

Next, one needs to employ the leader's behavior to create support. If the leader isn't convincingly behind the change, it hasn't got a chance.

You must use symbols and language. They really do work. At Xerox we had our little quality cards that people tucked away in their wallets and purses and there's no doubt that they helped seduce employees into joining the crusade. At Corning everyone who goes through quality training gets a gold apple quality pin. It doesn't matter what you use, but use something.

Then you need to define the points of stability, to make sure that it's clear what isn't changing. Some things, of course, ought to and must remain the same. If you tell people what they are, you avoid having people waiting for the other shoe to drop when there is no other shoe.

You also have to create dissatisfaction with the status quo. Otherwise, why are people going to work hard to disrupt it? And you can't wait around until everyone feels pain from the marketplace, because then it's too late. So you need to use some induced pain. You have to throw a few punches here and there. One good way is to use competitive benchmarking to inform people of how badly they're doing.

And you have to build participation in the planning and implementation of the change. Long ago, there was a piece of research on work in a pajama factory. One group of workers was allowed to participate in bringing about change. A second group had change imposed on them. The first group outperformed the second. The reason is, if I participate in creating the change, I'm going to understand it better, and I'm going to have ownership. We really pushed this hard at Xerox. Which is not to say that you invite participation no matter what the change. You don't have all employees troop into a room and raise their hands if they're in favor of buying an air cargo company. They don't have the expertise to make a decision like that.

You must reward the new type of behavior you're trying to achieve. You surely can't tell people to do one thing and then punish them when they do it or else you'll drive them crazy.

At the same time, you have to provide the time and opportunity for people to disengage from the current state. Change is like a loss to people, and so they will pass through the normal state of mourning. After it embarked on some pretty significant change, Mountain Bell once staged an actual funeral for the old organization. Maybe that sounds silly, but it helped employees adjust.

It's indispensable that you develop and communicate a clear image of the future state, as we did with the Green Book.

And you have to be sure that you use multiple leverage points to achieve change. There are two axes to change—a technical axis and a social axis (meaning the people and the culture). Many managers try to drive change through the technical axis alone, and it doesn't work because the people aren't being touched.

Finally, you must employ a transition management and structures and eventually collect and analyze feedback.

It should be self-evident that total quality management represents a huge change, and it throws a long shadow on an organization. Thus it is foolish to think it will happen overnight. In fact, it will not happen anywhere near as swiftly as most managers would like. Most of the time, it seems to move through a company at geological speed. It's a safe bet that the change in most organizations will take five to seven years. We've seen it time and time again—at Alcoa, American Express, AT&T, Weyerhaeuser, Corning, Johnson & Johnson, Nestle, and, of course, Xerox.

Not surprisingly, that five-to-seven-year time frame is offputting to a lot of chief executives. They would like to see the change tomorrow, and if they have to they'll settle for it taking a year. But the thought of waiting more than five years is disconcerting. Yet if you don't accept this timetable going in, you will never accomplish your goals. That we can guarantee.

If you think about it, it becomes obvious why so much time is necessary. A lot has to happen. How you are going to compete must change. You must change the way you look at your output. You must change the nature of what the work is. You must change people's skills and attitudes. It takes time to change the formal organization and time to change the informal organization.

The length of time required is also a function of the size and the complexity of the organization. You could change one plant a lot faster than an entire company. You can change a small business faster than a big company, but not as fast as a plant.

Through our own hands-on experience, we have arrived at eight insights related to total quality management and large system change.

1. Pain and crisis are necessary. There are no successful examples of change at a large corporation without a major crisis and pain. You simply wouldn't undertake the effort otherwise.
2. Quality must be a way of thinking about the business. It usually takes awhile for people to get it. It certainly took awhile at Xerox.
3. Quality requires a change in the total system—both social and technical.
4. Quality must also be a cultural change.
5. Consistency is necessary in the organization and over time. There are two broad models for implementing quality in the United States. There is the Xerox model, where you push the same tools and nomenclature through the organization. And there is the model where different divisions do different things. You lose a lot of power without consistency. You need to fight the battle of "semantics hill," as we like to say.
6. Senior management has to play a critical role.
7. Unit managers also need to play a critical role.
8. Learning is very important.

There are several broad conclusions to be drawn from these insights. Accomplishing such fundamental change is tough and requires a lot of work. It's a senior management job that can't be delegated. You certainly shouldn't do it unless it's really required, you're willing to make the investments over time, you are ready to stick with it, and it's important to your business.

At Xerox we used this vehicle because we tried a lot of conventional things—cutting out fat and diversifying, for instance—and we realized we weren't even close to solving our problems. If you happen to be in a situation where the supply of your product is limited and demand exceeds supply, you don't need to do any of this. All quality books say that whatever your situation, you should immediately institute system-wide change. Well, the truth is, you don't necessarily have to do this. For some chief executives, that ought to be refreshing news.

It ought to be pretty obvious that it greatly undermines your credibility if you start a quality effort and then a year later you back off from it. Therefore we built an implementation template for total quality management from our experiences.

You must start with the chief executive officer. There are four basic models of CEO behavior.

1. Business as usual. He doesn't get involved at all, but regards quality as a function in the organization.
2. Delegation. Quality is a program. He delegates it and supports it where people want to do it.
3. An agenda item. Quality is one of the few core CEO themes and drivers over a period of years.
4. The agenda item. Quality is the overriding concept and core paradigm for all initiatives and activities in the organization.

To succeed at total quality management, you have to use either 3 or 4 as your model. Xerox chose 4. Choosing 1 or 2 will get you something, but neither will ever get you total quality. It is not something that the top can tell the middle to tell the bottom. You have to walk like you talk.

Having chosen the CEO model, you need to get some lead users. You can't just start the Normandy invasion. You have to have some guerrilla warfare. At Xerox we had Fuji Xerox and some of the efforts Frank Pipp had undertaken in manufacturing.

Early on, you need to do some diagnostics. You have to figure out where the pain is. You have to get the senior management on board (the Leesburg process). Then you have to figure out the implementation strategy and plan to do it. This was our Green Book. The plan must reflect the CEO's commitment, the diagnosis, the experience of lead users, and the senior management.

Rarely does everything work out the way you expect. So you should undertake a broad assessment, probably two years into the process, not four as we waited to do at Xerox. Then learn from it and tinker with the strategy as needed, as we did by emphasizing customer satisfaction as our top priority. And never stop looking in the mirror. You must repeatedly continue to assess yourself and learn. The process never ends.

Beyond the Magic Leader

CHANGE IN A CORPORATION is a drama on a large scale, and the central actor in that drama is the chief executive officer. He, more than any other person or even group of people, determines the final act.

So who do we cast for this prominent role? While leadership in general has attracted a flurry of attention over the years, the more elusive subject of leadership during periods of profound upheaval has only recently been studied. It seems clear to us that a very special brand of leadership is vital during times of wholesale organizational change. We refer to it as the magic leader.

A simplistic definition of a magic leader would be that he is charismatic. But we're talking about something much more complex than that. We don't simply mean someone who delivers rousing speeches and gives good sound bites on television. In fact, these are probably of not much import at all.

To our way of thinking, three major types of behavior distinguish the magic leader.

The first of these is *envisioning*. By this, we mean that the person articulates a compelling vision of the future that people identify with and get excited about. We all know some obvious examples: John Kennedy's idea of putting a man on the moon, Martin Luther King's "I have a dream" speech, Patton's speech about the spirit of fighting men.

By projecting such a vision, the leader furnishes a focus for the company to rally around. It is important that the vision be challenging, meaningful, and worthy of pursuit, but at the same time it must be credible. People must sincerely believe that it is possible to succeed in the pursuit of the vision. Otherwise, why would they pursue it?

While their personal styles inevitably differ, all magic leaders must somehow make their vision clear and compelling to others. And as they articulate this vision, they need to set high standards and make their own behavior a model of what's expected from those beneath them.

The second element of a magic leader is *energizing*. He has to be someone skilled at motivating workers to act. How does he do it? Again, different leaders have their own idiosyncratic styles. But the most common way is to demonstrate his own personal excitement and energy, and then to leverage that excitement through personal contact with sizable numbers of people in the corporation. At the same time, he also expresses confidence in his own ability to succeed. And he points out interim successes as evidence of progress toward the vision.

Finally, the magic leader must invest a great deal in what we call *enabling* the change. By this, we mean he provides broad personal support to members of the organization to help them attain the company's goals. It is not enough that workers are directed toward a vision and motivated by the creation of energy. They often need emotional assistance in accomplishing their tasks. The leader can deliver it by empathizing with others in the company and by showing total confidence in their ability to rise to the challenges.

Incidentally, we don't feel that magic leaders are born that way, or else it wouldn't do much good to list these characteristics. We believe all three sets of behavior are learnable, not simply observable.

On the face of it, magic leadership seems great to have. It is unquestionably inspiring and compelling. But it is also risky. It would be a mistake to assume that a magic leader is a cure-all. In fact, our observations indicate that you buy a whole bag of problems when you get a magic leader.

First of all, the magic leader may become the object of unrealistic or unattainable expectations, and be trapped by the obligation to perform one magical feat after another.

Then there is the matter of dependency and counterdependency. A strong and visible leader triggers markedly different psychological responses among employees. Some individuals, even entire organizations, may become overly dependent on him. If the leader isn't there, they feel that something can't work. No one else will initiate any action. On the other hand, others may become uneasy with a strong personal presence and devote considerable energy and time to trying to prove that the leader is wrong.

Another problem is that the magic leader's approval or disapproval becomes such an important commodity that people may grow hesitant to ever disagree with him. As a result, useful dissent gets suppressed.

What's more, people may feel betrayed if the organization doesn't change and flourish as promised. They get angry at the magic leader. Also, the leader frequently ends up disenfranchising the next level of management in the organization because no pronouncement, directive, or initiative is viewed as completely valid unless it has his personal stamp. The organization starts to believe that no one else can make things happen. As a result, the magic leader may end up underestimating his management.

Finally, there are limits to what one person can accomplish, however magical he may be. And so the leader may find himself hemmed in by the expectation that the magic will continue forever. Like a magician, he has to keep pulling rabbits out of a hat or his credibility is shattered. The question throughout the organization becomes, "What have you done this week?"

What does this add up to? The Delta Consulting Group and Columbia University studied some two hundred and eighty-five companies during a fifteen-year period and found that forceful, larger-than-life leadership at the top is critical to successful change. But they also found that the story is a little more complicated than the mythmakers would have us believe. The ghosts of would-be heroes stalk the corridors of executive suites throughout America. There are any number of charismatic leaders who failed to guide their organizations through the traumas of tumultuous change.

Why is it that some succeed while others fail? The answer is that magic is not enough. Unless the magic leader has developed complementary leadership in the ranks below him, his efforts to bring about change may badly disrupt the organization—or even wreck it.

Effective reorientations are characterized by the presence of another type of leadership which makes sure that individuals behave in the way they are required. We call this second type of leader the "instrumental leader." His strengths are structuring, controlling, and rewarding. He concerns himself less with the grand gestures and more with the myriad mundane matters necessary to nourish change. Usually the people who are great magic leaders don't like to tackle these areas. What we're saying is, to drive change you need two types of leaders because you can't find all these things in one person.

The truth is, while change is an essential fact of organizational life, not all change requires extraordinary leadership. Most change is incremental. It's fine tuning that enables a company to adapt to an organization in flux. But sometimes the organization needs to undertake strategic change. Management asks basic questions: who are we, what business are we in, how do we compete, and what values are uppermost? The answers may set the stage for a fundamental recasting of the organization's philosophy and rationale.

When strategic change dramatically severs an organization from its past, we call it framebreaking, because the frames of reference and definition that had long served the organization are ruptured, and a new structure begins to take shape. Framebreaking is normally a response to environmental and competitive upheavals so dramatic that they threaten the organization's survival. Some obvious examples are the turnabout of Apple Computer, Navistar (formerly International Harvester), and Chrysler.

More often, an organization can adapt with less dramatic, though still profound, changes in its strategy, structure, people, and behavior. In these instances, the changes are relatively gradual and the organization that emerges retains continuity with the past. We refer to such changes as organizational framebending. Xerox, Digital Equipment, NCR, and Kodak are among the many companies that have bent their frames but not broken them.

The magic leader crops up more often as a framebender than a framebreaker, largely because senior management rarely survives the corporate meltdown that leads to framebreaking. Successful framebending is virtually impossible without strong and visible leadership. But in most instances the magic leader's complement is the less visible but equally critical instrumental leader, who puts the changes into effect.

Yet even the best combination of magic leader and instrumental leader can achieve only so much by itself. The companies most successful at change have nurtured skilled leaders at all levels. Unless it already exists, such institutional leadership has to be painstakingly developed with the active participation of the magic leader. A good starting point is to assemble a senior team made up of, say, the people who run the major business units. The top leaders should meet with them regularly, spending as much time as possible with them, so that they truly become a team with an emotional commitment to the new vision. The idea is to make them owners of the process, rather than management centurions executing a set of orders.

The next step, no less crucial, is to extend the boundaries of senior management so that the top thirty to one hundred managers, depending on the size of the organization, also become owners. Ultimately, organizational change succeeds or fails because of the day-to-day activities of employees and managers beyond the reach of top management.

As far as we're concerned, it does no good to glorify the leader as savior. Magic leadership is essential for strategic change, but it is likely to fail without complementary operational and institutional leadership. Organizations need to think harder about developing leaders at all levels so that executive succession brings the right mix of people to senior management ranks. At best, they will then ensure the day-to-day leadership that will keep the institutions from tumbling into crisis in a turbulent environment. At worst, they will provide the magic leaders who can pull them through the next wrenching change. And there's nothing wrong with that.

The CEO and His Consultant

IN USHERING IN SIGNIFICANT change in a corporation, a chief executive can use all the help he can get. He needs his management team. He needs his family. And we're thoroughly convinced he needs some outside perspective and expertise.

Why would any top executive worth his salt go to a consultant for help? What happens when he does?

First of all, consulting is a broad, umbrella term that covers a lot of sins, so to speak. Most people don't understand precisely what it is.

Basically, three kinds of consulting go on, and we think the best way to illustrate them is to borrow the three distinctions coined by Peter Block, a consultant who has written widely and well on the profession. He lays out these models in his book *Flawless Consulting: A Guide to Getting Your Expertise Used.*

The first model is the medical or expert model. In this type of work, the consultant comes in, studies a problem, and tells the chief executive what to do. He is afforded free reign, and virtually becomes a part of the manager's staff. In essence, the CEO is admitting that he doesn't have the knowledge to figure out the solution and to fix it, and so he places himself completely in the consultant's hands and just asks that he be kept posted on what he's doing. The role of the manager in this model is limited to evaluating the work after it's completed. The manager isn't expected to develop the necessary skills so he can handle the problem if it recurs. In effect, the consultant gives management a couple of shots and suggests some pills to swallow.

Then there is the pair-of-hands model. In this arrangement, the consultant is hired as an extra pair of hands for the management team. This most commonly occurs when management has identified a problem and a solution to it, but it doesn't have the time or resources to deal with it. And so a consultant is retained to perform the work. It could involve doing a study or some task like programming. The role is not to solve a problem but to complete an identified job. It is a very passive role. The consultant is given specific marching orders and control rests totally with the manager. In this model, of course, the consultant is totally dependent on the manager having made an accurate diagnosis and having come up with a sound solution. For if things don't pan out, the consultant usually gets heaped with the blame.

Finally, there is the collaborative model. In this situation, the consultant and the client engage each other in a relationship, but the client does not relinquish ownership of the problem. And thus you solve it together. That is what Delta Consulting does. It is the least common form of consulting and the least rewarding economically. It is highly time-consuming and labor-intensive. It's almost a teaching type of role. You're trying to transfer knowledge and if you do it well you may do yourself out of a job. For then the student becomes the teacher.

Why should anyone engage such a consultant?

This question gets asked a lot, because to some managers it's a sign of weakness that they need to hire a consultant and to rely on him in any significant way. If a manager is good enough to rise to the top of a large corporation, why should he need anyone else's advice, particularly an outsider's?

Well, managing is hard and has gotten a lot tougher. So managers find they need help. And that help is often all but impossible to find inside the organization, especially if the issue is organizational in nature. If you want to change an organization, then that's the worst time to go searching for inside advice. People within the company are all armed with their own agendas. Bob Allen, the chairman of AT&T, once said that asking phone company people to describe the organization was like asking fish to describe the ocean. You need to be outside it to really see it for what it is.

Another problem: it's hard for a CEO to get useful answers from people beneath him in the organization. And so he turns to outsiders with expertise whom he trusts. A consultant brings experience. He's been there before. Whereas a manager may become the CEO for the first time in his career, a consultant may have seen dozens of CEOs come into their positions. Also, CEOs like to hear about how other CEOs deal with problems. Consultants can effectively introduce CEOs to other CEOs so they can share thoughts. There's a network value involved.

Moreover, consultants serve as sounding boards at minimal cost. If a chief executive tells one of his key executives, "Hey, I'm thinking of doing a reorganization," and the other executive sees that he receives a huge promotion out of it, he says, "Terrific, when do we start?" And then if the CEO ultimately decides against doing it the way he had spelled it out, he's got a touchy problem. Managers are great CEO watchers. They are always looking for signals. So a consultant allows for a private audience in which ideas can be discussed and kept secret from the rest of the organization.

A final, not insignificant factor is that the consultant has no career aspirations or corporate agenda within the company. His only hope is to continue to get more work. And that freedom facilitates the consultant being a source of honest criticism and feedback. The CEO doesn't have a boss to watch over him. The board of directors doesn't really serve that purpose. And so the consultant is able to step in and fill that role.

Needless to say, for a consultant and a CEO to be able to work together in a meaningful way, they have to trust each other. One of the key questions the CEO has to ask himself is, Does this consultant care about my being a successful CEO? The answer has to be a ringing yes. Picking the wrong consultant is like choosing a dishonest auto mechanic. You get told there are thirty things wrong with the car when there are only two. The CEO has no other good way to double-check on the accuracy of the problems confronting him unless he finds a trustworthy consultant.

What's more, it's important that a consultant avoid becoming a conduit for other people to funnel information to the CEO. You can't have managers thinking, "I'll tell him this so he can pass it on." People ought to tell the CEO themselves. CEOs should get as much data as they possibly can directly from the source.

And a CEO has to like being with the consultant. It's a fairly intimate relationship. If there's no rapport, why spend so much time together? Any seasoned consultant knows he does his best work when there is harmony with the CEO and he sincerely cares about his success.

Which is not to say that there isn't a potential danger lurking in this last point. If he becomes too intimate, the consultant may tend to pull his punches to detrimental effect. Because he wants the CEO to like him, he may start to see things through the CEO's glasses and not his own. If you're honest, you have to risk being thrown out of the CEO's office.

We can cite one fairly recent example. In this instance, the CEO's skills were not all that impressive and his ability to lead was not great. His cronies were no better. He decided he wanted to undertake a quality effort but it flopped because people simply didn't have faith in the leadership. For months, a consultant from Delta told him that he needed to change his management team, but he was incapable of making the decision to fire people. After the most interminable amount of time, he looked at the data he was presented with and said, "I'll have to think about this some more, and so let's meet next month." The Delta consultant said, "No, we're wasting our time. We're meeting with you and thus colluding and making it seem like we're making progress when we're not."

This is what has to be done sometimes as an honorable thing. If you're not having an impact, you have to walk away from the business.

In another case, a CEO wanted to set up an office under him of three equal senior executives. Delta told him that in this particular case it was a lunatic idea. The three guys didn't like or respect one another and harbored radically different views of the world. They also saw each other as competitors for the top job. The advice ended the consulting job. The CEO did go on to create the office and it never worked. Two of the executives left, and the one who remained was clearly the worst of the lot. Being right isn't enough sometimes, but you need to take these kinds of risks.

The message we're trying to get across is that the CEO has to be able to take criticism, hard as it is to do. Some CEOs find themselves saying, "Hey, this consultant never has anything good to say." It may seem that way sometimes, but it's the nature of the work.

What does a collaborative consultant actually do?

Well, he needs to have a lot of time alone with the CEO. There are no shortcuts. A few phone conversations and some faxes won't suffice. Delta usually insists on monthly meetings, often with no prescribed agenda.

A lot of times, the consultant will attend the company's major management meetings, where he can see how things play out and talk with others beyond the CEO. Time and again, the consultant finds himself trying to be used and influenced. Sometimes it's patently obvious. The same ploys and the same games get used over and over again. But whatever information he gathers can be useful, so long as he knows what he's getting. There are always going to be feelings of resentment, distrust, and fear. That comes with the territory. It can take a couple of years for a management team to accept a consultant fully into a company, even if the CEO trusts him right away. You can't order trust.

A key thing a consultant has to remember is this: each relationship is different. You don't want to remake people, because you're not going to be able to do that. You can't change someone in his fifties who's been rewarded and told he's successful for the way he's behaved. You need to try to help someone become a stronger force within the context of his own particular style.

Not the least important characteristic of being a good consultant is picking the right clients. A consultant is only as good as his clients' success. He can't be any better, and he *can* be worse.

A Uniquely American Solution

XEROX PURSUED TOTAL QUALITY management because it was the right approach at the right time. And it paid dividends in spades. Now scores of companies, persuaded that quality ought to be their best friend, are trying to practice this very same concept. In fact, at a recent gathering of representatives from nearly fifty companies, more than 80 percent of them reported that they had kicked off total quality programs.

That's all well and good. But we may be missing the point. The key to American competitiveness is not to mimic others but to play to our own competitive strengths.

Why did TQM, an American invention that initially sprang from Bell Laboratories, take root so well in Japan? Much of the reason is that its inherent values fit so ideally with Japanese values: discipline, conformity, and identification with the enterprise. TQM stresses duty and obligation to the group rather than the individual, and consistency rather than variation. That's the Japanese way to the tee.

American workers, on the other hand, subscribe to some sharply different values: innovation, entrepreneurialism, autonomy, teamwork, and diversity. Indeed, the dream of many American workers is not to rise through the ranks to middle management of a large corporation, but to strike out on their own and start a business, to leverage their own creative energies, and to grab a piece of the action for themselves.

So where does this leave us? It implies that opportunities for true competitive advantage lie in directions markedly different from those now in vogue. Granted, total quality management is an extraordinarily powerful tool, but we're kidding ourselves if we think we'll ever be better at it than the Japanese.

There's no denying that you need quality to play the game in today's world. It's the ticket of admission. But it's not the way to win anymore than defense alone is the way to win a football game. Xerox can't beat Canon on quality alone. Quality is a big step. In many industries, it may indeed be required to survive, but it ultimately may not be sufficient to succeed.

Remember, one thing quality doesn't do is change the inherent nature and structure of the work in a corporation. Rather, it assumes that they are sound. But are they? We don't think so. In the long term, we believe that some big payoffs for corporations will come from rethinking how they organize work, information, and people—in other words, from entirely new architectures.

We believe we need to take a much broader view of organizational design. For we're convinced that architecture itself can be a remarkable source of competitive advantage. Year after year, many cherished assumptions of design are being disproved, and still more will be. The biggest one to fall is the much trumpeted advantage of economies of scale.

One way we like to think of this change is that people have moved away from load-bearing walls to structural steel. Load-bearing walls used to restrict builders from going beyond a certain height. When structural steel came along, buildings could rise to unheard-of levels. Right now, corporations are likewise discovering some wondrous new building materials that can elevate them higher than they ever thought possible.

A simple way to look at organization design is in terms of information processing. A core task of organization design is the processing of information. Most of what moves around Xerox and most companies is not copiers or refrigerators or pretzels but information—written, spoken, and electronic information. Classical organization theory says that the way to coordinate information among groups is through hierarchy. You carve up work into the smallest possible groups and then create supervision and coordination. This is what is known as machine bureaucracy. Today we have exceedingly steep hierarchies, and they have some serious drawbacks. Fishy odors have been emanating from them for years. Their costs are high, they are lethargic to react, and the jobs created by them for lower-level people are often miserable.

But now there's an attractive alternative to machine bureaucracy because of information technology. It provides things like electronic mail and knowledge-based systems that obviate the need for hierarchies. Information technology enables companies to coordinate behavior without control through the hierarchy. It allows for autonomous units to be created that are linked together through information. It allows more "loose coupling" without running the risks of lost coordination and control.

Hierarchy is load-bearing walls. Information technology is structural steel—a new way to frame a building.

Recently, we've seen a whole host of leading companies bringing in truckloads of structural steel, including Procter & Gamble, Corning, Hewlett-Packard, Digital Equipment, AT&T, and Xerox. All of them are experimenting with and learning about new work architectures to create new ways of working. The basic idea they're developing is to organize around self-managing "micro-enterprise units"—work units or teams that encompass an entire end-to-end work process linked to a product or service. These units are microcosms of the full enterprise, but are endowed with great autonomy to structure and manage themselves. At the team level, they operate without supervisors, design their own work processes, cross-train to create multifunctional people, and share in the financial benefits of their efforts.

These are some of the types of entities that are evolving as part of the new designs:

• Autonomous work teams. These are self-managing groups, given real power, that undertake whole pieces of work. They've done this in factories for a while but the concept is only now being applied to offices. Procter & Gamble pioneered the idea in this country. It started using it in the 1960s, and has designed all its factories around it.

• High-performance work systems. These are sets of autonomous teams linked by technology into total work systems designed to support autonomy. In other words, whole factories can be created around these teams.

• Alliances and joint ventures. These are done at the tops of organizations and allow you to leverage your true competitive advantage and combine with others who have complementary advantages. Corning's strategy is a perfect example of this. As a rule, we are not very good at it in this country. The Europeans are much better, and the Japanese are learning. But Americans are steadily coming around and doing more and more ventures.

• Spin-outs. This means creating new entities outside of the parent company—in essence, staking entrepreneurs. 3M and Corning do a great deal of it. If you pursue this aggressively, you will ultimately wind up with sets of spin-outs.

• Networks. These constitute combinations of different forms—joint ventures, subsidiaries, spin-outs—with various tight and loose linkages. Scale without mass is achieved. Examples are Corning, which actually describes itself as a network, or Benetton, the clothing chain. Benetton doesn't own its stores or manufacturing facilities, but is simply an information conveyor. We think we'll see a lot more networks, partly because you can't do everything well.

• Self-defining organizations. These are organizations capable of rapid change that can reconfigure in response to or in anticipation of change.

• Fuzzy boundaries. This refers to reducing the boundaries between the inside and outside of the organization. It means including customers and suppliers as part of the organization. Customers then actually become codesigners of products. When Delta Consulting works with clients, it puts them on its electronic mail system. So are they inside or outside the organization? Xerox is engaged in a host of projects with customers in which they help to design new machines.

• Teamwork at the top. This means creating teams to actually run businesses. Sets of people thus play the traditional chief operating officer role. It boils down to a matter of managing diversity with different skills.

By moving toward these approaches, we can get well away from the machine-bureaucracy, steep-hierarchy model of organization that has been part of our heritage for close to a hundred years and move toward fresh models built around autonomous teams. We're seeing it already in places like AT&T's Capital Corporation, Corning's administrative center, and Xerox's customer service teams.

The results are astounding. Data collected from a wide range of applications suggest that costs can be shaved from 25 to 50 percent, while increasing quality. Interestingly, these micro-enterprise units are highly responsive to the use of quality improvement tools, since they can apply these tools to an entire work process rather than a small slice of the work.

Workers, of course, can't help but be encouraged by these developments. More autonomy and self-management lead to an increased sense of worth for them. Many employees have said they feel that their company is drawing on more of their potential. These approaches tap into something that brings together the best of teamwork and the best of individualism. We like to call it "rugged groupism."

We all know that America faces a critical competitive challenge. If we're going to confront it, then we have no choice but to create radically more effective organizations. Quality, high-performance work systems, and strategic organizational design all offer great potential. But the true answer will be the creative integration of these approaches. That is what we think is a Uniquely American Solution.

At a recent seminar in Japan for a hundred and fifty Japanese managers and consultants, one participant made a very telling remark. He said that he had toured some American plants that were using new work architecture and he was astonished at the enthusiasm, knowledge, and abiding commitment of the workers. In fact, he said he felt these factories outshone most Japanese plants. As a Japanese manager who now had to devise effective ways to cope with this tough new competition, he said he found the self-managing organization "the most frightening thing that I have ever seen."

To say the least, this is encouraging. There's no reason to keep trooping to Japan to learn how to manage. Many of the answers to our future are right here.

From Decline to Competitiveness

NOT LONG AGO, the German journalist Joseph Joffe, writing in *The New York Times*, commented that:

> The rivalry of nations in the democratic-industrial world has moved from the battlefield into the economic arena. Nobody expects the Germans to invade Alsace again: now they pay for the pleasure of owning the choice plots there, just as the Japanese are buying, not bombing, Pearl Harbor.

These comments articulate an obvious, but nonetheless important observation. We have entered a period of intensified international economic competition. While this global rivalry is not explicitly violent and does not occur on physical battlefields, it is still a very real conflict with profound stakes. There are battles to be won and lost. There are very tangible casualties in terms of disappearing jobs, damaged or destroyed companies, and abandoned industries.

Recently, we happened to find ourselves on the Amtrak Metroliner, riding between Washington, D.C., and New York. Amidst the other business people buried in their paperwork, we barely noticed the scenes passing by our window. At one point, however, we looked up from our work and found ourselves shocked by the panorama. As we moved north from Philadelphia towards New York, we were moved by the mile after mile of abandoned or decaying industrial buildings. They stood in stark, silent contrast to the scenes we had witnessed not long before when the two of us shared a ride on the Bullet Train between Tokyo and Osaka in Japan, and were impressed by the bustle of activity and the economic vitality that we saw out of that train window. It was almost as if a special message was being sent to us, that our country is in dire danger of losing on the economic battlefield of nations.

That loss is one that gravely concerns us, as it should others. Our country has been built on the foundation of opportunity that stems from growth. The unique idea of America concerns freedom, opportunity, and the individual. At the core of this is the notion that each individual has an opportunity to excel and succeed, regardless of his or her origins, based on the person's efforts and capabilities. That boundless hope comes from the large and growing opportunity space that our economy and our institutions have provided. Long-term economic decline, which starts to limit and indeed shrink that space, therefore poses a threat to our way of life, our values, and ultimately the idea of America.

Therefore, the global industrial competitiveness of the United States must be a concern of all in this country. While we began to awake to this reality in the 1980s, we have tended to do too little too late. The coming years will be decisive.

Our experiences in general, and with Xerox specifically, have led us to think about several elements that influence competitiveness. As with Xerox, there are important factors that are internal to or specific to an individual company. At the same time, one cannot discuss competitiveness without mentioning that there are very real and significant factors that influence competitive effectiveness but are *external* to the single firm. Four seem particularly significant:

> First, there are *structural factors* in the business environment of the United States that may make it difficult for companies to compete. These factors include changing patterns of ownership, the dynamics, expectations, and time frames of the capital markets, and the objectives of institutional investors, all which may make it harder for firms to engage in long-term economic warfare against tough global competitors. Over time, we need to find ways to provide patient capital and create ownership structures so that the interests of owners will align with the longer-term perspectives that are needed to achieve global advantage.

Second, there are *political factors* in the United States that undercut efforts to compete globally. In particular, we're referring to the crisis in education, the lack of concerted government action to stimulate competitiveness, and our antiquated ideas of antitrust law. We must have an educated, skilled, and motivated work force, or we will never succeed. We also need relationships between business and government that help to promote the interests of American companies on the global scene and that recognize the existence of global markets and global competition. Our government should be a partner and supporter of our business enterprises, much as the governments of Japan and France are.

Third, there are *economic factors* in the United States, including the balance of trade, and in particular the Federal deficit, and its impact on cost of capital, that impair the ability of firms to access the funds they need to support competitive initiatives.

Finally, there are *international political-economic factors,* and in particular the behavior of Japan in relation to this country, that make competition on a "level playing field" near impossible.

Now, we could discuss these four factors at length. Our objective simply is to note that part of the answer lies outside the actions of individual firms, in the arena of public policy.

While these external factors are consequential, we do see different companies that are significantly more effective competitors than others, even within the same industry. It appears that the actions of individual companies still explain a lot of the variance in competitive effectiveness. That's clearly what we learned at Xerox, and many other companies have proved that also.

Anyhow, the external factors are complex, problematic, and not amenable to quick fixes. In the near to medium term, corporate leaders have the greatest leverage on the internal factors that influence competitiveness—the characteristics of our organizations that determine how well they can anticipate, cope with, respond to, and master this evolving environment of global economic competition. We intend to focus, therefore, on the internal determinants of competitive success. The core question we want to address is: "What are the critical factors that will enable companies to become radically more effective?"

The simple answer is to look again at our handbook for decline that we discussed earlier, since each chapter has an obvious corollary. We can push our thinking further, and look at what would be called the root causes in quality terms. What are the critical success factors for competitiveness—the necessary and sufficient conditions for success? We believe there are four.

The first critical success factor is *strategy*. A basic requirement for competitive success is viable competitive strategies. Many of the best international competitors, and in particular the Japanese, have been markedly superior in the ability to gain focus and generate strategic momentum over a period of years. They have identified clearer targets (often us), and more specific objectives. They have executed more sustained efforts to achieve those objectives, particularly in their intent to gain global market share.

Therefore, qualitatively different and better strategic thinking and execution are required. In particular, we need to start thinking about global competition, global markets, and the game of global chess that our competitors are engaged in. The leadership of each of our enterprises needs to work to understand carefully what are the unique core competencies that the company brings to the table, and what can truly be sources of sustained competitive advantage. Drawing from the concepts of quality, our strategic thinking must start with the customer and work back until we identify the things that we uniquely can do for or provide the customer better than anyone else. Ultimately, the process of developing strategy may be as important as any particular concept. Specifically, we need to stop separating the thinkers from the doers. Recently some companies have made significant progress in strategy formulation and implementation by having the executive team actively engaged in a process of collaborative strategy development, much as we did when we applied quality concepts to the Xerox strategy in the "Xerox '95" exercise.

The second critical success factor is *quality*. There is now evidence about quality from companies like the Baldrige winners, and in particular companies such as Motorola, Xerox, Milliken, General Motors,

IBM, and Federal Express, and from other firms that have had comparable quality efforts and achievements, such as Corning and Alcoa. Sustained strategic level work on quality can make a significant difference in the capacity to compete in tough global markets, and can lead to the recapturing of lost market share. These companies, and others, have done so through the implementation of "total quality management"—a top to bottom, end to end, strategic, organizational, and cultural change.

We've learned a lot about total quality strategies over the last decade or so. Many of these leading firms have recognized that quality has become a necessary, but not sufficient element of competitiveness. In many industries, providing a quality offering (one that meets or exceeds the customer's requirements the first time and every time) has become the daily ticket of admission or the means for survival. This means that quality is critical, but by itself it is not the assurance of success. Rather, innovation, design, and speed have become the leading edge differentiaters. At the same time, without quality, one cannot continue to be a player.

Another thing we've learned is that the most difficult problems in implementing total quality strategies are not technical, but behavioral. Quality technology is not that new, sophisticated, or complex. It is the challenge of changing the behavior of tens of thousands of people each day toward the customer, toward the product, toward the work process, and toward each other, that is the major challenge in implementation of total quality. Not surprisingly, we've also learned that this change of behavior is tough to accomplish; it takes time (often years), and it requires the intimate and intensive involvement of the senior management.

The third critical success factor, and one that is just gaining recognition, is *organization design*. Competitive success requires successful innovation and speed. The capacity to innovate quickly is emerging as a critical determinant of marketplace success.

Innovation and speed lead us to think about radically different ways of organizing enterprises. Most of our major corporations are organized based on the paradigm of the machine bureaucracy and the theory of scientific management, both of which evolved during the early part of this century. That approach to organizing has become so pervasive that it has become reflexive, or implanted in the genetic code. Intensive competition is forcing us to reexamine this paradigm, and advances in information technology are just beginning to create the potential for new ways to organize, manage, and coordinate work.

We believe that an important opportunity for improvement of competitiveness in the 1990s will be the discovery, invention, and application of what we're calling new architectures of work and organization. In particular, we will need to devise forms that play to the inherent competitive advantage of the American culture and the diverse American work force, rather than mimicking the successes of others, such as the Japanese. It will require boldness and an ability to think outside the boxes and lines that define organizations today.

The fourth and final critical success factor is *organizational learning*. Even those with great strategies, total quality, and innovative organizational architectures don't always get it right the first time. They make mistakes. The best competitors do have a unique capacity to reflect upon and understand the meaning in those mistakes very quickly, and turn insight into action; they are learning-efficient organizations. They learn from customers, competitors, and suppliers. They learn from success and they learn from failure. They encourage the notion of "productive failure" as a key ingredient of the learning process. They recognize that the sources of success in the past are often the seeds of failure in the future.

Competitive effectiveness will therefore require companies to invest in the development of their capacity to learn. It will require significant improvements in the capabilities of individuals, groups, and whole organizations to reflect and gain insight. The key ingredients are the structures, processes, and environments that enable and encourage learning, but also empower people to translate learning into action.

Reflecting on these four critical success factors—strategy, quality, organization, and learning—another implication emerges. It is difficult for executive teams to work on these issues if they are consumed by running the day-to-day operations of the enterprise. Building competitive effectiveness will require significant reallocation of senior management time, and to do that will require the empowerment of managers down in the organization.

In summary, we find ourselves, in this last decade of the century, in the midst of profound change. The basis of the rivalry of nations is shifting to economic terms, at least in the industrial world. Competitiveness has become a critical national concern for us. Both the external and internal determinants of competitiveness require our attention and demand action.

The 1980s witnessed the financial restructuring of much of corporate America. If we are to succeed, the 1990s will need to witness the strategic, managerial, and organizational restructuring of our firms, and the development of new architectures for the enterprise. That's our challenge.

Appendixes

INTRODUCTION

Our description of the development of Leadership Through Quality at Xerox is, of necessity, abbreviated. In a book such as this, it would be impossible to provide a detailed description of each event that occurred. It would also be inappropriate to relate all of the concepts, models, and tools that were either developed or used during the early days of the quality story at Xerox.

Some readers, however, will want to have more information about some of the material that we cover concerning the development of Leadership Through Quality, particularly the material in Chapters 9, 10, and 11. We've included some selected documents that should provide additional detail and information.

APPENDIX ITEMS

Organization Model

In 1982, when Nadler first began working with Kearns, his analysis of the Xerox organization was done using a model of organization developed by him in 1975 while on the faculty at Columbia University, working with his colleague Michael Tushman. This model is described in Chapter 9, but is perhaps better understood through the graphic description included in Appendix 1.

Change Management Model

The basic model that Nadler used to develop the implementation strategy and architecture for Leadership Through Quality, as discussed in Chapter 9, was first published in an article by him in 1981. At the core is Richard Beckard's view of change as a movement from a current state to a future state, through a transition state. In Nadler's integration of the change management research literature, he proposed three basic organizational change problems: power, anxiety, and control. He then identified a set of practices that appeared to be associated with the more successful management of change. Appendix 2 is a summary of these twelve change management principles.

Key Events in the Development of the Leadership Through Quality Change Strategy, 1982–1984

From October 1982, when Nadler and Kearns began to work together on an organizational change strategy, through February 1984, when the Kearns "family group" was the first management team to be trained in quality, many events occurred. We described some of the highlights in Chapters 9, 10, and 11. For those who desire a more structured description of the events, Appendix 3 includes a flowchart of the key events during this period.

Xerox Corporation: Leadership Through Quality—Definition

In December 1982, one of the key questions that people asked about quality was "What is it?" During a trip by Nadler and Norm Rickard to visit management training classes at the Leesburg Center, Nadler developed a definition of Leadership Through Quality (at that point still called Commitment to Excellence). This approach, called the "Three Circles," continued to be useful and ultimately found its way into the Green Book. Appendix 4 is the final version (from the Green Book) of the Three Circles diagram.

Summary of Key Decisions

The first senior management quality meeting, held at the Xerox Leesburg Training Center in February 1983, was designed to be a high-involvement, participative event (see Chapter 10). The objective was to involve the twenty-five most senior managers of the corporation in shaping the quality strategy and its implementation. The basic device used to structure the participation was a set of thirty-four questions that the core planning group (Nadler, Rickard, Tragash, Dukenski, and Kelsch) developed. During the two and a half days, the group of managers worked in various large and small group settings to develop and agree upon answers to these questions. Through that mechanism, they shaped the strategy and developed their own feelings of ownership. Appendix 5 lists the thirty-four questions that were developed for Leesburg.

Xerox Problem Solving Process

One of the core activities in quality improvement is problem solving. Prior to the development of Leadership Through Quality, Hal Tragash had been involved in setting up employee problem solving teams throughout

Xerox. Tragash found that teams would be more effective if they shared a common set of tools and thus a common language around problem solving. He decided to use a six-step process, based on generally accepted methods for effective group problem solving. In 1982–83, as Leadership Through Quality was being shaped, Tragash successfully argued that there would be value in having the top of the organization use the same problem solving tools that had been found to be valuable at the bottom of the organization. The six-step Xerox Problem Solving Process (PSP) was adopted as one of the core tools of quality, and eventually all Xerox employees were trained in this approach (see Chapter 10). Appendix 6 is the Xerox Problem Solving Process.

Xerox Quality Improvement Process

In addition to the PSP, the original quality implementation team (formed in April 1983) determined that there was a need to build another tool, a basic guide to quality improvement. This Xerox Quality Improvement Process (QIP) provided a map for people to look at any existing work process or to design new work processes. It helped to operationalize quality and provide people with a road map for the application of quality tools to real work settings (see Chapter 11). Appendix 7 lists the steps in the Xerox QIP.

Xerox Quality Training Sequence

A major investment in quality was made when the senior managers at Leesburg committed to train every Xerox employee in quality. In actuality, the quality training was composed of a set of different training modules and experiences. These are described in Chapter 11. Appendix 8 provides an overview of the quality training sequence that formed the basis for the training provided to more than one hundred thousand employees.

Appendix 1

Organization Model

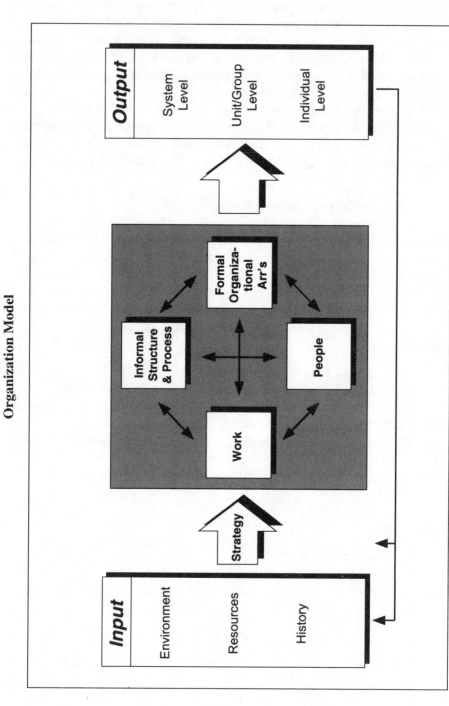

Adapted from Nadler, D. A. & Tushman, M. L. "A model for diagnosing organizational behavior:
Applying a congruence perspective," *Organizational Dynamics* (Autumn, 1980).

Change Management Model

Core Problems in Organizational Change	Change Management Implications	Practices Associated with Effective Management of Organizational Change
Power – Intensified nonproductive political activity stimulated by changes in the informal organization.	Shape the political dynamics associated with the change.	1. Get the support of key power groups.
		2. Use leader behavior to support the direction of change.
		3. Use symbols and language.
		4. Build in stability.
Anxiety – Dysfunctional responses by individuals to the uncertainty and potential threat posed by change.	Motivate people to act constructively.	5. Create dissatisfaction with the status quo.
		6. Employ participation in planning and/or implementing change.
		7. Reward needed behavior in transition and future states.
		8. Provide time and opportunity to disengage from current state.
Control – Loss of managerial control as the current state is disassembled before the future state is in place.	Manage the transition state, as well as the current and future states.	9. Develop and communicate a clear image of the future state.
		10. Use multiple and consistent leverage points to change behavior.
		11. Employ transition management structures.
		12. Build in feedback and evaluation of the transition.

Adapted from *Concepts for the Management of Organizational Change*. New York: Delta Consulting Group Inc., 1981.

Appendix 3

Key Events in the Development of the Leadership Through Quality Change Strategy, 1982–1984

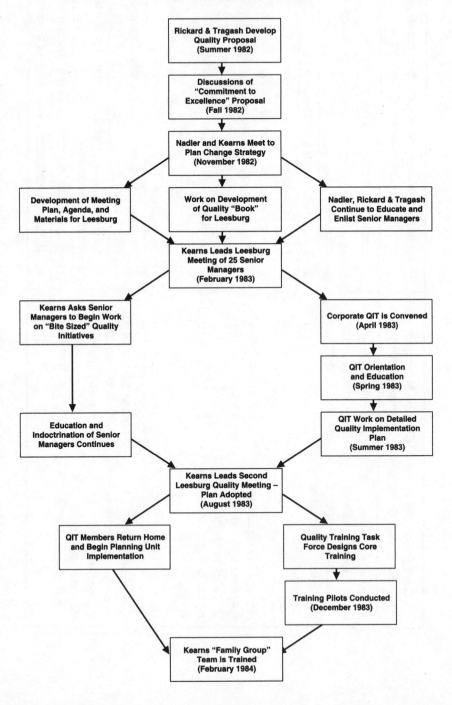

Xerox Corporation: Leadership Through Quality—Definition

Tools

- The Xerox Quality Policy.
- Competitive Benchmarking and quality goal setting.
- Systematic defect and error prevention processes.
- Training for Leadership Through Quality.
- Communications and recognition programs which reinforce Leadership Through Quality.
- A method for measuring cost of quality (or its lack).

Leadership Through Quality

Quality Principles

- Quality is the basic business principle for Xerox to continue to be a leadership company.
- We will understand our customer's existing and latent requirements.
- We will provide all of our external and internal customers products and services which meet their requirements.
- Employee involvement, through participative problem solving, is essential to improve quality.
- Error-free work is the most cost-effective way to improve quality.

Management Actions/Behavior

- We will assure strategic clarity and consistency.
- We will provide visibly supportive management practices, commitment, and leadership.
- We will set quality objectives and measurement standards.
- We will establish and reinforce a management style of openness, trust, respect, patience, and discipline.
- We will establish an environment so each person can be responsible for quality.

Reprinted with the permission of the Xerox Corporation.

Appendix 5
Summary of Key Decisions

Definitions

1. Is there agreement on the principles, tools, and management actions on which the definition of Commitment to Excellence is based?
2. Is there agreement on the proposed definition of Commitment to Excellence and its implications for the way in which Xerox people accomplish their work?
3. By what name should Xerox's total quality strategy be known?
4. Is the proposed problem-solving process accepted as basic to the concept and part of its definition?

Objectives

5. Is the description of the mature state complete, and are these expectations appropriate?
6. Do we believe that five years is a realistic time period to achieve this state?
7. Do we believe that the activities described will result in the improved business results (e.g., increased market share and customer satisfaction, improved profits, and increased employee job satisfaction)?
8A. How specific should the expectation levels be for 1987?
8B. Should the Quality Implementation Team be asked to develop more specific expectations for their operating units as part of the unit implementation plans?
9. Is the time required for planning the implementation and for training senior executives really necessary before launching quality improvement? Or should we start sooner?
10. Should all operating units begin at the same time, or should efforts be concentrated on the major units with the others selecting the pace based upon need and capacity?

Training

11. Is there agreement on the need to train *all* employees on the Commitment to Excellence?
12. Is there affirmation of the tops-down training implementation?
13. Is there support for the "family group" approach to training?
14. Is there concurrence with the recommended training objectives?
15. Is the training task force an appropriate vehicle to develop Commitment to Excellence training?

Communications

16. What is the process called?
17. Will the process be titled identically throughout the Corporation?
18. Will Corporate develop communications guidelines? Will the operating units develop their own communications strategies?
19. Will Corporate pre-announce the process?
20. When will the process be announced?

Setting Standards and Measurements

21. Will the process for incorporating quality into the management process be established as proposed?
22. Given that Competitive Benchmarking and customer satisfaction surveys are under way, should new methods be utilized to define external customer requirements (e.g., a more formal process for collecting customer visit information by executives, Tech Reps, and Marketing Reps)?
23. Should guidelines for a process to establish internal customer requirements be developed by the Quality Implementation Team?
24. Should a Quality Policy be established, such as the one in the Xerox Quality Improvement Process?
25. How should units develop the cost of quality? Annually? What level of precision?
26. How will quality be incorporated into the management process? For example,

    a. the objective setting process
    b. management MBOs
    c. ensuring all employees know their roles in improving quality
    d. the planning (Operating Plan and Business Plan) process
    e. operations reviews
    f. all decision-making processes
    g. the quarterly CMC quality reviews
    h. Any others?

Rewards and Recognition

27. Are the proposed principles appropriate?
28. What actions will senior management take to demonstrate its involvement and support of a quality rewards and recognition system?
29. When should this system be in place and functioning?

Quality Implementation Structure

30. To what extent is there agreement on the proposed implementation and structure for quality?

The Role of Senior Management

31. Is there agreement on the need for consistent and sustained effort on the part of senior management to assure the successful implementation of Commitment to Excellence?

32. Is there agreement and commitment on the "Guidelines for Quality Management" regarding the managerial behavior needed to make/help/let it happen?

33. Is there approval for periodic survey research to monitor and evaluate managerial practices required to sustain the Commitment toExcellence over time?

34. Is there support for focusing on our own teamwork to better understand the quality of our team management process (how well we work together) as a critical ingredient in the success of our Commitment to Excellence?

Appendix 6

Xerox Problem Solving Process

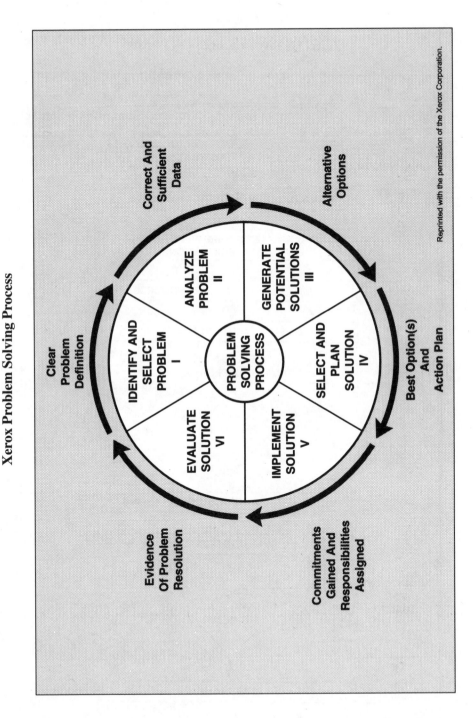

Reprinted with the permission of the Xerox Corporation.

Appendix 7

Xerox Quality Improvement Process

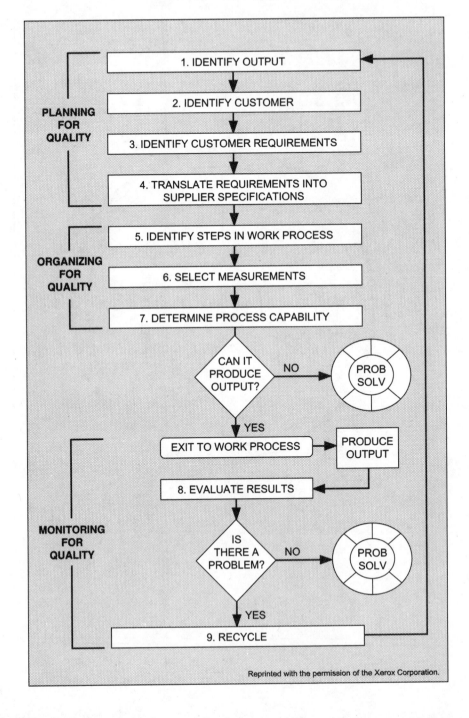

Reprinted with the permission of the Xerox Corporation.

Appendix 8

Xerox Quality Training Sequence

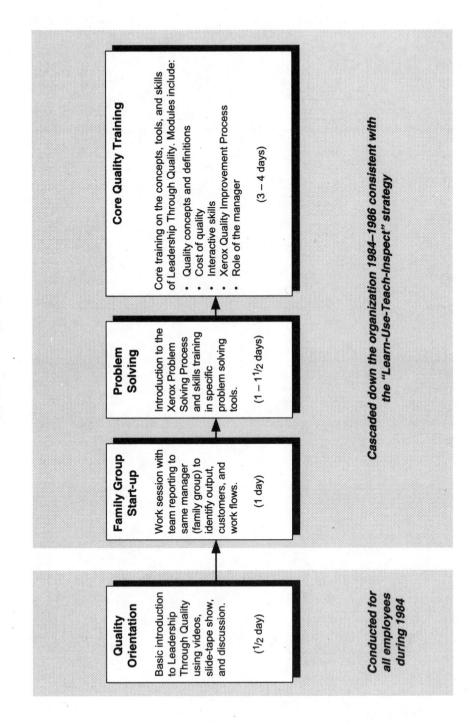

Quality Orientation

Basic introduction to Leadership Through Quality using videos, slide-tape show, and discussion.

(1/2 day)

Family Group Start-up

Work session with team reporting to same manager (family group) to identify output, customers, and work flows.

(1 day)

Problem Solving

Introduction to the Xerox Problem Solving Process and skills training in specific problem solving tools.

(1 – 1 1/2 days)

Core Quality Training

Core training on the concepts, tools, and skills of Leadership Through Quality. Modules include:

· Quality concepts and definitions
· Cost of quality
· Interactive skills
· Xerox Quality Improvement Process
· Role of the manager

(3 – 4 days)

Conducted for all employees during 1984

Cascaded down the organization 1984–1986 consistent with the "Learn-Use-Teach-Inspect" strategy

Acknowledgments

WE WERE FORTUNATE TO HAVE the help and assistance of many very generous and talented people in putting together this book, and they deserve recognition and thanks for their contributions. A number of people were very helpful to us in reconstructing the story of Xerox in the 1960s and 1970s, as well as the Xerox quality story. They consented to be interviewed and they shared freely and extensively from their notes, files, records, and memories.

Specifically, Bob Schneider and David Curtin, both now retired from Xerox, were extremely helpful in allowing us to build a narrative of Xerox in the sixties and seventies. David Bliss, now a managing director at Delta Consulting Group Inc., was tremendously valuable in providing us with a flavor of Xerox at the levels below Kearns in the seventies and early eighties, drawing on his more than twenty years with the company.

Hal Tragash, now at Rhône-Poulenc Rorer Pharmaceuticals, and Norm Rickard, still at Xerox, contributed immensely by sharing their notes and recollections of the early days of Leadership Through Quality. John Kelsch was a great help, drawing on his wonderful sense of history and his objective and reliable views of the company over time. Jeff Heilpern, also a managing director at Delta, shared valuable perspectives from the 1987 Xerox quality assessment.

Jim Sierk, now chief quality officer at Allied-Signal, and John Cooney, still at Xerox, assisted by providing perspectives of the Xerox Baldrige team. A number of current and past Xerox executives were also gracious in sharing their views and helping us find key information, including Frank Pipp, Wayland Hicks, and Paul Allaire, the current CEO and chairman of the company. Joe Cahalan, director of communications for Xerox and a member of the original Quality Implementation Team, aided us in locating pictures and other archival information.

For facts about Xerox, especially its early history, we are indebted to the books *My Years with Xerox: The Billions Nobody Wanted* by John H. Dessauer; *The Making of a Public Man* by Sol M. Linowitz; *American Samurai* by Gary Jacobson and John Hillkirk; and *Fumbling the Future* by Douglas K. Smith and Robert C. Alexander, as well as articles by David Owen in *The Atlantic* and John Brooks in *The New Yorker.*

There have been some other friends of the effort who have provided us with significant support during the preparation of this volume. Barbara Martz helped us get the project started and connected us with key resources. Jack Hilton has been both a cheerleader and perceptive critic. Our executive assistants, Lucy Clarke at Xerox, and Kathy Mahon at Delta, were indispensable to us, and managed to carve out the time in our schedules to do the work involved with the book.

We are also grateful to our wives, Shirley Kearns and Elizabeth Nadler, who read various drafts of this book and offered incisive criticism and many helpful suggestions.

At HarperCollins, we owe our thanks to Mark Greenberg, our original mentor there, and Virginia Smith, who so skillfully and enthusiastically saw us through publication. For his continuous support, we thank our agent, Philip Spitzer.

Finally, we want to express our tremendous appreciation to Sonny Kleinfield, who worked closely with us in all the stages of the development of this manuscript. Working alone, the two of us would have created a clear, credible, authoritative, and dull manuscript with limited appeal. Sonny worked with us to help discover the story and the drama, and he brought to life many of our words.

Obviously, while we appreciate the assistance of all whom we've named, we accept the responsibility for the views expressed here.

Index